Bid Writing for Project Managers

*To Mark E, Neil M, Richard P, Lois P, Dave S and Pam V.
You guys first showed me the essentials a long time ago, and
I'm very grateful.*

Bid Writing for Project Managers

DAVID CLEDEN

GOWER

Published by
Gower Publishing Limited
Wey Court East
Union Road
Farnham
Surrey, GU9 7PT
England

Ashgate Publishing Company
Suite 420
101 Cherry Street
Burlington,
VT 05401-4405
USA

www.gowerpublishing.com

British Library Cataloguing in Publication Data
Cleden, David.
 Bid writing for project managers.
 1. Proposal writing in business. 2. Letting of contracts.
 I. Title
 658.7'23-dc22

 ISBN: 978-0-566-09214-5 (hbk)
 ISBN: 978-0-566-09215-2 (ebk)

Library of Congress Cataloging-in-Publication Data
Cleden, David.
 Bid writing for project managers / David Cleden.
  p. cm.
 Includes index. ISBN 978-0-566-09214-5 (hbk) -- ISBN 978-0-566-09215-2
 (ebook) 1. Project management. 2. Letting of contracts. 3. Proposal writing in business. 4.
 Business planning. I. Title.
 HD69.P75.C5223 2010
 808'.066658--dc22

                                                                                         2010032977

Printed and bound in Great Britain by the
MPG Books Group, UK

Contents

List of Figures		*ix*
List of Tables		*xi*
List of Abbreviations		*xiii*
Preface		*xv*

Chapter 1	**Zen and the Art of Bid Writing**	**1**
	In the Beginning	1
	What is a Bid?	3
	Back to Basics	6
	Laying the Foundations for Success	8
	Common Reasons Why Proposals Fail	10
	Summary: Zen and the Art of Bid Writing	13

Chapter 2	**The Anatomy of a Bid**	**15**
	The Job of the Bid	15
	Anatomy of a Winning Proposal	17
	Five Stages in the Bid Life Cycle	21
	Summary: The Anatomy of a Bid	27

Chapter 3	**Planning to Win**	**29**
	Planning the Bid	29
	The Bid Process	35
	The Bid Writer's Toolkit	38
	Summary: Planning to Win	43

Chapter 4	**Analysing the Requirements in Depth**	**45**
	Ignore the Requirements at your Peril	45
	Reviewing the ITT	46
	Key Themes	47
	Finding the Key Themes	48

Differentiators and Discriminators 53
Research 57
ITT Analysis Checklist 59
Summary: Analysing the Requirements 60

Chapter 5 **Developing the Bid** **63**
Identifying the Business Objectives 63
Checklists for Developing the Bid Solution 67
Does the Client Understand the Problem? 69
Innovation 71
Summary: Developing the Bid 74

Chapter 6 **Establishing the Project Framework** **75**
The Role of Estimation in Bidding 75
What Needs Estimating? 82
Prerequisites for Good Estimation 87
Summary: Establishing the Project Framework 95

Chapter 7 **Estimation Methods** **97**
Ground Rules For Estimation 97
Commonly Used Estimation Methods 110
Due Diligence on Estimates 123
Summary: Estimation Methods 126

Chapter 8 **Realistic Costing and Pricing** **129**
Price Versus Cost 129
Cost Principles 131
Building the Cost Model 132
Key Stages of Financial Review 134
Factors Affecting the Price 141
Summary: Realistic Costing and Pricing 142

Chapter 9 **A Structured Approach to Writing the Bid** **143**
Why Structure Matters 144
Choosing the Right Structure 144
How to Develop the Proposal Structure 150
Reviewing the Bid Structure 158
Summary: A Structured Approach to Writing the Bid 160

Chapter 10	**Getting the Message Across**	**161**
	At the Heart of Good Communication	161
	Getting to the Point	164
	Patterns of Argument	166
	Assuming Too Much	170
	Objectivity	172
	Bad Habits to Avoid	173
	Summary: Getting the Message Across	175
Chapter 11	**The Management Solution**	**177**
	Developing the Management Solution	177
	Writing the Management Solution	181
	Executive Summary	192
	Summary: The Management Solution	193
Chapter 12	**Quality Control**	**195**
	Reviewing the Bid	195
	Planning Your Reviews	200
	Managing the Review Process	201
	Polishing As You Go	202
	Summary: Quality Control	205
Chapter 13	**The Transition to a Project**	**207**
	Producing the Finished Proposal	207
	Preparing for the Next Stage	208
	Learning Lessons	211
	Final Steps	215
	Summary: The Transition to a Project	217
Appendix A	*A Bid Checklist*	*219*
Appendix B	*Glossary*	*233*
Index		*241*

List of Figures

1.1	What is a bid?	5
1.2	How bid responsibilities map onto the project	7
1.3	The successful bid rests on three key principles	9
1.4	The role of the project framework	12
2.1	Winning – what does it take?	18
2.2	The five stages of the bid life cycle	22
2.3	One offering but many different solutions	24
3.1	Hitting the wall	32
3.2a	A bid process (stages 1 to 3a)	36
3.2b	A bid process (stages 3b to 5)	37
4.1	The relative value of key themes, differentiators and discriminators	54
5.1	The relationship between what the client needs and what the supplier can offer	64
6.1	Estimation underpins the entire planning process	77
6.2	Estimation is one of four key stages in establishing the project framework	78
6.3	The time–cost–quality triangle	85
6.4	An alternative representation of the time–cost–quality relationship	86
6.5	Estimates, targets and commitments	87
6.6	The estimation model tracks any changes in the requirements	93
7.1	Task decomposition is the first (and crucial) step in estimation	99
7.2	The theoretical spread of possible outcomes	101
7.3	Using error bars to show the estimation range and confidence level	102
7.4	The cone of uncertainty	103
7.5	The ripple-down effect caused by a last-minute change to the requirements	106

7.6   Estimation using expert judgement   113
7.7   Estimation using consensus expert judgement   117
7.8   Estimation using count and calibrate   120
7.9   Estimation using comparison   122
8.1   Key stages of costing activity in the bid process   135
9.1   An example proposal structure captured in mind-map
       form   152
9.2   A page from an example storyboard   155
10.1   Stating key themes explicitly as notations in the margin   165
10.2   A pattern (or writing template) for a simple factual
       presentation   167
10.3   A writing pattern for an argument made by deductive
       reasoning   168
10.4   A writing pattern for presenting and justifying a working
       hypothesis   169
11.1   An example of an outline project schedule   186
11.2   An excerpt from a detailed project schedule   187
12.1   A typical mix of reviews during the creation of the bid   198
12.2   The decreasing value of reviews   201

List of Tables

2.1	The client's view of what makes a winning proposal	19
2.2	The multidisciplinary skills of the bid writer	20–21
3.1	A useful task prioritization scheme	34–35
3.2	Bid artefacts	38–41
4.1	How to structure a key theme	52
4.2	A generic example of a structured key theme	53
4.3	Another example of a structured key theme	53
4.4	Different ways to differentiate your proposal	55
4.5	Four areas which may require further research	57–58
6.1	Sources of estimation error	90–91
7.1	Estimation assumptions for producing a report (example)	107
7.2	The suitability of different estimation methods	110–111
7.3	Getting the best from expert judgement	112
7.4	How good is the estimate? A checklist	124–125
8.1	The vital differences between cost and price	130
8.2	Cost principles	131–132
8.3	Key aspects of your cost model	132–133
9.1	Using active headings to communicate with the reader	149
9.2	The main topics in a storyboard template	156–157
10.1	The characteristics of strong writing	163
10.2	Some tips on avoiding assumptions	171
10.3	The consequences of MILI: Make It Look Important	173
11.1	What questions does the Management Section address?	183
11.2	Guidelines for presenting the project schedule in the bid	188
11.3	Guidelines for documenting bid assumptions	190
12.1	Three different types of review	196
12.2	Guidelines for managing the review process	201–202
13.1	Preparing for the next stage: after the bid submission	208–209
13.2	Guidelines for trade-off discussions with the client	211

List of Abbreviations

BAFO	Best and final offer
CV	Curriculum vitae
ITT	Invitation to tender
MILI	Make it look important
MSP	Managing successful programmes
PQQ	Pre-qualification questionnaire
PRINCE	Projects in controlled environments
RUP	Rational unified process

Preface

So: Another book on project management?

Not really. Although this book is aimed at managers, particularly those with some experience of commercial projects, it is not a book about how to run a project. Plenty of other books already cover this topic, trust me.

A book for sales people, then? How to win over the client and secure a deal?

Again, not really, although you will find several chapters on how to put forward a persuasive argument and get your messages across in a proposal.

Alright, then. Is it an introductory guide for those new to bid writing? Will I find help with organizing a bid team, prioritizing the work and structuring the proposal? Will it tell me what to include in a bid and what to leave out?

Getting warmer.

Mostly this is a book for managers about to engage in writing a commercial proposal which, if successful, will result in a contract to deliver a project or programme of work. But it's not just a handbook of bid writing. It contains some advice which might just save your project from disaster six months down the line. Allow me to explain.

First let's consider for a moment the precarious state of project delivery. We know that a sizeable number of projects hit difficulties. Research shows that about 25 per cent of projects fail or are cancelled before completion. (See, for example, *The Chaos Report*, a biennial survey published by the Standish Group.) A much larger number (about 50 per cent) run significantly over budget or schedule, and often both. Only a quarter of projects actually succeed. This has been happening for years and the situation doesn't seem to be improving. What's going on here? Why is it so hard to run a successful project?

The Ingredients for Success

A successful project has several key ingredients. First you must have the right set of skills (and the people) to do the job. We will call these the *core competencies*. For example, to build a house you need bricklayers, carpenters and plumbers who all know their trades. You also need a site foreman who knows in what order jobs need doing and will make sure things are done properly. Similarly, a project needs a team of people who know their jobs, and a project manager to keep a weather eye out in case the unexpected happens.

Secondly, you need good management processes which will keep the project on track. These will help to ensure there is effective communication between the client, the team, any subcontractors and the project stakeholders. They will help the team develop a good understanding of the tasks to be carried out, what these depend on, their priority and how long each task will take – in other words, a realistic plan. They will also provide an effective way of monitoring progress, spotting problems at an early stage and solving them.

Let's call these things the *delivery processes*. In our house-building analogy the site foreman is like the project manager. He or she applies delivery processes to monitor the building work, checks each stage against the architect's plans and solves any problems that arise.

Sometimes delivery processes are grouped together and called a 'methodology'. Different methodologies abound, often with impressive-sounding acronyms such as RUP, PRINCE2, MSP, etc. There is little doubt that following a recognized methodology greatly improves a project's chances of success. Which one you choose is less important than choosing one and sticking to it.

Is that it? With these things in place, are we assured a successful project?

No. We are still missing an important third ingredient: the project's *conceptual framework*.

The Conceptual Framework

All projects begin with someone somewhere having an idea. It might be a modest idea: *let's add some new features to an existing product*. Or it might be more ambitious: *let's create something that has never been done before*. The point is, many key aspects of a project are determined in this very early stage, long before a project manager is brought on board or the first task of the project is mapped out. Decisions are taken, expectations are set and objectives are formed – and once formed, they are hard to shift.

In a commercial setting, the client will prepare an 'invitation to tender' (ITT) which enables suppliers to bid for the work. The ITT summarizes the client's business objectives, provides detailed requirements of the work to be done and will usually state the timescale and other constraints which the supplier must work to. There then follows a bidding process in which a number of suppliers show how well they can meet the terms of the client's ITT and state their price for doing the work. The client selects one of the bidders and a contract for the work is placed. At this point the project begins.

Decisions made about the conceptual framework shape the outcome of the project. If the conceptual framework is misjudged, the project may be flawed from the outset – although not necessarily in obvious ways because hidden problems may not appear until much further downstream.

This book is about how to build the conceptual framework of the project during the bid stage. More importantly, it's about building it *right*. The seeds of too many project failures are sown in the proposal. Get the conceptual framework right, and you stand a much better chance of delivering a successful project.

Of course, before this can happen, you must write the *winning* proposal. That means presenting a compelling argument to the client, and communicating the strengths of your solution and delivery approach effectively. And it also means organizing your bid resources to make the best use of what you have available.

These are the three goals of this book: to show how to establish a viable project framework, to organize for success and to persuade the client to award you the contract.

How to Use this Book

Time is the biggest enemy of anyone working on a bid, so here are some suggestions for getting the most out of this book.

Chapter 1 sets out the rationale of bid writing for project managers. If you already understand the importance of developing a viable project framework during the bid stage, you may want to skip ahead. But remember – these activities are the foundations upon which the project will succeed or fail.

If you have the luxury of some time before working on a bid:

- Read the introduction and bid background chapters (Chapters 1 and 2). These will put the bid tasks in context.

- If you are new to the bidding process, particularly the planning and management aspects, Chapter 3 introduces the key concepts.

If you have already started work on a bid and are looking for some help:

- Chapter 4 onwards follows the key stages in the bid process.

- Which chapter to start with depends on how far through the bid process you are.

- You may want to familiarize yourself with the bid process diagram (Figure 3.2a and b) and consult the glossary (Appendix B) if you encounter any unfamiliar terms.

If you have just received an ITT from a client:

- Read Chapters 5, 6 and 7 first to make sure you begin building the framework of the proposal in the right way.

It is important to remember that creating the proposal doesn't sit in isolation from the project that hopefully follows from it. The work doesn't end when the bid is submitted. Chapter 13 looks at the preparations needed to smoothly transition from bid to project. Many of the subsequent project issues arise from a poor transition, so this is an important stage.

Finally, to assist those working to a very tight deadline:

- At the end of each chapter there is a summary of the essential points. Just reading these summaries will give you a feel for the most important areas to focus on.

- Appendix A contains a bid checklist which maps to the bid process introduced in Chapter 3. You can use this as a reminder or to check your progress as you work through the bid stages.

Good luck and best wishes for a successful bid!

David Cleden, January 2011

1

Zen and the Art of Bid Writing

You cannot teach people anything. You can only help them to discover it within themselves.

Galileo Galilei (Italian astronomer and physicist, 1564–1642)

In the Beginning

Matthew's boss calls him the archetypal 'safe pair of hands'. With nearly a decade of solid experience, Matthew knows what is expected of him as project manager. The first few weeks on the new project are hectic but exhilarating. He meets with his new team and together they start to map out key stages of the project. Matthew is pleased that an early brainstorming session on risks really seems to get everyone fired up. Everyone relaxes over a few drinks in the pub after work and it is clear to Matthew he is leading a team of dedicated individuals with a broad range of skills.

Matthew also meets with the client to discuss the requirements, and all goes well. Not unusually for a government-funded project, there is a large group of stakeholders with diverse interests. At the first monthly Project Board meeting Matthew's project report is upbeat, and demonstrates that good mitigation plans are in place for a small number of risks that have been identified.

But a week later, his technical lead brings him a problem. She has been analysing the requirements in more detail and has discovered that an important off-the-shelf component in the proposed solution simply won't meet the requirements. Adapting the component will be time-consuming and potentially risky because the necessary skills don't exist within the team. Sourcing an alternative will be both time-consuming and costly.

A couple of days later, Matthew has a disturbing conversation with one of his subcontractors. It emerges that no binding subcontract was ever agreed for this part of the work. Extra time will be needed to agree terms with the subcontractor, delaying a critical milestone. Worse, the subcontractor is now pitching a higher price than originally budgeted for. Unforeseen delays and budget overruns are now threatening Matthew's project.

His technical lead brings more bad news. She has found further problems in the requirements document. Their original proposal to the client states compliance with a number of important requirements which, it now becomes clear, can't be met by the proposed technical solution. This news is a potential show-stopper.

Matthew holds a requirements workshop with the client, aiming to negotiate away the problematical requirements. Not surprisingly, the client is initially reluctant to reduce the scope but is persuaded to trade off these requirements for additional (and more affordable) functionality in other areas. But yet another problem emerges. The workshop reveals that there are big holes in the client's requirements; important things have been overlooked in the Invitation To Tender. Worse, several of the client stakeholder groups are unhappy with the proposed solution, feeling that they were excluded from the bid evaluation process. The client's internal politics are awkward; some of the stakeholders may not sign off on the design unless their views are taken into account.

Matthew knows these problems are solvable, but it means new and unexpected effort (for example, carrying out a more detailed requirements analysis which will add months to the schedule). He initiates change control procedures to recover these extra costs and the relationship with the client deteriorates rapidly. They thought they were contracting for a turnkey system but are suddenly facing long delays and significant cost increases.

By the end of month three, Matthew's highlight report is awash with critical issues and forecast overruns. After such a promising start, where did it all go wrong?

SEEDS OF FAILURE

In Matthew's case, as with many projects, the seeds of failure were sown long before the project manager was appointed. A combination of poor decisions during the bid and failure to do important groundwork led to problems laying dormant for some months. Let's examine some of them.

- *Feasibility of the solution.* The bid team proposed a solution which in several important respects didn't meet the client's requirements. Almost certainly time pressure was a contributing factor. Nobody felt they had enough time during the bid to properly analyse what the client was asking for and determine which solution (or indeed, if *any* solution) would meet these requirements.

- *Commercial agreements.* Failing to get subcontractors 'signed up' during the bid stage was an elementary mistake. It left Matthew's organization exposed, taking on the risk of delivering something outside their immediate control without transferring part of that risk to the subcontractor.

- *Missing or misunderstood requirements.* In a large or complex bid, it can be easy to overlook the significance of certain requirements. It is one of the reasons why requirements tracking tools are a good idea. This ensures that each requirement maps on to some element of the solution. It means nothing gets forgotten and there are no nasty surprises when the project is delivered to the client.

- *Lack of vision or understanding on the part of the client.* It is not uncommon for a client to have an incomplete picture of what they want the project to deliver. This is fine if a project methodology is selected which takes this into account, for example by working iteratively to gradually refine the requirements. But if the project is organized to deliver only what was asked for during the bidding process, it can be a recipe for disaster.

Each of these problems originated in the bid stage. Undoubtedly, preventing these sorts of problems during the bid stage is *hard*. There is never enough time, or enough people, or the right skills available, or enough information from the client to properly understand what is needed. But laying the foundations of the project during the bid is crucial. It is the single biggest factor in determining the success of the project.

What is a Bid?

There are many kinds of bids, just as there are many kinds of projects. The bidding process is a key sales activity for most service- and product-oriented organizations. The principles of bid writing apply equally across the scale from the very small to the very large project.

Principally, we will focus on a *commercial* bid, usually resulting in one of several possible suppliers being awarded a contract to execute a project or programme of work. However, many of the principles to be discussed remain valid outside of a commercial context, such as when pitching for an internal project or undertaking work on a non-commercial basis.

THE BID (OR PROPOSAL)

The *bid* is the supplier's response to a client's concept for the project; the answer to the questions posed by the client. It is also referred to as a *proposal* and we will use the two terms interchangeably. The bid is a binding document, initially evaluated by the client to determine if the work should be awarded and if it is, it becomes a commitment on the part of the supplier as to what will be done.

THE ITT

To keep things simple we will use the term 'ITT' (Invitation To Tender) or 'tender' as the catch-all for the client's description (or concept) for the project. You may be familiar with other variants such as: Request For Proposal, Request For Quote, Invitation To Bid, and Invitation To Quote, etc. Each refers to information issued by the client to prospective bidders which, in theory, completely defines the work to be done.

On a large bid, there may be several stages of bidding. For example, an initial response to a Pre-Qualification Questionnaire is often used to select a longlist of bidders who will then respond to a full ITT. Following evaluation of proposals, bidders are whittled down to a shortlist who may then have to submit further refinements to their bids, culminating in what is often termed a 'Best And Final Offer' (BAFO).

As we step through the principal bid stages, we will encounter some key terms which have specific meanings. A full glossary is provided in Appendix B. Combining these elements, a picture of the generic bidding process begins to emerge (see Figure 1.1).

Although there is only one client project team, there are usually multiple supplier teams, each vying to win the work. This is a competition that only one supplier can win – the one who demonstrates their abilities and aptitude for delivering a compliant solution at an acceptable price. Even in the case of a sole supplier bid (i.e. where there are no competitive pressures), the benefits of following a good bid process still apply.

This picture of the bidding process also gives us some clues about where things can go wrong. The ITT is critical because it contains the detail of what the project must achieve. However, formal procurement processes often forbid contact with the client during bidding except through closely controlled channels to ensure that no supplier is given favourable treatment. Without an open dialogue with the client, errors and omissions in the ITT may propagate into the project leading to problems down the line.

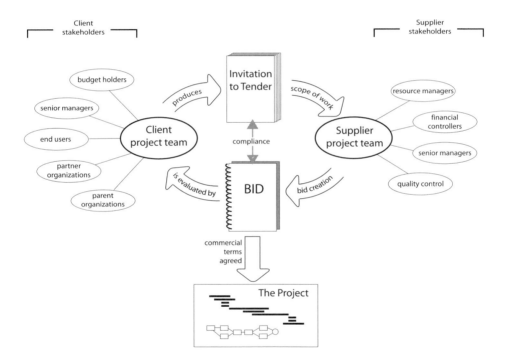

Figure 1.1   **What is a bid?** *In a commercial setting, the ITT and the bid sit at the interface between the client and the supplier. A project is formed around the commercial agreements struck on the basis of a successful bid*

Notice that the set of project stakeholders often extends beyond the immediate teams involved in the project from the client and supplier organizations. Both parties have other masters that must also be served. Active stakeholder involvement naturally varies from bid to bid but good communication between all stakeholder groups is very helpful (if permitted within the rules of the procurement).

Compliance is an important consideration for every bid. Begin by assuming the bid must meet all the requirements laid down in the ITT. However, submitting a non-compliant bid can sometimes be a smart move. Perhaps the client has overlooked something and you can see a better way of doing things, thereby stealing a march on the competition whose proposals will look dreary and unimaginative by comparison. Or perhaps you have realized that what the client is asking for can't be achieved – in which case you can score points for your foresight and honesty, and help the client avoid a nasty problem before it occurs.

Back to Basics

Sometimes it is good to be reminded of the obvious, particularly when the consequences are far reaching. How, precisely, does a successful project manager manage a project? This is an important question because if we don't know the answer, we cannot expect to write a bid which will lead to successful delivery of the project.

So – back to basics. Figure 1.2 illustrates a project manager's six key responsibilities. Notice how each of these has its roots in tasks which are begun during the bid stage. Critical decisions are being made which will have profound implications once the project is underway.

This *project framework* is usually driven by the needs of the bid – for example, most clients want to know when key milestones will be reached, so preliminary planning must be done even though many aspects of the project will be uncertain at this stage. Similarly, the client may want to understand what risks are entailed, so the bid team must carry out risk analyses and write these up in the proposal. Although driven by what the client asks for in the tender, these items are actually creating the project framework. If the bid is successful, this project framework is transitioned into the operational project. In other words, a large part of the preliminary planning (or 'project start-up' in PRINCE2 terms) is fixed and agreed with the client during the bid stage. Naturally, getting this right goes a long way towards ensuring project success later on.

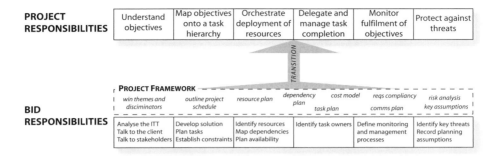

Figure 1.2   **How bid responsibilities map onto the project.** *Key activities performed during the bid create the project framework which becomes the basis for executing the project*

However, problems arise when too much effort goes in to making the bid as attractive as possible without sufficient thought for what is feasible, i.e. making promises to the client that can't be kept. We will look at these key elements in more detail.

KEY ELEMENTS OF THE PROJECT FRAMEWORK

Understand the project objectives

A better understanding of the objectives increases opportunities for the project team to resolve problems and come up with more innovative solutions. This requires a thorough appreciation of not just the tangible project objectives but awareness of how these fulfil broader business objectives. The tender documents must be analysed in detail but are only a starting point for developing this understanding. Omissions and apparent contradictions can be revealing.

Map objectives to a task hierarchy

The sole purpose of the task hierarchy is to deliver the objectives in the most efficient way. It determines how the project is divided into discrete, manageable activities, what inputs are expected and what outputs are generated. These are the fundamental building blocks of the project. Assembling these in the correct order will ultimately lead to the delivery of the business objectives.

Orchestrate the deployment of resources

Fundamentally, planning determines what must be done, when, in what order and how long it will take. The difficulty for the bid team is that much of the detail may be uncertain or will take too much time to fathom. Yet without this information, good estimates are impossible. For instance, it is easy to promise in the proposal to meet the client's delivery dates but much harder to demonstrate you have the resources to commit to these dates.

Delegate and manage task completion

Effective management of project tasks heavily depends on identifying individuals with the right skills. Many clients require key members of the team to be named in the bid, so it is important to choose team members carefully.

Monitor fulfilment of objectives

A large organization will usually have tried-and-tested reporting, monitoring and communication processes. You may have 'boiler-plate' text which can be lifted from previous proposals to describe how these control processes work. But the client may be looking for something extra, or may expect you to adapt to his particular circumstances. It is a case of being attentive to what the client is looking for and adapting what you already have to offer.

Protect against threats

The reality of a project can be so different to how it was planned that the most important risks aren't even conceived of during the bid stage. Risk management is a vital part of every bid – but it can also be a sink-hole of time and effort if done poorly. To be truly effective, the bid team need to see beyond superficial risks to the root of the uncertainties.

Laying the Foundations for Success

THREE KEY PRINCIPLES

Having looked briefly at some of the difficulties, what emerges are three key principles for writing a successful bid (see Figure 1.3).

- Organize (to get the best from the bid resources).

- Persuade (to encourage the client to award you the work).

- Establish the project framework (to set the project up right).

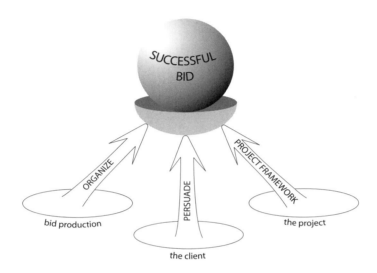

Figure 1.3 **The successful bid rests on three key principles.** *Organization is fundamental to a successful bidding process, persuasion is necessary for the bid to succeed and establishing the project framework is the key to a successful project*

Organize

The bid must get written on time. There are no excuses if you miss the submission deadline, and no prizes for coming second. A great deal of preparatory work needs to be done even before any words are written. The bid is a mini-project in its own right.

Persuade

It is not enough to have an excellent solution and a rock-solid delivery strategy: you have to convince the client of this. It sounds obvious, but don't assume the client will recognize all the brilliant aspects of your solution. Point them out.

Emphasize the strengths, and explain how you will counter any weaknesses. In short, know how to communicate your solution persuasively.

Establish the project framework

The contract you sign with the client will bind you to the project framework so it is important to get it right. The project team will have to live with the decisions being made now, and they won't thank you for forgetting obvious tasks or setting them impossible challenges. (And if you are the nominated project manager, you will be the one inheriting these problems.)

Building the framework of the project is a lot like planning, but with subtle differences. In a framework, the spaces are just as important as the structure: they provide flexibility. Whilst the gross dimensions of the structure are tied down, the fabric and the finishing details may still be varied. The framework must be a solid construction but it is not the finished artifact.

When creating elements of the project framework during the bid, keep two important questions in mind:

- Is it feasible? (If not, you will either need to look harder for an alternative approach or decline to bid).

- Do you need to commit to this level of detail at this stage?

Remember that the plan that you submit in the bid can never be as detailed as the plan created during project start-up. A detailed proposal is always to be welcomed, but it needs to be based on solid planning, not hurried guesswork.

Common Reasons Why Proposals Fail

If you have been involved in bid writing before, you will probably have experienced the frustration of pouring heart and soul into a bid only to have the client select a competitor's proposal – and not know why. Suppose we could eavesdrop on those clients. How might they justify their selection?

- 'The bid was non-compliant. It was an automatic rejection under the terms of our evaluation strategy.'

- 'The bid arrived after the specified deadline. It had to be returned unopened.'

- 'The supplier had not substantiated claims made in the proposal.'

- 'The supplier did not demonstrate a sufficiently detailed understanding of our requirement.'

- 'The solution was over-engineered. It gave us more than we really needed, at a price we couldn't justify.'

- 'The proposal did not represent the best value for the functionality offered.'

- 'The structure of the proposal was confusing, making it hard to find relevant information.'

- 'The supplier misunderstood our key requirements.'

- 'The proposal described a generic solution which didn't take into account our special circumstances.'

- 'The solution was attractive, but we were concerned about the viability of the proposal. Not enough analysis of the risks was presented.'

- 'Errors, omissions and inconsistencies in the proposal caused us to question the supplier's level of professionalism.'

Notice that only one of these explanations mentions price, and then only obliquely. Clearly price is important but it is only one of many factors, and doesn't always have the influence that many people assume.

Many of these failures arise from not following a well-defined bid process. Common problems are poor structure, not addressing all aspects of the ITT, failing to undertake thorough reviews, and missing deadlines. These things are easily fixed, as long as checklists are followed and simple planning processes are adhered to. (A bid checklist is provided in Appendix A for guidance.)

Other problems are more subtle and stem from failures to properly understand what the client hopes to achieve, or a failure to communicate your solution convincingly.

But succeeding at the proposal stage is no use if it builds in failure of the project. The bid needs to hold in balance the desire to meet all the client's requirements (or perhaps even to exceed them) with the need to define a project framework which is both feasible and commercially deliverable (see Figure 1.4).

Here is the dilemma: if a 'sales' mentality dominates, we run the risk of promising what can't be delivered. Conversely, an overly cautious stance may turn the client away and lose the sale. There is a fine line to tread, which requires a number of different skills to be brought into play. We will look at the specific skills needed for this balancing act in Chapters 9 and 10.

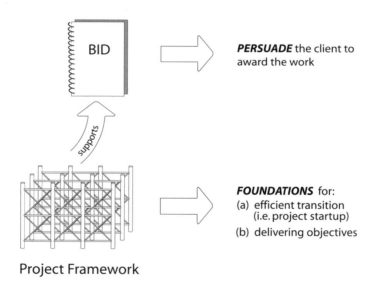

Figure 1.4   **The role of the project framework.** *It creates two main benefits. First, it provides much of the management content of the bid, and a strong framework will assist in persuading the client to award the work. Secondly, the framework establishes the project, leading to a better planned and less risky project*

ON THE BLACK RUN

Executing a project can feel like starting from the top of a ski slope. The objective is to stick to an agreed route, pass through a number of gates, avoid crashing into obstacles along the way and reach the finish line as quickly as possible.

As a project manager, which would you rather do? Shove off from the starting gate as soon as possible (after all, one of the objectives is to reach the end in the shortest time), scan ahead for any obstacles, try to figure out where the course goes so that you can slow or make turns in time – and hope no one has strung any wires across your path.

Or: spend a little time on preliminaries. Check the equipment over (and make sure you have the right equipment). Look at some maps to work out an optimum route and where potential dangers lie. Perhaps talk to someone who knows the territory or has been down the run ahead of you. If time allows, walk the route or survey it from a nearby vantage point.

Of course, the second option is the rational choice. Unfortunately, the problem on many bids is that events often conspire to drive us towards option 1. There is too little time, or the right people aren't available, or the pressure to win the work at all costs is overpowering.

In these circumstances, it is still possible to write a winning bid. The only problem is the ticking time bomb left behind for the project manager to discover much later.

Summary: Zen and the Art of Bid Writing

- This chapter introduced the key aspects of commercial bidding. *The bid is where the foundations of project success are laid.* Not only must the bid persuade the client of its worth, it must embody a feasible and commercially viable solution.

- Keep the three principles of a successful bid in mind: *organize, persuade* and establish the *project framework*.

- Following a good *bid process* will help avoid common failures. (See Appendix A for a checklist.)

- The *project framework* is set during the bid. The desire to win the contract leads to a temptation to make promises that will be difficult for the project to deliver.

- Bids are almost always written under *time pressure*. But skimping on the details of the project framework is only storing up trouble for later in the project.

2

The Anatomy of a Bid

In the modern world of business, it is useless to be a creative original thinker unless you can also sell what you create. Management cannot be expected to recognize a good idea unless it is presented to them by a good salesman.

David M. Ogilvy, advertising executive,
co-founder of Hewitt, Ogilvy, Benson and Mather, 1911–1999

Ogilvy was right. It isn't enough to have the right answers or the best solution or the most innovative approach – you have to be able to persuade the client of this truth. He recognized that quality and substance are only half the battle; without a compelling sales message, the client may go elsewhere. Since Ogilvy built one of the world's leading advertising firms on the back of this truth, we would do well to heed his words.

The Job of the Bid

At its heart, the bid is a sales document. This is why bid-writing is often harder than other types of business writing. Most business writing tends to be factually objective. It aims to convey factual information effectively and impartially. For example, a technical report must summarize as succinctly as possible the outcome of a particular activity or situation so that important decisions can be made. A progress report should strive to be a balanced view of achievements and setbacks, again so that key decisions can be taken on the basis of the facts presented.

A proposal has a different job to do. In fact, it has two quite separate jobs, which maybe explains why bid-writing can be difficult to get right. Like a technical report, the proposal has a factual basis. It must convey sufficient information to satisfy the client's interest in the product or service being offered. (What work will be carried out? What deliveries will be made? What payments will be expected? What external dependencies will threaten the schedule?)

The proposal must also be persuasive. It may do this subtly, perhaps by highlighting just how many features there are in your product – or more blatantly by highlighting your rivals' weaknesses. The persuasiveness of your bid takes it beyond the realms of the purely factual, objective report. However, only a light touch is needed because nothing turns a client off faster than hectoring or bragging.

Some people find it hard to write bullishly about their strengths, preferring to 'let the facts speak for themselves'. The trouble is, very often the facts don't speak for themselves. The result tends to be, not surprisingly, a very dry and factual proposal where it is far too easy for the client to miss the significance of these facts. The client must be told (or even better, shown) their significance: what is obvious to you may be far from obvious to the client.

Then there is the risk of losing out to a competing supplier whose proposal is lively and enthusiastic and stylishly presented. It is human nature to respond well to someone showing warmth and passion for a subject, particularly one close to your heart. When there is not much else to separate your bid from the competition, these subjective elements of the proposal are the ones that will count.

WHAT DOES IT TAKE TO WIN?

Suppose a client issues an ITT for a mid-size project. For the sake of argument we will define a mid-size project to be worth something in the region of £5 million. That might easily attract expressions of interest from at least 30 organizations. Some of these will fall away when they study the details of the ITT. A shortlisting process might further reduce the numbers to ten credible bidders. Of these, let us say three are likely to struggle to meet key criteria and will be eliminated during the bid evaluation.

That leaves seven credible bidders in the running. To be credible, most if not all, will have proposed solutions which are fully compliant with the client's requirements. There may be variations in price, approach, delivery methods, chosen products, etc. but by definition each of these seven solutions are capable of meeting the client's objectives. At a pinch, any one of them would do.

So how does the client decide? Once the basic elements of the requirements have been met, the client has the luxury of selecting the winning supplier on the basis of subtleties. He or she will be asking does this supplier really understand my objectives? How easy will it be to work with this organization? Will they value my business or will I have to take a ticket and get in line when we need to talk? Can I believe what this supplier tells me? Can they provide evidence to back up their claims? Little things will matter. Little things may be the difference between winning and losing.

The message to the bid team is clear:

- *Fulfilling* the client's requirements is mandatory – but won't guarantee you will win the work.

- *Telling* the client how you will stand out from the crowd is mandatory – but also won't guarantee a win.

- *Showing* the client what makes your solution unique is highly desirable – and *may* just make the difference between winning and losing.

Anatomy of a Winning Proposal

THE WIN–LOSE GAP

The difference between winning and losing is small. Obviously, if you get the fundamentals wrong, the proposal will fail. But even with the fundamentals in place, it is your attention to the less important details that often decides the winning bid.

Figure 2.1 shows how competing organizations are typically whittled away during the bid process. After initially expressing an interest, in this example three bidders decide not to proceed after completing a detailed analysis of the requirements. At the first stage of selection (e.g. where all the bidders have submitted a proposal for evaluation), one supplier is eliminated. Four suppliers are invited to refine their proposals following dialogue with the client, and resubmit.

Of these, one supplier is unable to meet the revised criteria set by the client. However, the three remaining suppliers all have compliant solutions – any one of them should be capable of executing the work successfully. Although the client is spoilt for choice, the individual suppliers are each looking for a way to distinguish their bid from the competition.

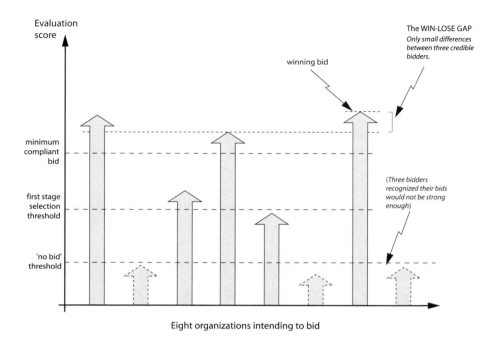

Figure 2.1   Winning – what does it take? *Out of the eight organizations intending to bid, ultimately only one can be successful. The remainder will be eliminated at various stages in the procurement process*

In the final analysis, the difference between winning and losing is likely to be very small. Price could be a factor, but so could the 'value added' elements of each bid. What won't tip the balance is simply meeting all of the client's requirements. All three suppliers have already met that criterion.

Throughout the development of your bid, ask yourself how your client will react. Will they see a winning proposal, or just another also-ran? Table 2.1 describes some of the things that can make a difference.

Table 2.1   The client's view of what makes a winning proposal

The also-ran proposal ...	The winning proposal ...
has a section called *Understanding the Requirement* which mainly repeats material in the ITT. The bid emphasizes the importance of understanding my needs, but doesn't provide any tangible evidence of this understanding.	demonstrates that you know my business. You understand my problems, the environment I work in and what I need from my suppliers. You have demonstrated this through your insightful analysis of my requirements which, in places, even goes beyond what I asked for in the ITT, straight to the heart of the issues that will help my organization run more effectively.
contains all the pertinent information but doesn't present this in a logical structure. The contents page lists only the highest level headings, forcing me to hunt through the entire document for a specific piece of information.	is structured in a logical and consistent way, which lets me go straight to the information I need without first having to read the entire bid.
says the right things but offers no proof or guarantees that they can be delivered. (For example, your proposal emphasizes the value and need for partnership working, but gives no indication how this will be achieved. You say the right things, but I'll need more than this if I'm going to trust you.)	backs up the key messages of the proposal with tangible evidence (perhaps through project references or illustrative examples or references to supporting material in an appendix).
lifts a solution that has worked in the past and offers it up as the right answer. It is weak on the specifics of how this solution will address my unique situation.	recognizes that this requirement is unique. Even though it may be based on a tried and tested solution, the proposal shows how this solution is tailored to fit my particular needs.
is workmanlike. It addresses all the areas I asked you to consider in the ITT, but goes no further.	communicates your enthusiasm for achieving a positive outcome. It demonstrates that you share the same goals as me, and will remain committed right to the end of the project.
addresses the requirements exactly as stated in the ITT. The proposal delivers exactly what I had asked for; no more and no less.	challenges assumptions made in the ITT where there is ambiguity. The proposal probes weak requirements and may even suggest alternatives that I had not considered.
explains (perhaps at great length) how good your organization is and what great value for money you represent, but fails to show how that relates to the needs of my organization.	focuses on my organization and its problems and what you can do to solve them. It addresses the issues on my terms, in language that I understand.
has the appearance of a hasty effort, thrown together in a short period of time, relying too heavily on the dictum that it is the content that matters, not how it is presented.	looks professional – is grammatical and correctly spelled, neatly presented, and has been thoughtfully laid out.

THE MULTIDISCIPLINARY CHALLENGE

One of the things that makes bid-writing difficult is that it requires many different skills. Table 2.2 shows the range of typical roles for a medium-sized bid. On a large bid team, specialists can be employed to provide these skills, but large bids are relatively uncommon. For every big proposal, there are dozens of smaller bids put together by one or two bid writers as dictated by the economics of the situation. Except in the largest organizations, it is simply not feasible to employ a big team of specialists assembling the technical parts of a proposal to order. More often, the team is small and working under severe pressure.

With so many different facets to the job, a proposal writer must often be a jack of all trades.

Table 2.2   The multidisciplinary skills of the bid writer

The role ...	The skills ...
Project manager	Scheduling and controlling the assembly and production of the bid (and on this kind of project, missing the delivery deadline is not an option). Knowledge of project management techniques will also be needed for the management sections of the proposal.
Human resources manager	Encouraging and motivating the bid team. A motivated team will not only be more productive, but the enthusiasm will be indirectly communicated through the quality of the resulting bid and in any face-to-face meetings with the client.
Researcher	The more you know about the client, their requirements and their business environment, the better you are able to form a solution to match these needs.
Salesman	Able to play to the strengths of your offering and compensate for its weaknesses. A client will need convincing; it is the job of a salesman to be persuasive.
Writer	The style of the proposal must be authoritative, informative, clear, concise and grammatical.
Editor	You cannot afford to submit first draft material. The proposal is an example of the standard of work you will produce for the client; don't give a second-rate impression. A good proposal must be honed from early drafts like a sculptor chipping away at a block of stone to reveal a work of art.
Illustrator	Everyone knows a picture is worth a thousand words. Using a diagram or two to convey important ideas will have twice the impact of a page of text.
Analyst	The client doesn't always express their requirements accurately in the ITT. Sometimes you will need to do further work to understand what they meant, and what is really needed.
Technologist	You must understand the essence of the technical solution (even if you are not technical). If there are technical specialists involved in the bid, you must still keep a grip on the overall technical solution and be able to explain how this will meet the client's requirements.

Table 2.2   *Concluded*

The role ...	The skills ...
Designer	The most obvious solution is not necessarily the best one. You may need to explore and discard several options before discovering the ideal solution.
Innovator	The solution contained in your proposal must stand out from the crowd. It must grab the client and convince them that your solution is the only one that really *works* for them. The way to do this is to give them something they weren't expecting (in a nice sense!)
Opportunist	Occasionally, opportunities present themselves where you can offer more than you have been asked for. Perhaps there is a synergy between your product set and the client's environment – exploit it. You need to be alert to these opportunities; they can be a major discriminator between you and your competitors.
Bean counter	You must be constantly worrying how your proposal will be scored. Look for any way to make the life of the evaluator that bit easier. Don't give them any excuse to mark the proposal down.
Perfectionist	The details matter and they need to be right.
Pragmatist	Accept that there will never be enough time to do everything you would like, so prioritizing the most important tasks is essential.
'Big picture' guy	Someone needs to visualize the proposal in its entirety. Details are important, but so is the ability to step back from them and spot any gaps in coverage. Your proposal needs to be accessible to a wide audience, some of whom may not have time to look at all the detail.
Accountant	Costing the proposal and understanding where the contingency and profit lie are essential if the proposal is to be commercially viable.
Risk analyst	Any piece of work will have some risk attached to it. The more you understand the implication of these risks, the better you can plan to prevent them. A good risk-management strategy will give the client confidence that you know what you are doing.
The client	You must be able to see things from the client's perspective; their issues, worries and objectives. Your proposal will usually be evaluated by a number of people, so the situation is complicated by multiple personal views as well as the corporate perspective.

Five Stages in the Bid Life Cycle

The bid life cycle begins with an *analysis of the opportunity*. Before committing resources to a bid we need to have confidence that it is a viable proposition. Is it both technically and commercially feasible?

Assuming it is, what will it take to win the contract? We need to *formulate a strategy to win*. This means answering questions such as: what are the critical requirements? What precisely is the client looking for?

Then comes the hard work: first in *creating a feasible proposal*, and secondly in making sure it meets all the *quality standards and compliance criteria*.

Once the proposal is finished and signed off, we enter the production stage: *bid assembly and dispatch*. Since there is usually little time left ahead of the submission deadline, it is important this is planned for well in advance.

Finally comes a vital but often overlooked stage – the *transition to the project* (assuming we have indeed produced the winning bid). This is where the knowledge and insights gained by the bid team must be transferred to the incoming project team, otherwise we risk handicapping the project, possibly irrecoverably so.

Figure 2.2 shows the five key stages in the bid life cycle. These same stages are just as important for a 10-day job as for a multi-million pound bid. All that changes is the scale of effort involved at each stage.

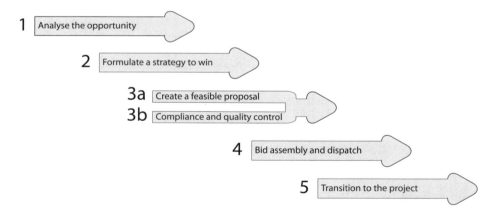

Figure 2.2   **The five stages of the bid life cycle.** *Each stage is relevant no matter how large or small the bid is. For the smallest of bids, they may last only hours. On a large bid, they may be measured in months or even years*

ANALYSE THE OPPORTUNITY

Businesses are always hungry for work. Without a steady stream of new contracts, an organization will quickly go out of business. That means trawling for opportunities wherever they can be found and being prepared to venture into new territory if the opportunity arises. But not every opportunity will be the right one. Better to find this out quickly before too much time and effort has been spent. This is the key goal of this stage. Is this the right opportunity for our organization? Are we really capable of meeting the objectives? Is it a sound commercial proposition? You should expect some opportunities to fail to qualify.

An efficient business will be able to qualify a prospect early on. Those that don't make the grade must be discarded, no matter how enticing. Remember that bid resources are finite and must therefore be used with care.

FORMULATE A STRATEGY TO WIN

Don't be fooled into thinking that a bid is a repeat of something you have delivered before. Every bid is different: a different client, different business environment, different objectives, different constraints. There is always something that makes each bid unique. Recognizing this uniqueness means formulating a delivery strategy that is tailored to these specific circumstances, even though the core of what you offer (e.g. a product or standard set of services) remains the same.

There is an important difference between the *offering* and the *solution*. Your offering is the off-the-shelf thing that you supply: perhaps a product or a service-based offering or a type of specialist consultancy. But your offering is not really what the client is interested in. He or she wants a solution – something that meets their own objectives, fits into their business environment, doesn't interfere with existing processes and will, over time, provide some tangible benefits. Whilst the offering may be the major ingredient, the way that the offering is deployed, tailored, integrated, managed, customized and configured is what really matters. This is your solution and it is uniquely yours.

Take a look at Figure 2.3. In each case, a supplier tries to provide the same offering to two different clients. However, two different solutions need to be prepared by tailoring the offering to meet specific client requirements. In this way, each solution addresses different aspects of how the project will be executed – elements which are unique to each client. One of the key tasks of the proposal is to describe both the offering *and* the solution to show that there is a good match to the client's requirements.

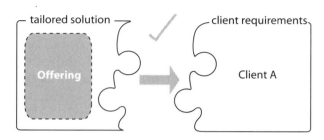

The offering is the core of the proposal but needs packaging as a tailored solution to meet the client's requirements.

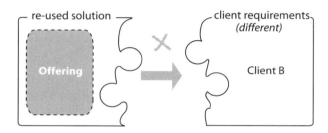

Reusing the bid solution for a different client almost certainly won't be acceptable even if the offering is the right one for the job.

Figure 2.3   **One offering but many different solutions.** *Each solution is specifically tailored to the needs of a client and forms a wrapper around the common core offering*

Offering

An offering is the product, service or skill set which your organization sells. Offerings can be described without reference to specific clients. There are many different types. For instance, the offerings of a product-based company are the *products* that appear in the sales catalogue – the laptops, disc drives, shrink-wrapped software or whatever. Part of your offering may be the *technical expertise* needed to configure and deploy your off-the-shelf components.

Systems integrators or consultancies will have offerings based solely on the *skills and knowledge* of their staff, for example the ability to design customized solutions or the know-how to implement enterprise management applications. *Outsourced facilities* is yet another kind of offering.

Notice how the *highlighted* words define what you offer (i.e. the 'offering') but don't reveal how you do it. This is the job of the solution.

Solution

The solution is the unique customization, configuration or delivery approach you are proposing to the client. It is the totality of what will be delivered. The offering only says what the client is buying, but the solution describes how it will be delivered and made to work, specifically:

- how the offering will be tailored;

- the delivery process;

- installation and roll-out across the business;

- seamless integration into the client's other business activities;

- how support will be tailored to the client's needs;

- how the benefits of the solution will be measured.

It is easy to distinguish between the offering and the solution. Your organization will have only one set of offerings – the things that it does or produces – but each client will demand a different solution. Being able to properly convey both aspects is a key requirement of the bid.

CREATE A FEASIBLE PROPOSAL

Creating a feasible proposal is the underlying theme of this book. Some of the most common causes of project failure are 'programmed in' during the bid stage: unrealistic objectives, faulty assumptions, poorly understood constraints, badly estimated tasks, etc. If the proposal isn't feasible, no amount of clever project management later on is going to recover the situation.

Developing a feasible proposal demands some important skills:

- Scoping – revealing the nature of a task in its entirety and then figuring out what must actually be done to complete a particular task.

- Estimation – poor estimation methods lie at the heart of many project disasters.

- Architecting a plan – this requires skill in prioritizing, sequencing and establishing sensible contingency measures.

- Risk management – keeping the analysis practical and timely is often the challenge.

- Creative thinking – this may be the deciding factor both in winning the work and in delivering it with commercial success.

COMPLIANCE AND QUALITY CONTROL

Many proposals are unsuccessful because they don't give the client what they asked for. This may be a straightforward omission, for example failing to comply with specific instructions on how to bid, or providing a response which doesn't address all of the client's requirements. It may be more subtle – perhaps failing to fully appreciate the client's perspective, thereby providing answers to the wrong questions.

The compliance stage ensures that the client's bid instructions are followed to the letter, checks that the proposal addresses all of the client's requirements (and is presented in a way that the client can relate to) and verifies that the supplier's own quality control standards have been followed.

BID ASSEMBLY AND DISPATCH

Fundamentally, producing the winning proposal means getting the job done. Miss the submission deadline and it makes no difference how well you followed the bid process. The client doesn't know how hard you worked or how organized you were (or weren't). All they get to see is the end result. So bid production must always take priority. Put your project management skills to good use to plan, coordinate, prioritize and manage all the constituents of the bid.

TRANSITION TO THE PROJECT

The final stage is all about giving the delivery project the best chance of success. It may not always be possible to arrange for continuity of staff between bid team and project team, but there are other ways to transfer the knowledge: good bid documentation, organization of materials, thorough briefing sessions and above all, a willingness to discuss risks and problem areas that the project team may not otherwise discover for themselves until it is too late.

Summary: The Anatomy of a Bid

- The writing of a bid is a balance between *salesmanship* (i.e. convincing the client that your solution offers best value for money) and feasibility (i.e. ensuring that what is offered can be delivered by the project team).

- The *win–lose gap* for competitive bids is often very small. If all other factors are equal, an enthusiastic and motivated bid team will quickly be apparent to the client and is a key factor in success.

- A fully compliant bid should be sufficient to put the supplier into the final stage of the competition – but no more. Success will be determined by other discriminators and any *added value* that can be offered.

- The bid team need *multidisciplinary skills*. Depending on team size, individuals may be challenged to perform a number of different roles.

- Know the difference between your *offering* (your standard products or services) and your *solution* (the unique packaging of your offering to meet the client's objectives).

- Every bid comprises five main stages:

- Stage 1: *Analyse the opportunity.* Not all bids are worth pursuing. Disqualify weak opportunities as early as possible.
- Stage 2: *Formulate a strategy to win.* Every bid is unique, even if there are superficial similarities. The *offering* and the *solution* are different things.
- Stage 3a: *Create a feasible proposal.* Balance the desire to impress the client against the need to stay 'grounded' by what the project team can actually deliver.
- Stage 3b: *Compliance and quality control.* Check you are giving the client what they have asked for and are following your own organization's guidelines.
- Stage 4: *Bid assembly and dispatch.* Get the job done in time. Put project management skills to good use to plan, coordinate, prioritize and manage the inputs to the bid.
- Stage 5: *Transition to the project.* Think how best to transfer knowledge and information to the incoming project team.

3

Planning to Win

Planning is an unnatural process; it is much more fun to do something.
The nicest thing about not planning is that failure comes as a complete
surprise rather than being preceded by a period of worry and depression.
Sir John Harvey-Jones, UK businessman and author, 1924–2008

So far, we have identified the need to establish a solid project framework during the bid stage and seen how this influences project success. We have also recognized that the bid must be persuasive and well-structured, or there won't ever be a project to worry about. In the following chapters we will look at the techniques which enable this to happen. First, we must look at what it takes to plan and organize the winning bid.

Even if you are not the bid manager, personal organization is essential. You will need to understand your role in the bid plan, when you need to deliver your contributions to the bid and how these will be reviewed and incorporated into the final proposal.

Planning the Bid

Producing any proposal is a mini-project in its own right. It requires most of the planning, monitoring and controls that a fully-fledged project does. If the bid is anything more than a simple quote, someone must assume the role of Bid Manager. It is down to the Bid Manager to plan, organize, lead and coordinate all the work leading up to the submission of the proposal to the client – and sometimes beyond.

THE BID MANAGER'S RESPONSIBILITIES

It is best to think of the Bid Manager as the project manager for the duration of the bid work. Their responsibilities begin with the receipt of the ITT (sometimes even earlier) and only end when the contract is won or lost. In the intervening period the Bid Manager will need to cover a lot of ground:

- Evaluating the ITT; getting a bid/no-bid decision from the stakeholders.

- Creating and maintaining the proposal structure.

- Agreeing the win themes and proposal discriminators.

- Arranging for research into any weak areas of the proposal.

- Managing the bid team and delegating tasks effectively.

- Organizing (and sometimes contributing to) the writing, editing and polishing of the text.

- Coordinating presentational material (e.g. production of graphics, tables, schedules, accounts, marketing materials, etc.).

- Arranging formal bid reviews and the sign-off of key stages.

- Producing the proposal package (e.g. overseeing printing of the required number of copies, packaging and delivery).

- Getting a debrief from the client (win or lose).

- Transferring knowledge and responsibilities to the delivery team (if successful).

- Learning lessons and improving the process for next time.

Planning really is the key to success when writing a proposal. If you cut corners or peak too early, you may deliver the bid on time, but it will be substandard and probably won't be the one accepted by the client. Adding material at the end of the bid life cycle to 'beef the proposal up' is rarely as effective as steadily building the proposal throughout the bidding period. Focus too hard on one particular area or fail to allocate effort proportionately, and the bid will be patchy and incomplete. On a long bid (say a month or more), it is important to get this balance right.

The art of preparation and planning is knowing in advance what needs to be done and what resources it will take. You can only do this if you have a properly defined bid process to follow. Without one, you may forget important things, run out of time, or waste precious effort on non-essential tasks.

JUST DO IT ... (A CAUTIONARY TALE)

The day the ITT hit his desk, George leapt enthusiastically into action. Skim-reading the key chapters, by lunchtime he already had the major sections of the proposal mapped out. He knew he ought to assign a technical architect to develop the detailed solution and a project manager to draft the project plan, but that would take a couple of days to organize and the bid was due in a fortnight. George didn't want to wait. He was pretty sure he knew what the client needed. He could get the bulk of the proposal written himself and draft the others in for the finishing touches.

At the end of four days, George had an impressive amount of material assembled and ready in final draft. He had written the Executive Summary which emphasized the client's key themes. He had made ballpark calculations to come up with a price which seemed reasonable and he had pulled in detailed spec sheets from tried-and-tested products used on a previous bid. With a week to go, George was feeling confident that the bid was 80 per cent done.

Then it all started to go wrong. The technical architect pointed out some awkward requirements George had overlooked which weren't covered by the products he had selected. Soon after, the project support office informed him that the client's delivery milestones were unachievable with the resources at hand. When George went back and looked at the ITT in more detail he realized he had misjudged the essence of what the client was asking for. Worse, having spoken to the account manager, it was clear George's price was far beyond the client's budget. With only a few days left before submission, most of what George had produced was useless.

No doubt you spotted many of George's mistakes. Involving others in an early review might have teased out subtleties in the ITT. Design problems could have been spotted early on, avoiding the dead-end solution that George pursued. Early development of a cost model would have highlighted difficulties in achieving the budget. More effort in understanding the client's objectives and developing a suitable delivery strategy would have kept the proposal focused. Unfortunately, without a plan to make best use of the bid resources, the efforts of George and his small team were disjointed and counter-productive.

George's fatal mistake? He threw planning out the window in favour of just getting on with it.

DEADLINES – HITTING 'THE WALL'

At some stage in your bid, you may encounter 'the wall'. This is the point when you can clearly see that the sum of the uncompleted tasks exceeds the total time remaining. It is the realization that something has to give. It is also a key decision point (see Figure 3.1).

What to do? There are really only two solutions. The first is to find a way to gain more time, i.e. push the deadline further away. In practice, this can only be done if the client is willing to grant an extension to the bidding period. At best, it provides a temporary reprieve and even then, you still may not get everything done. The bid plan should never rely on an extension being granted – but there is no harm in seizing the opportunity if it arises.

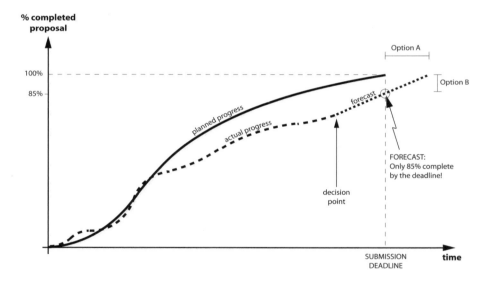

Figure 3.1   **Hitting the wall.** *A decision is needed as soon as it becomes clear the bid is forecast to miss the submission deadline. Option A: seek an extension to the bidding period from the client. Option B: reduce the scope of the remaining work. (This is where your earlier planning and prioritization will pay off.)*

The second way is to reduce the amount of work to be done. You can do this by ruthlessly prioritizing tasks and concentrating on the highest priorities first – these must be the things that will make the biggest difference to your proposal. Writing a bid is invariably a time-limited exercise so you need to ensure that the highest-value tasks (i.e. those that will score you most points in the proposal evaluation) are done *first*.

EXTENDING THE SUBMISSION DEADLINE

If you are struggling to keep to your bid schedule, requesting an extension may give you the extra time needed to complete fundamentally important parts of the proposal. Before doing so, consider the following points:

- How will the client view a request for an extension? Will it be seen as an indicator of your organization's poor management or inability to deliver to schedule?

- Are there reasonable grounds for an extension? If so, your request needs to emphasize the advantages to the client, i.e. more time enables a more considered response to be provided, which clearly benefits the client.

- Expect your competitors to use the extra time to improve their bids. Requesting an extension might actually be giving competitors a greater advantage.

- Make sure your bid plan doesn't rely on seeking an extension if some of the tasks overrun. It is better to assume the client will refuse an extension and then be pleasantly surprised, not the other way round.

PRIORITIZING TASKS

There has yet to be a bid that can't be improved with just a little more time spent on it. But time is always in short supply. Planning the bid will demand hard decisions to be made; you simply won't be able to do everything you would like. So make sure the things you spend time on are the things most likely to have a positive influence on the client.

Assume you *will* run out of time. If you clearly prioritize each task during the initial planning stage, you will have minimized the impact on the bid. Work methodically from highest to lowest priority. The things you haven't been able to do are therefore the things that will make least difference.

The assessment of priority boils down to one question: what impact will this have on the client's evaluation of my bid? Look critically at each task in your plan and ask yourself what contribution it makes to this goal. Then, if (when!) you begin to run out of time, the priorities will guide you on what to skip and what to focus attention on. It is up to you how many priority levels you work with, but more than five or six will begin to be a burden to manage. Table 3.1 describes a typical prioritization scheme.

Completing your level 1 priorities is really the absolute minimum for your proposal to even be considered by the client. Level 1 and 2 priorities together will typically result in a mid-ranking proposal. In other words, your production plan must ensure you have resources to complete all your level 1 and 2 priorities, with something to spare.

Achieving level 3 priorities should put your bid among the leading contenders. Level 4 priorities are the icing on the cake or, if you prefer, your chance to 'go the extra mile'. These give the proposal a final polish, perhaps by offering the client some additional value over and above a narrow interpretation of their requirements, or demonstrating your professionalism in the attention shown to the details.

Table 3.1   A useful task prioritization scheme

Priority Level	Meaning
Level 1	The outputs from these tasks are *mandated* by the client in the ITT or Statement of Requirements. If Level 1 tasks are not fully completed, the proposal will be judged non-compliant. Examples of level 1 priorities: • inclusion of material under all section headings specified in the ITT • clear and complete definition of what is being offered • presentation of price information • compliance with tender packaging and labelling instructions • timely delivery of proposal to the client! Unsurprisingly, failing to complete level 1 tasks means a high probability of the proposal being rejected.
Level 2	The outputs from these tasks are *expected* by the client. Failure to provide them is likely to result in a lower evaluation mark than would otherwise be the case. Examples of level 2 priorities: • demonstration of your understanding of the client's business context • satisfactory level of detail provided under all section headings • estimates underpinning a competitive price • summary of relevant track record, skills and experience

Table 3.1   *Concluded*

Priority Level	Meaning
Level 3	These tasks have a strong likelihood of *positively discriminating* your bid from your competitors. Examples of level 3 priorities: • innovative approaches and solutions • addressing quality control issues • illustration of value from the client's perspective • attention to stylistic detail (e.g. consistency, absence of spelling mistakes, clear and distinctive style, use of meaningful diagrams) • logical structuring of information
Level 4	Outputs from level 4 tasks *reinforce* your key themes and provide convincing justification for your bid. Examples of level 4 priorities: • tangible evidence to support claims made in your proposal • amplification of important messages • innovative approaches and ideas, some of which may go beyond the client's requirements • demonstration of enthusiasm and commitment
Level 5	Level 5 tasks are *distraction* tasks: things which seem important or urgent but don't significantly add value. A poorly designed bid process will often impose bureaucratic tasks of limited value. Avoid doing any level 5 tasks if at all possible.

The Bid Process

The bid process governs the way the bid team prepares, develops and delivers the proposal to the client. If well thought out, the bid process is a blueprint for success.

Most successful proposals are not the result of chance. They have been created by following a well-honed bid process, designed to guide the bid team in the right direction. Those who choose not to follow a bid process trust to their instincts and a large dose of luck that 'things will come right' for them.

The point of having an established bid process is that it ensures that the right things are done at the right time and that nothing gets forgotten. It removes the element of chance. Even though each proposal is unique, the bid process ensures quality and consistency. It asks the same pertinent questions, although the answers are different in each case.

The bid process is a guiding framework but it is not a prescriptive join-the-dots formula. Original thought and hard work are, unfortunately, still required. However, the bid process will marshal these activities to greatest effect.

Figure 3.2 illustrates a typical high-level bid process. Most of these elements can (and probably should) be broken down into more detailed activities that fit with your organization's preferred way of working. You may already have a well-developed bid process which may differ in some of the details. That is fine – nevertheless it is important that all of the elements in Figure 3.2 appear in some guise or other, or you may be missing crucial steps in the process.

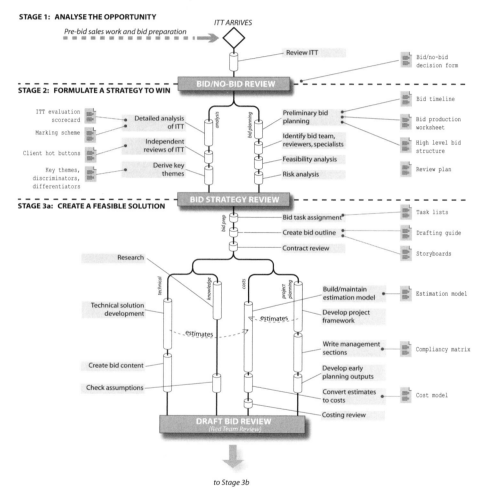

Figure 3.2a   A bid process (stages 1 to 3a). *The benefit of a bid process is that all tasks and decision points are clearly identified, enabling interim goals to be set and the bid writing work to be prioritized and planned*

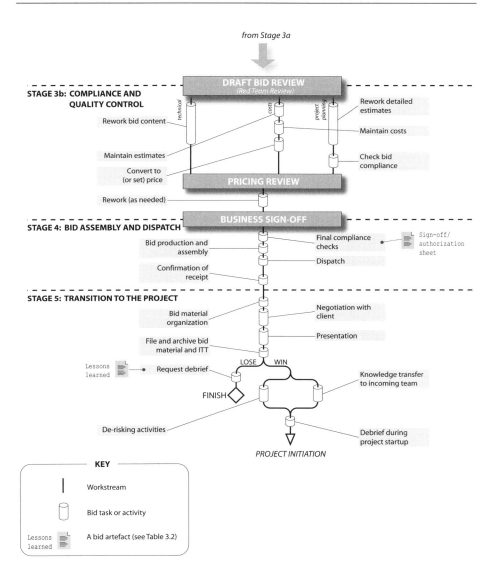

from Stage 3a

DRAFT BID REVIEW
(Red Team Review)

STAGE 3b: COMPLIANCE AND QUALITY CONTROL

technical

costs

project planning

Rework bid content

Rework detailed estimates

Maintain costs

Maintain estimates

Check bid compliance

Convert to (or set) price

PRICING REVIEW

Rework (as needed)

BUSINESS SIGN-OFF

STAGE 4: BID ASSEMBLY AND DISPATCH

Bid production and assembly

Final compliance checks

Sign-off/ authorization sheet

Confirmation of receipt

Dispatch

STAGE 5: TRANSITION TO THE PROJECT

Bid material organization

Negotiation with client

File and archive bid material and ITT

Presentation

LOSE   WIN

Lessons learned

Request debrief

Knowledge transfer to incoming team

FINISH

De-risking activities

Debrief during project startup

PROJECT INITIATION

KEY

| Workstream

Bid task or activity

Lessons learned   A bid artefact (see Table 3.2)

Figure 3.2b   A bid process (stages 3b to 5)

The Bid Writer's Toolkit

Any kind of craftsman needs a good set of tools to do their job well. The bid writer is no exception to this. Some of the 'tools' are obvious – space in which to work, a minimally disruptive working environment, computers, printers and photocopiers, etc. Beyond these essentials, there is much that can be done which will save considerable time and increase the chances of producing a winning proposal.

Working from a liberal definition, 'tools' can mean anything from reference material, information repositories and Internet access to word processing and graphics software. The point about tools is that they are there to save time, ensure consistency and provide a support environment for the tough job (yours!) of writing the winning proposal.

Your chosen bid process is an important part of this toolkit. It comprises a number of interim outputs or 'artefacts'. These are stepping stones on the way to the finished proposal – not necessarily sections of the proposal itself, but necessary pieces of work which result in a more polished bid than would otherwise be the case.

In the following chapters we will make reference to a number of bid artefacts which are introduced in Table 3.2. These form an integral part of the bid process. Together they help the bid team to make best use of available resources and focus on the things that will have the biggest impact on the client.

Table 3.2   Bid artefacts

Type of artefact	Meaning and use
Bid/no-bid decision form	*Establishes whether it makes sound economic and business sense to spend the time needed to write the proposal.* This form helps you evaluate the chances of success objectively by highlighting areas of weakness. Writing a proposal is labour-intensive and you can't bid for everything. Save your resources for the most promising opportunities. Knowing when to bid is the most important decision in the whole process.
ITT evaluation scorecard	*Assesses the completeness of the client's tender documents.* It is a mistake to assume the client always produces a well-defined tender. Begin by taking a critical look at the ITT. What is missing? What is the client not telling you? Does the client's requirement make sense? You need to know if you have been given enough information from which to produce a credible bid.

Table 3.2   *Continued*

Type of artefact	Meaning and use
Marking scheme	*Helps with understanding how your proposal will be evaluated by the client.* Many clients use a formal marking scheme to eliminate substandard bids and create a shortlist where more subjective measures come into play. Knowing the relative weighting of marks against each section of your proposal means you can focus on these areas to greatest effect.
Bid timeline	*Keeps track of how the bid is developing against the key milestones.* All bids, no matter how small, need careful planning. If you misjudge the pace of bid production and run out of time, you will almost certainly have failed. A bid timeline can help you stay on track. Break the work down into manageable chunks and monitor how you are doing against these interim deadlines.
Client hot-buttons	*Identifies the issues that really matter to the client.* The ITT is crammed full of things that the client says he wants, but you can be sure that some areas are more important than others. Knowing what these are lets you focus on the client's 'hot-buttons' and make sure there is no doubt about how you will satisfy them. Hot-buttons are often unintentionally well-disguised. This worksheet helps you find them and make sure they feature prominently in your proposal.
Key themes	*Consolidates key sales messages and makes sure these are reinforced throughout the proposal.* Key themes are the parts of your bid that should have the evaluator nodding and putting a metaphorical tick in the margin. They may be things the client has specifically asked for, or things he didn't realize he wanted until he read them in your bid. There may even be a subset of themes which are unique to your bid (i.e. discriminators or differentiators) – something which your competitors won't be able to offer.
Discriminators and differentiators	*Emphasizes to the client what makes your proposal unique.* Discriminators and differentiators are what set your bid apart from the competition. Many of the bids submitted will share key themes, but your discriminators are unique; they are the reasons why the client will prefer your bid to all the others. True discriminators tend to be few and far between: if you have them, be sure to make the most of the opportunity. Chapter 4 provides more detail on these.
Bid production worksheet	*Makes sure the instructions in the ITT are followed to the letter.* Sometimes an ITT will provide a checklist to follow (e.g. 3 volumes, prices contained in Section 8, no more than 10 pages for the executive summary, submit five bound copies, etc.) These instructions may be scattered through the ITT. Although you spot them on the first read-through, by the time of submission, they might have been forgotten about. Gather these instructions into one place (i.e. the bid production worksheet) and then you can check them off before the bid is submitted.

Table 3.2 *Continued*

Type of artefact	Meaning and use
High-level structure/detailed proposal structure	*Delivers a well-structured proposal that is both readable and logically organized.* Mapping out the structure gives you a feel for the scope of the proposal, where most effort is needed and how to allocate the sections amongst the team. It is invaluable for the rest of the team to see where their contribution fits and helps to avoid duplication. Begin at the top level section headings and then work out the detailed breakdown in each section. Expect the structure to change as the bid strategy evolves.
Storyboards	*Summarize key sections of the proposal. These can be refined before the labour-intensive writing work begins.* The objective of your proposal is to convey the appropriate information as clearly as possible to the client. Storyboarding techniques help to ensure a logical sequence and guide you in linking your facts with the recurring themes of your proposal. Many people find it helps to be very clear on the messages to be conveyed *before* starting writing. Working from a storyboard keeps the text focused on the facts and free from padding. On a large bid, storyboards enable all team members to get a clear overview of the detailed proposal structure.
Drafting guide	*Provides consistency of style, format and tone.* It is easy to waste a lot of time reformatting contributions from different writers, eliminating differences in style and generally smoothing out the inconsistencies that arise when several people are working on one document. By adopting a drafting guide at the start of the bid, many of these problems can be avoided.
Cost model	*Contains a detailed breakdown of costs for every element described in the bid.* A lot of otherwise excellent proposals fail because the bid pricing is left to the last minute. Unless you are fortunate enough to be offering services from a priced catalogue, pricing your solution can be a tricky and time-consuming affair. The job of the cost model is to let you understand what the *cost to you* will be and this figure needs to be as accurate as you can make it. The *price* offered to the client is a subjective sales decision.
Review plan	*Gives the bid reviewers advance warning of what contributions are expected from them.* The review plan identifies the type of review, when the material will be ready, when review comments are needed and who (or what type of person) will be doing the review. If your bid schedule doesn't allocate time for an effective review before submission, you are seriously damaging the quality of your bid.
Compliancy matrix	*Proves to the client you have provided everything that has been asked for.* This is a failsafe device in case the client can't find specific information in your bid. Its main purpose is to cross-reference each requirement in the ITT to the response in your proposal. It should leave the client in no doubt that you have answered *in full* every question that has been asked.

Table 3.2   *Concluded*

Type of artefact	Meaning and use
Sign-off/authorization sheet	*Makes sure the bid passes the necessary internal approval stages in good time.* Most organizations have policies on who needs to sign off a proposal before submission. This may be related to the financial value of the bid, the type of work, or other factors which are specific to your organization. Make sure these people have been primed to play their role and that the sign-off doesn't delay submission. Having a sign-off sheet is also a good way to record these decisions for posterity.

Remember: these are only suggestions for what should be included in your bid process. Which ones you use (and how you apply them) will vary according to your circumstances. Try them out and see if they work for you, but don't be afraid to modify or discard anything that isn't making the bid process effective.

THE BENEFITS OF USING A BID PROCESS

The good … Here are just some of the benefits of adopting a formal bid process:

- *Roles*: everyone involved in the bid understands what is expected of them.

- *Planning*: without a clear bid process, it is hard to plan the work and the bid may run out of time.

- *Efficiency*: the bid process saves times by ensuring the right things are done at the right time.

- *Prioritization*: right from the start, assume you will not have sufficient time to do everything you would like to. The bid process will help to prioritize and focus the team's efforts on the things that will have the biggest influence on the client's evaluation criteria.

- *Completeness*: important things won't get forgotten. The bid process makes sure your proposal addresses all of the client's requirements and that the bidding instructions are followed.

- *Creativity*: a good bid process allows for creativity which is what gives your bid an edge – 95 per cent of your proposal will be indistinguishable from your competitors, so the creative elements will make a real difference between success and failure.

- *Reusability*: once created, the bid process can be reused efficiently and effectively many times. (This doesn't alter the fact that every bid is different, even though the process that creates each bid is the same.) Once you have a refined bid process, your success rate will increase.

The bad … If you don't already have an established bid process, you will need to consider carefully what is right for your situation. Here are some of the pitfalls:

- *Start-up costs*: if you don't yet have a bid process in place, it can be a lot of work to set up. Don't try and do this at the same time as responding to an ITT. The bid process needs to be firmly established *before* you write a bid.

- *Cumbersome*: don't allow your bid process to become unwieldy or bureaucratic. If in doubt, ask yourself, 'How is this contributing to the overall quality of the proposal I submit?' If you are doing things for no tangible benefit, drop them from the bid process.

- *Flexible*: the bid process must encourage creativity in the bid team, not stifle it. Don't allow your bid process to become rigid and inflexible. Good ideas should always be welcomed. Look out for early warnings, such as: 'We can't take this approach because the bid process won't allow it.'

- *Comprehensible*: you and your team must be able to understand the process in terms of what needs to be done and why. If the process is unclear and confusing, its benefits are lost. Keep the process (and the supporting worksheets) as simple as possible.

STARTING FROM SCRATCH

If you don't have an established process, you will either need to build on existing informal methods or start from scratch – but don't leave this until you have an important bid to write. Creating or modifying your bid process must be treated as a separate activity to bid-writing. Writing a proposal is stressful enough without this additional burden.

Above all, keep your bid process streamlined. Anything which doesn't result in an improvement in the quality of the bid or a production efficiency is a distraction and should be discarded.

Here are some suggestions on how to begin defining your bid process:

- Involve others who are regularly involved in bid-writing. It makes sense to share ideas and concerns and reach a consensus before imposing a process on others.

- Prioritize the key elements of the bid process into three groups:

   1. Simple changes which can be easily introduced and which will have some measurably positive effect.
   2. Changes which will have a large effect (e.g. through improving the quality or efficiency of the bid process) but which require significant resources to implement.
   3. Everything else.

Set a timetable for making changes to the bid process, according to the priorities above. Don't be too ambitious: the essential elements can be put in place quite quickly, but other parts of the process may take some months and will need refining through trial and error on several bids.

Summary: Planning to Win

- *Plan the bid work* as you would any other project. The duration of the bid may be relatively brief, but the same kind of plans and controls will be needed. Don't be tempted to rush ahead just because the timescales are short.

- Devote careful thought to *prioritizing the bid tasks*. Every piece of work needs to be justified in terms of the value it will add to the finished proposal.

- *Be pragmatic* if you recognize you are likely to hit 'the wall'. You may have to cut some lower-priority tasks, or consider asking for an extension to the submission deadline.

- *An established bid process will save time* and help create a high-quality proposal (e.g. by making sure that important things are not forgotten).

- A good bid process *takes time to establish.* Don't try to develop or refine the process while in the middle of a bid. Plan this as a separate activity.

- A bid process is not about filling in forms and worksheets. It is about the *information, the thought processes and the decisions* which naturally arise from compiling the various bid artefacts.

- There must be room in your bid process for *creativity*. Following the bid process is not a joining-the-dots exercise; it must empower the team, not constrain them.

4

Analysing the Requirements in Depth

What we do not understand we do not possess.
Johann Wolfgang von Goethe, German poet and novelist, 1749–1832

Once the chores of initial planning and organization are done, the strength of the bid will depend on understanding exactly what it is the client wants. Unless you are lucky enough to have had extensive contact with the client before the tender process began, your main (and perhaps only) source of information will be the ITT.

No matter how overwhelming the urge to begin writing the proposal, there is a great risk of wasted effort until the ITT has been properly analysed. The client's requirements are central to the construction of the proposal. Until these are fully understood, it is difficult to build any aspect of the project framework.

This chapter looks at how to analyse the requirements in depth and how to begin structuring the key messages.

Ignore the Requirements at your Peril

Many project failures can be attributed to early misunderstandings between the project team and the client. These give rise to differences between what the client expects and what the project team actually delivers. Many such misunderstandings trace their roots back to the bid stage. It is therefore important to pay close attention to the ITT provided by the client for two very good reasons:

1. Without in-depth analysis of the ITT, it is unlikely the proposal will be selected by the client. Either an inappropriate solution will be offered or, if subtle clues are missed in the ITT, the bid won't address important themes and will fail to appeal to the client.

2. Even if a flawed proposal were successful, since the ITT has not been analysed properly, the basis for the project is still invalid. The project team may begin work on an altogether different premise to the client's. It may take quite a while before someone notices the different assumptions, expectations or goals, by which time it may be too late to avert disaster.

As a project manager, you will certainly have a vested interest in avoiding the second scenario. If you are also the bid manager, then the success of your bid is closely linked to the first scenario. Indeed, whatever your role, analysing the requirements in depth is absolutely fundamental otherwise the resulting bid will be unfocused and lack persuasion.

Reviewing the ITT

It is good practice for everyone involved in the bid to review the ITT. Furthermore, it is *essential* for the bid manager to do so – probably many times over. This can be tedious, so the process may be helped by having specific goals in mind, i.e. particular information or themes to be alert to. These then determine how the bid is structured and developed in later stages.

Here are some suggestions (by no means an exhaustive list) for what to look for in the ITT:

- What are the key themes (e.g. issues likely to be of particular importance to the client)?

- What are the risks (a) for the client, and (b) for you, as supplier? These might need to be broken down into different areas, e.g. technical risks, business risks, management risks, etc.

- What is the project dependent on? There are usually external dependencies on third-party organizations (e.g. other suppliers, subcontractors, or partner organizations), as well as dependencies on the client.

- What are the key planning dates (e.g. client milestones, delivery dates, contractual dates, payment dates)?

- What are the deliverable items?

- What are the client's goals?

- How will the client judge the success of the project? What are the ultimate business objectives?

- What are the quality standards to be achieved? Are these objective or subjective?

- Who are the client stakeholders? These are the individuals or organizations with a vested interest or influence over the project, e.g. end users, management boards, shareholders.

Key Themes

In every proposal there are a handful of important points that summarize or characterize your bid. It may be an emphasis on a particular aspect of the client's requirement, a strength in the product or service you are offering, or an innovative approach you are proposing to take. When all else has been taken note of, these are the messages you would like the client to remember.

Understanding (and making good use of) key themes is one of the differences between a workmanlike proposal and a winning proposal. A workmanlike proposal answers all the questions, but it lacks energy, boldness and enthusiasm. Key themes will help you make the most of the inherent strengths of your solution:

- Defining your key themes forces you to understand the particular features of your bid that will be attractive to the client. Once these are clear in your mind, it will be easier to communicate them.

- Writing down the key themes helps to ensure that everyone involved in the bid understands the importance of these themes and shares the same vision of the solution.

- The key themes serve as a reminder of the messages that need to be emphasized during bid-writing. Subtly, and in as many different ways as possible, you need to make sure the key themes are repeated in each major section of your proposal.

- Key themes are an excellent way to get newcomers up to speed on the bid. This is very useful for proposal reviewers who may not have time to review all the background material.

WHAT ARE KEY THEMES?

Key themes exist at a higher level than requirements. Being able to meet a particular requirement probably doesn't constitute a key theme. However, meeting a whole group of requirements in a particularly innovative or cost-effective manner does.

Note that key themes are not necessarily unique to your organization or your bid. Expect at least some of your competitors to be offering a solution with the same key themes.

A key theme is:

- A point that deserves special emphasis in your proposal.

- An aspect of the solution which you know is particularly important to the client.

- A particularly innovative, cost-effective or attractive part of the solution to be brought to the client's attention.

- Something that the client has a particular interest in or will be alert to.

Finding the Key Themes

There are three main sources of key themes:

- Themes that the client highlights as important. (These are obvious to all bidders. Expect these to feature in all credible proposals.)

- Hidden messages in the ITT. (These may not be spotted by all bidders, so may give rise to a competitive advantage.)

- Strengths of your offering which are pertinent to the client's requirement. (Possibly unique to your bid.)

THE CLIENT'S THEMES

Some key themes are easy to spot. Sometimes the client will highlight issues of fundamental importance in the ITT. They are often found under headings such as evaluation criteria, points for special consideration, key concerns or something similar, but generally they won't be hard to find.

Don't ignore these obvious themes and assume that the client will know how well you can address them. You should count on your competitors emphasizing the strengths of their solution in relation to these key themes. Even if you can't differentiate your proposal on these themes alone, it is important that they are all covered in your solution. Suppose the client's ITT particularly stresses the importance of assigning an experienced project manager to handle the service delivery. Since this theme is obvious to all bidders, you are unlikely to gain advantage over your competitors just because you put forward an experienced project manager. However, failure to do this (and equally importantly, failure to emphasize this person's relevant experience in the bid) will result in a lower scoring during the evaluation.

HIDDEN THEMES

Hidden themes come in various guises:

- Themes which are important to the client but are poorly expressed in the ITT.

- Unconscious themes – patterns of requirements which the client probably hasn't realized is an underlying theme.

- Undiscovered themes – things which the client may not have thought about or may not be aware of.

Poorly expressed themes are common in large ITTs particularly when many people have contributed to the documents or the ITT has been hurriedly prepared. The client understands very well the importance of these issues but for whatever reason, hasn't been able to write it down cogently.

A revealing exercise is to write in the margin next to each requirement one keyword which best sums up the topic of the requirement. When you have gone through all the requirements, examine the pattern that emerges:

- Which keywords occur most frequently? (Is this the topic of a hidden theme?)

- Is there a grouping of similar keywords? (Is there a theme based on the relationship between these keywords?)

- Is there a lot of duplication? (Does this indicate emphasis on a particular theme?)

- Are there keywords missing that you would have expected to see? (Does this imply a different emphasis, or has the topic been overlooked by the client?)

Poorly expressed themes will often become apparent if you have other sources of information, e.g. from a bidders' briefing or through informal contact with the client. You can then go back to the ITT and identify the themes more clearly with the aid of this background information. If you are not sure you are interpreting a hidden theme correctly, you may want to seek clarification from the client. (Note: Bear in mind this carries the risk of giving away a useful advantage if the client's clarifications are routinely circulated to all bidders.)

The clues to *unconscious themes* will be scattered throughout the proposal. The client isn't being intentionally vague about these themes; they genuinely have not seen the underlying patterns in the detailed requirements. Your ability to highlight the 'big picture' issues to the client will demonstrate your analytical abilities and insight. If done well, you can show that you understand the client's requirement, the business context and can see past the details of the requirement to the fundamental issues.

'Keywording' requirements will also help identify unconscious themes. Be alert for patterns or repetitions which the client hasn't explicitly acknowledged in the ITT. It can sometimes help to compare the way the requirements have been grouped and structured with similar ITTs you have received in the past.

Contrasts may leap out: areas which appear to have been missed or given only sketchy coverage, different priorities assigned to groups of requirements, different solutions proposed for similar requirements.

What has given rise to these differences? The client may have good reason for producing the ITT in this way, in which case you must avoid antagonizing him by suggesting ideas that have already been rejected. Or the client may not have considered these possibilities (or perhaps not understood some fundamental issues about his own requirements) in which case you may be able to score highly on insight and originality.

Undiscovered themes are opportunities for you to demonstrate the value of your organization's knowledge and skills. It allows you to suggest different aspects of the solution and explore opportunities which the client doesn't know about. Undiscovered themes are rare and a lot depends on whether you, as a supplier, are well placed to provide insights into the client's business. However, these are great themes (if you can find them) because they are clear examples of your bid 'adding value' above and beyond the narrow limits of what the client has asked for.

Inevitably, there are dangers. You need to be sure that these suggestions will be welcomed by the client. Could they be seen as over-complicating the situation? Is there any evidence that the client may have considered and rejected such ideas? Further analysis of the requirements may be needed to be sure of your position.

YOUR STRENGTHS

Begin by assuming that the client does not have a good appreciation of your organization's strengths. Even if you think they do, can you be sure that everyone evaluating your proposal will be sufficiently knowledgeable and share this appreciation? The proposal will need to tell the client – or better still, demonstrate – all of your relevant strengths.

Making unsubstantiated claims is to be avoided. It is easy to talk up your organization's abilities and experience and many bidders will do so. Unfortunately, nothing is likely to irritate a client more than an endless series of grand claims with no real evidence to back them up.

Always try to:

- Offer tangible evidence for every key theme, i.e. documented facts to back up claims made about your offering, skills or track record.

- Keep away from unnecessary superlatives, i.e. try to present your strengths impartially.

- However, don't undersell your capabilities – present all the relevant evidence.

Table 4.1 shows one way to structure a key theme.

Table 4.1   How to structure a key theme

Structure	Detail of message
Key theme definition	A concise statement of your key theme.
... which means:	A list of the main implications and benefits which this is likely to give the client.
... which depends on:	The assumptions and dependencies on which this theme is based.
.. and is demonstrated by:	Tangible evidence to back up the assertion in the definition part of the theme.

If you follow this breakdown, you will avoid making empty promises to the client. You will be able to show how the theme will make a positive difference to the client, any preconditions for successful delivery and, most importantly, how you can demonstrate the truth of what you are saying.

The choice of your key themes must be based on your judgement of the client and his or her needs. Generally, the more specific the detailed themes, the better. A couple of examples of fairly generic themes are shown in Tables 4.2 and 4.3.

Table 4.2   A generic example of a structured key theme

Structure	Detail of message
Key theme 1:	'Our management style and culture encourages openness with our clients and forges an effective working relationship built on mutual trust.'
... which means:	The client has visibility of project issues at an appropriate level of detail. Sometimes there may be bad news as well as good. There is give and take by both parties. If things are starting to go wrong, there is quicker detection and correction of the problems.
... which depends on:	A robust agreement on the scope of our responsibilities as supplier and client (i.e. a strong contractual baseline). This gives both parties the confidence to properly engage in project issues, rather than focusing on protecting interests and positioning for best advantage.
... and is demonstrated by:	Frequency and nature of progress reporting. (Refer to Reporting Plan) Our style of working. (Refer to Management Plan) Management processes, as documented in our ISO-accredited quality procedures. Project references (attached) and customer testimonials (referenced).

Table 4.3   Another example of a structured key theme

Structure	Detail of message
Key theme 2:	'A risk-averse approach is embedded in the core of our management processes, not offered as an "add-on" activity.'
... which means:	Management of risk is built into the plan, so it won't get sidelined or forgotten as the project wears on. We use recognized industry-standard risk management strategies.
... which depends on:	Both parties need to agree an effective process by which risks are detected, monitored and controlled. Some risks will require the client to respond proactively – which may have implications for the availability of client staff.
... and is demonstrated by:	Draft management deliverables which have been prepared as part of the bid and have addressed the major areas of risk. A preliminary risk register has been created as part of the bid. Our management plan containing a clear and concise description of our approach to managing risks. Our nominated project manager has recognized qualifications in risk management.

Differentiators and Discriminators

Key themes, differentiators and discriminators are closely linked, but exist in a kind of hierarchy of usefulness, as Figure 4.1 shows. Although similar-sounding, there are important differences between a differentiator and a discriminator. Both are very valuable to your bid.

What do we mean by these terms?

Key theme: of particular importance, a point to be emphasized.

Differentiator: something which serves to distinguish between similar objects.

Discriminator: a thing which constitutes or marks a unique difference or enables fine distinctions or differences to be observed.

DIFFERENTIATORS

A differentiator is any tangible element that will make your bid stand out from the crowd. It may be a particularly compelling key theme or it could be some aspect of the bid itself: a brilliantly logical structure, an attractive design theme running throughout the bid, client testimonials, a personal commitment from your CEO . . . anything that helps set your bid apart from the competition. The point of a differentiator is to make an impression on the client.

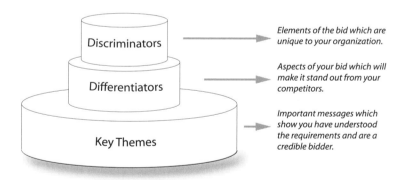

Figure 4.1   The relative value of key themes, differentiators and discriminators. *Missing key themes will see the bid marked down. You must assume your closest rivals will also elaborate many of the same key themes. Differentiators will earn additional marks in the bid evaluation. With enough differentiators, you may pull ahead of rival bidders. If the client values your discriminators and you are the only one able to offer them, then your bid stands an excellent chance of winning*

Suppose a key element of your solution is the delivery of a new accounting system. You also know that the client is worried by training issues – how long will it take staff to become familiar with the new system, and at what cost to the business? To differentiate your bid, you might decide to show an annotated sequence of screenshots of the user interface, or even provide a video clip of someone working through a particular scenario. This 'worked example' illustrates how easy the system is to use and will allay the client's fears over usability. The client didn't ask for this in the ITT, but this material will help to differentiate your bid from others that haven't thought to do this.

It is quite likely that some of your sharper competitors will have similar ideas. No matter – the important thing is that you don't lose ground when the proposals are evaluated. Bidders who simply respond exactly to the requirements are limiting their chances of success – they risk losing out to those who stretch for ways to differentiate their bid.

There are lots of way to differentiate your proposal from the competition. Be alert to opportunities and try to think creatively.

Table 4.4   Different ways to differentiate your proposal

Differentiator	Detail of message
Solution development	Invest more time and thought in how you develop the solution. Show that your solution is more thoroughly developed and will not just meet the client's expectations but exceed them in some important respects.
Innovation	Some (but not all) clients will be impressed by innovation and creativity. How far you take this is a judgement call, but at the very least, it will show that you have thought more deeply about the client's requirements.
Presentation	Pay attention to the style and layout of your proposal. A professional-looking document makes a better impression than a badly structured document littered with spelling mistakes.
Empathy	Try to 'connect' with the client. Make the client feel that you understand their requirements better than your competitors. Be the 'easy' option to choose: easy to work with and easy to trust.

DISCRIMINATORS

Discriminators are key themes on steroids. A discriminator is an aspect which is unique to your organization, i.e. something that only you can offer the client. Unlike your key themes (common to all serious bids) and differentiators (possibly shared with your main rivals), a discriminator will give you an edge over the other bids. Literally they will discriminate your proposal in one or more important respects from the rest of the competition.

Let's look at a simple example of a discriminator. Suppose the client wants to co-locate all customer service functions into a single call centre. Some basic research reveals that the client already uses a telephone switch for which you are the sole reseller. Here is a great opportunity: as sole reseller of the existing equipment you have a discriminator. You can offer a solution based on the client's legacy infrastructure in a way that no other organization can.

Of course, the client could decide to scrap your legacy system and replace it with a more powerful model rather than upgrade the existing equipment. Your job in the bid is to present the arguments for upgrading (e.g. cost-effectiveness, proven reliability, less disruption, etc.). If you have judged the situation well, this discriminator puts you in a strong position.

Discriminators are comparatively rare. There may not be any in your bid – in which case you will have to rely on doing an especially good job with your key themes and differentiators, and trust that your competitors don't have any discriminators either.

To make the most of any discriminators:

- Draw attention to your discriminators in the Executive Summary (or proposal introduction) and make reference to them in the relevant sections of the bid. Discriminators will give your bid a real edge so you can't afford to have the client's evaluation team miss them.

- To be effective, you need to say *what* the discriminator is, *how* you can prove, justify or demonstrate its validity, and *why* this is important to the client (e.g. because it reduces risk, increases the client's return on investment, etc.).

- Educate the client to recognize bogus discriminators in your rivals' bids. For example, if you are the sole authorized reseller for a software product, point out the risks of choosing an unauthorized supplier: untrained staff installing the product, no formal support, no scheduled upgrades, etc.

Research

Do you have enough information to develop the bid strategy? The answer will depend on how much you already know about the client, the nature and extent of the relationship, and the specifics of what is being requested in the ITT. More than likely, you will need to research some aspects to support solution development or bid-writing.

Research needs to be done holistically as you progress through the various stages of the bid. Use research as a support tool for your bid. If you are proposing a challenging or innovative solution, you will need to research its feasibility. Encourage the bid team to think creatively when addressing the requirements. Ideas should be continually popping up and some of these will trigger their own lines of research. What if we outsourced the testing phase instead of doing it ourselves? (What companies specialize in doing this? Are their prices competitive? Are there similar projects where this has been done?)

Table 4.5   Four areas which may require further research

Research area	What you need to know
The client	The more you understand the client's situation, the better you are able to pitch your proposal. This can mean going far beyond the apparent boundaries of the work, perhaps understanding the organizational politics and the health of their business sector. Do you know: • Timescales and internal drivers within the client's organization? (Is somebody's promotion or job on the line over the success of this project?) • Who are the stakeholders in each of the key areas: financial, business, and user communities? • Does the client have preconceptions over technology, suppliers, products, etc.? • How will the client judge the success of the work? • How knowledgeable is the client in this area?
The requirement	Some ITTs are comprehensive documents, which have been carefully thought through and pretty much stand on their own. Others are hasty, ill-conceived or downright confusing. In either case, your competitors will be starting from the same point, but can you go further and gain further insights into the requirements? • Why has the client begun this procurement? • Is this a 'follow on' from an earlier contract? • Is the requirement open, i.e. might there be many possible solutions which satisfy the requirements? • What is the budget? • Are there elements to this work which are outside the client's direct control?

Table 4.5   *Concluded*

Research area	What you need to know
Your offering	Unless you are a small organization in a niche market, no single person will have a sufficiently detailed knowledge of all aspects of your offering. • Which people have the most relevant knowledge within your organization? • Do any of your staff have relevant experience with this client? Do they have personal contacts? • Have staff worked on a similar project before, perhaps with a previous employer? • Is the delivery process for your core offering as well documented as the technical aspects? (Do you understand the risks and all the things that could go wrong?)
Your competitors	You must know where your strengths and weaknesses lie in comparison with your competitors so that you can highlight strengths and downplay (or mitigate) your weaknesses. (And you can be sure your competitors will be trying to do the same.) The more you understand what the competition is up to, the greater your chances of beating them. • Who are your competitors on this bid? (This may not be easy to discover.) • What are your competitors' main strengths and weaknesses? • How have your fared against these competitors on recent bids? • Are your competitors teaming with other specialist suppliers or subcontractors?

SEEKING CLARIFICATION

What do you do if your analysis of the ITT highlights some unanswered questions? There are two choices. You can raise the issue with the client or you can try to find out the answers on your own.

Sometimes the easiest way to find an answer is to ask the client, particularly if your questions relate directly to something that is unclear or missing in the ITT. Some clients actively discourage this kind of contact – chiefly because of the risk of legal challenges to the procurement process if the client inadvertently assists one bidder to the detriment of the others. Most ITTs will state whether the client is willing to be contacted and the process for doing so. If not, a polite enquiry should resolve the matter.

- Don't make a nuisance of yourself by asking for too many clarifications (particularly if most are trivial) or by drip-feeding your clarification requests.

- Group your clarifications into two categories: 'need to know' and 'nice to know'. Need-to-know clarifications are ones that will materially affect the solution or the way you format/present the bid. Try to find a different way to answer the 'nice-to-knows'.

- Follow to the letter the guidelines in the ITT on seeking clarification. If you try to bend the rules, not only do you risk irritating the client but you send a message about how you will interact with the client if you win the work.

- Is there anything about your request for clarification that might give away an important advantage to your competitors? If you are seeking to confirm an innovative line of thought, you might lose its advantage by telegraphing the idea to the other bidders. A better course of action might be to document your working assumptions in the proposal and negotiate around this point once you have been safely shortlisted by the client.

- Check how clarifications will be circulated to other bidders. If this is being done by email, it is possible that other bidders may see your organization's name. (In some situations, you may not want competitors to know you are bidding.)

- Look carefully at the clarifications other bidders are submitting. What can you deduce from their questions?

ITT Analysis Checklist

By the end of your analysis of the ITT you should be able to tick off the following points:

- *Scope*. The scope of the work the client requires is clearly understood.

- *Stakeholders*. The client's stakeholders are identified (i.e. those with a role to play in the evaluation of proposals or an involvement in the product or service to be delivered).

- *Business context*. The client's business goals are clear and any constraints or dependencies which might affect the project have been identified.

- *Entry requirements*. Has the client specified any special criteria which the supplier must have in order to be selected?

- *Formal requirements*. The client's requirements are clearly laid out and are substantially complete (i.e. sufficient as a basis on which to prepare a proposal).

- *Key themes*. The different types of key themes have been identified.

- *Bidding instructions*. The instructions for bidding are clear.

- *Reference documents*. All the documents and sections referenced in the ITT have been provided by the client.

- *Submission timetable*. The timetable for bid submission (and any preceding events such as briefings, interviews, etc.) are clearly defined.

- *Feasible solution*. Your offerings upon which the solution will be developed appear to be a good match to the client's requirements (insofar as this can be determined at this early stage in the process).

- *Risks*. Preliminary risks have been identified (from the client's perspective and from your perspective as supplier).

- *Success criteria*. The success criteria for the project and the acceptance criteria for individual deliverables are understood.

- *Resources*. There is sufficient information to understand what resources will be needed to deliver the project (manpower, specialist skills, physical resources, etc.).

Summary: Analysing the Requirements

- Don't put off the *detailed analysis of the ITT*. The earlier this is done, the better its influence on your bid strategy.

- Use an *ITT checklist* to check if there are any major gaps in the information you need for the proposal.

- Read the ITT with *specific goals* in mind. Make sure this is active not passive reading. It is easy to miss important clues if you are just 'going through the motions'.

- *Be prepared to spend a lot of time* becoming familiar with the ITT. This may mean reading the documents many times during the course of the bid.

- Find the *key themes*. These may be clearly stated in the ITT, hidden away, or stem from knowledge which you bring to the table.

- *Write down your key themes* in a structured way; avoid empty promises.

- Keep a list of your *key themes* to hand throughout the bidding process. Refer to it constantly.

- Assume your competitors will submit competent bids. It is up to you to find ways to *differentiate* yourself from the competition. That may mean doing more than answering the questions posed by the ITT.

- *Discriminators* are things that only you can offer. Don't overlook them and don't be afraid to emphasize them; what is obvious to you is not necessarily obvious to the client.

5

Developing the Bid

We are continuously faced by great opportunities brilliantly disguised as insoluble problems.

Lee Iacocca, US automobile businessman, 1924–

In the last chapter we looked at the importance of really understanding the client's requirements. Having done so, we can now start to develop key aspects of the bid – principally by thinking about what kind of solution will best satisfy these requirements.

Creating the bid solution is also the first step in building the project framework. The benefits are obvious: establishing the building blocks of the project during the bid smoothes the eventual transition from bid to project and – because key aspects such as delivery schedule, feasibility and the management of external dependencies have been properly addressed – maximizes the chances of the project succeeding.

Identifying the Business Objectives

In a conventional bid-writing approach, the bid solution is a direct response to the ITT. The client's requirements are analysed in detail (as discussed in Chapter 4) and it is then a question of developing a solution to fit.

However, suppose we don't take the statement of requirements at face value. What other clues might there be to develop a winning solution? One way of looking at the ITT is to regard it as a re-statement of the client's business problems. These are the problems that first triggered the procurement process. The problem may be relatively straightforward as in: 'I need a specialist service to fulfil a specific need that can't be provided within my organization.' Or it may be more complex: 'How do I achieve a 25 per cent increase in organizational efficiency through investment in new technology and working practices?'

With further analysis, the client then identifies a set of requirements which address the underlying problems. These requirements are encapsulated in the ITT which, in turn, are analysed by potential suppliers who put forward a solution in the form of a proposal (see Figure 5.1).

Clearly, there is a risk of a mismatch. The specification of the problem by the client and the proposal of a solution by the supplier are frequently one step removed. Imperfectly specified requirements in the ITT may obscure the underlying business problems to the extent that there is no guarantee that meeting the requirements will ultimately satisfy the underlying business problems. Suppose the client has made a mistake in the analysis? The requirements in the ITT may be the wrong ones or may result in an inefficient solution. Even if a supplier satisfies every last requirement stipulated by the ITT, some aspect of the underlying problem may remain.

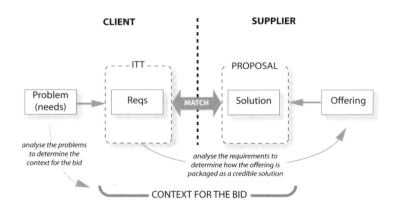

Figure 5.1   The relationship between what the client needs and what the supplier can offer. *Analysing the requirements will reveal how existing offerings need to be tailored. This results in the bid solution. But a fundamental understanding of the client's problems (or needs) provides the context for the bid*

ESTABLISHING CONTEXT

This affords an important opportunity for the supplier who can look beyond the narrow focus of the ITT and properly understand the context of the bid. Establishing the context will naturally take into account the underlying problems or needs of the client. This may require research, or further contact with the client (if permitted by the procurement rules), although often there are clues in the requirements which allow the business context to be reconstructed.

RECOGNIZING THE PROBLEM CATEGORY

Since many business problems originate either directly or indirectly from the need for business change, it is often helpful to categorize the bid context into one of two generic classes:

- The client wants to *implement a change*. The nature of the change is well understood: the client probably knows what solution is needed and has a good idea about how it should be delivered. During the bid evaluation, the client is looking for the organization best able to implement the change – probably in terms of quality, time and cost. Or:

- The client has *identified the need to change,* but doesn't fully understand the best way to achieve this change. Most likely, the client has a basic grasp of what is needed but may be out of their depth when it comes to appreciating risks and judging the best approach. Whilst the client understands the business goals to be met, it is not clear how best to achieve these goals. The proposal must advise the client as well as document the features of the solution.

Recognizing which category your ITT fits into is valuable because you can then tailor the proposal to suit. This may even mean addressing concerns that the client hasn't fully expressed in the ITT. Such insights will give the bid a competitive advantage but more importantly, will help the project ultimately deliver the business benefits.

So how precisely does knowledge of the problem category affect what goes into the solution?

IMPLEMENTING A CHANGE

A client who wants to *implement a change* is typically well prepared and has a good understanding of the work to be carried out. It is reasonable to expect a well-researched business case and preliminary assessment of risk. The client is likely to be familiar with the technologies and processes necessary to deliver the change, though they may not have the resources in-house to carry out the work. Such a project may well fit into an overarching programme dealing with different aspects of the proposed change, meaning that there will be external dependencies and constraints to take into account.

For a client in this situation, you won't need to devote as many proposal pages to explaining the intricacies of the solution, how the technology works and the associated risks. (However, don't ignore them completely. These topics need covering but can be dealt with at a high level.) You can assume the client is fundamentally knowledgeable and competent in the relevant aspects of the solution. Therefore the 'success factor' for the bid will be showing how your solution delivers maximum value for money.

This means placing emphasis on the 'how' instead of the 'what'. The client already understands what your offering is; it is the details of the solution that are needed. How will you tailor your offering? How flexible can you be in delivery? Can you accommodate specific requests, etc.?

This strategy brings project planning to the forefront of the proposal. Ironically, this kind of bid often fails because too much time and energy is spent explaining the offering (most of which the client already knows) leaving little coverage of the practicalities of delivery. It is much easier to draw together material which describes the core offering (e.g. product brochures, marketing literature or material from previous bids) whereas working out the delivery plan details – when and how to deploy resources, contingency planning, where the vulnerabilities lie, etc. – requires original thought.

IDENTIFYING THE NEED FOR CHANGE

A different strategy is needed for the client who has identified the *need for a change*. The hallmark of this scenario is usually found in the ITT which, whilst clear on the desired results, may be quite vague about *how* these are to be achieved.

This calls for subtle differences in the bid solution. You may need to spend more time explaining the issues and risks associated with the solution. Don't assume the client is familiar with technical issues (i.e. avoid jargon, or at least make sure there are clear definitions). Use conceptual diagrams to aid understanding. Plan to invest more time in rewriting the technical sections for clarity and ease of understanding than might otherwise be the case.

Significantly more time may need to be spent analysing the requirements before the most appropriate solution can be developed. This analysis may need to be summarized in the bid so the client can understand the reasoning behind the solution. You will also need to draw the client's attention to its benefits because the significance might not be obvious.

The development of the bid solution may suggest things that the client has not thought about, or highlight risks they were not aware of. You may be able to use this to your advantage, reassuring the client that these fresh problems have been addressed, reinforcing the message that you are a supplier that will support and advise as well as deliver.

If your bid solution contains a number of options, don't automatically expect the client to be able to choose one without detailed supporting information. A client who is not familiar with the nature of this kind of project will appreciate having alternatives clearly explained and the pros and cons laid out in detail.

Checklists for Developing the Bid Solution

The following checklists suggest how you might approach each class of problem. The main difference is one of emphasis: all the items mentioned should probably appear in your proposal regardless of the type of problem the client is addressing. However, emphasizing certain aspects in your solution will help gain the client's confidence and can be the deciding factor when the bid is evaluated.

CHECKLIST FOR AN 'IMPLEMENTING A CHANGE' BID

- Demonstrate you know what you are talking about (*show your understanding* not just of the client's requirements but of the technical solution in general).

- Be very clear on the details of *what will be delivered*. Since the client already understands what the work entails, they are likely to look for tell-tale details – and won't be reassured if they are missing.

- Highlight how your solution *delivers value* to the client. Once the client is satisfied with the details of the solution, they will need to compare your bid with your competitors to see which represents the best value. Don't leave the client guessing; be explicit about the value offered, and quantify this where possible.

- Explain the *strategy and process* for delivery. Very often the way in which the client's needs are met (i.e. the delivery process) will be just as important as the quality of the deliverables. This might mean providing a detailed delivery plan or introducing key staff such as the project manager and lead architect to the client to build confidence and trust at a personal level.

- Adopt a *price-sensitive approach*. By making your pricing modular (i.e. separately pricing key elements and any options) you will make it easier for the client to perform like-for-like comparisons.

- Look for things in the ITT which will *discriminate your bid* from the competition, and make sure these are emphasized. If there is something which you do better than the competition, make sure the client knows about it.

CHECKLIST FOR AN 'IDENTIFYING A NEED FOR CHANGE' BID

- Show that you *understand the client's business*. The client may be worried about losing control of the project by not having a sufficient understanding of the technologies involved. They will want reassurance that you understand the business needs as well as the technology that will deliver them.

- *Show your credentials.* If the client is uncertain how to implement the necessary changes, they will not want a supplier who is also on a learning curve. You must be able to demonstrate your track record through delivering similar projects.

- Have a good *risk mitigation strategy*. Although risks need to be carefully presented (i.e. a large and detailed risk log can be both daunting and off-putting to the client), generally the client will appreciate a response which clearly lays out the risks and shows that the supplier has a plan to deal with them. This must include well thought out mitigation plans for the major risks. Anyone can come up with a long list of things that could go wrong: you need to show that you have an effective way of dealing with them.

- Show that your organization (and specifically, your key people) *are easy to work with*. You may need to act as the 'client's friend' and guide them through the key project stages. Gaining the client's trust and confidence isn't easy, but the process begins during the bid stage. Once the client believes the project team understand what is needed and are committed to meeting the business objectives, you are well on the road to success.

- Choose *reference projects* carefully. If you have helped other clients through a similar transitionary period (even if the project deliverables were quite different) this will be a valuable reference for the client to pursue.

- *Be creative*, particularly if the requirements are very high level or vague. The client may be receptive to innovative approaches (and possibly even non-compliant solutions) if you have insights which can deliver the client's objectives more effectively.

Does the Client Understand the Problem?

The quality of the ITT – specifically the extent to which it addresses all aspects of the business requirement without contradiction or ambiguity – clearly has a profound effect on the job of the bid writer. There are many reasons why a client may issue an ITT that is less than perfect: lack of time, unfamiliarity with the tendering process, lack of knowledge (or thought) about what is required, inability to express the requirements clearly, and complex tendering rules.

When faced with such handicaps you will need to judge how much weight to place on each requirement – whether your solution must comply exactly or whether the client is receptive to alternatives.

First impressions of the ITT are often misleading. Some of the most detailed and seemingly comprehensive requirements often unravel when subjected to detailed analysis. Perhaps the client has lifted requirements from elsewhere or combined various requirements from similar (but significantly different) tenders which the organization has undertaken in the past. Very often it is not until the second or third detailed reading of the ITT that all the inconsistencies, omissions and deficiencies in the ITT become apparent.

What to do? As we saw in Chapter 4, there are two main possibilities:

1. *Seek clarification from the client.* Don't be afraid to challenge the client's requirements; it is in their interests to make sure their requirements are both comprehensive and comprehensible.

2. *Interpret and enhance.* In the absence of contact with the client, your only option is to interpret the ITT as best you can. The more thorough and detailed your analysis, the more convincing your arguments will be. You don't need to openly criticize the client's requirements, but it is helpful to show where there is confusion and inconsistency and how you have factored this in to the solution.

Golden rules for interpreting the client's requirements:

*   Document your assumptions. The client can quickly identify if any of these are wrong and take this into account in the evaluation.

*   Don't assume any more than you have to.

*   Keep the client's objectives in sight. (What are the business problems that are driving the ITT?) It is the client who determines the destination but you may be able to find a better path through the uncertain terrain to reach it.

*   Show your working. Make sure the client understands why you think they have missed some important requirements, or why there is a better way.

*   Isolate areas of real uncertainty and address them as options to the main proposal. If real doubt remains, these may need to be conditionally priced and subject to further clarification during contract negotiation.

CHANGING THE CLIENT'S MIND

Your view of how best to meet a requirement or deal with a particular risk may be at odds with the client's. You may judge that a particular requirement doesn't make sense or misses an opportunity to find a better way. This is a good thing – providing you are certain of your position and can justify it. Your insights may enable you to distinguish yourself from the competition. However, you must first prove your case.

It is no use asserting in the proposal that a requirement is flawed. Begin with the client's perspective; try to understand their viewpoint. Then you must build the case (with suitable justifications at each step) for your alternative solution. Bear in mind that, rightly or wrongly, the client will evaluate your proposal according to their own preconceptions. If these are misplaced, you first need to persuade the client of this and offer supporting evidence.

- Clearly identify the requirements you believe are misjudged (including the scope of the problem and their implications).

- Provide evidence of the flaws. This may mean analysing different scenarios or following a logical chain through to a conclusion.

- Highlight key weaknesses (i.e. flawed assumptions, incorrect dependencies, misunderstood facts, missed opportunities, etc.).

- Show the logical implications of a *better* interpretation of the facts.

- Highlight key differences and any consequences they give rise to.

- Summarize the proposed requirement or approach to be taken, emphasizing the benefits that accrue and the risks that are avoided.

Innovation

In proposal parlance, an *innovative bid* has a special meaning. It means a bid which offers an alternative approach to meeting the client's requirements. The client will be able to achieve the same objectives but not necessarily in the way that was envisaged in the ITT.

Many requirements are based on some model solution that the client has in mind. If you can identify a better model which still meets the requirements, then you may be able to submit an innovative bid. Although the solution is likely to differ in significant ways to what the client expects, it must still meet the business objectives as well as offering additional benefits. Suppose a client requests a bus timetable so that they can plan a journey into town. Instead we offer a door-to-door taxi service for the same price as the bus fare. It is not how the client intended to travel, but it provides clear advantages.

Innovation can be an excellent discriminator. If you have spotted an opportunity overlooked by your competitors, you can turn an open competition into a one-horse race. Once you have lodged an attractive idea in the client's mind, the other bids on the table may seem dull by comparison.

In reality, creating an innovative bid is not simple, and can be risky if it means interpreting key requirements differently. Nevertheless, it is always worth being alert for this kind of opportunity. Most clients will be happy to receive an innovative bid providing you have correctly interpreted their business objectives and can offer additional benefits.

But there is also a downside to an innovative bid. The solution is not formally compliant with the requirements and may be substantially different to the one the client had in mind. This does not matter if the client is persuaded of the benefits. However, some procurement rules and marking schemes may not be flexible enough to permit extensive innovation which means the bid may score poorly in the evaluation – not because the proposal is weak, simply because the evaluation criteria were set with a particular type of solution in mind. It pays to be certain of how the client will react to an innovative bid. If in doubt, ask (assuming the client hasn't barred communication while bidding is underway).

GOING THE EXTRA MILE

Figure 2.1 in Chapter 2 showed that there is often a small difference between the winning and losing bids. A fully compliant proposal is 'good enough' in the sense that it satisfies all the requirements, but may still not be good enough to win the contract. To write the winning proposal, often means providing additional value or 'going the extra mile'.

How? Thinking carefully about the bid strategy and solution before developing the bid is an important factor. So too is deciding where to focus attention (e.g. distinguishing between a client who needs to 'implement a change' and one who has 'identified the need for a change').

Another obvious factor is how much work goes into the proposal. If you spend 20 days on a proposal which your competitors cover in only 10, the difference should be apparent in the end result. The client will take this as an indication of your commitment and enthusiasm. It is an implicit promise: look how hard we have worked on the proposal; we will work just as hard for you if you award us the contract.

The bid team's mindset will also play an important part. If their goal is simply to get the proposal out the door and move on to something more interesting, they are unlikely to create a compelling proposal.

As always, the specifics will depend on the situation, but here are some ideas for going the extra mile:

- Create a 'concept' diagram which captures the essence of the entire solution on a single page. (If done well, this can often be the focal point of further negotiations. It will stick in the client's mind and it may be used as a reference point when comparing your solution to the competition.)

- Provide draft versions of key delivery documents. You should already have templates for project plans, service level agreements, change control procedures, etc. and you will have already produced a high-level plan. With a little more effort, you can insert a draft project plan in an appendix and score some points on the speed with which you will be able to start work.

- Select one issue which is at the crux of the client's requirement (e.g. a particularly complex problem, or a non-standard situation or something which you know is a hot-button) and elaborate your solution and approach. This could take the form of a detailed technical analysis, a mock-up of how the process will work or even a working prototype. You can't do this for all aspects of the work, but it is a representative example of the standard of work the client can expect if your organization is selected.

- Options. Are there additional features or benefits you can provide? These must offer tangible value and make sense within the context of the requirements, even if not specifically requested in the ITT. Spotting something that the client has overlooked in the ITT can give you a valuable edge over the competition – it shows you are thinking beyond the confines of the ITT and have truly understood the client's business objectives.

Summary: Developing the Bid

- Don't be tempted to start writing the proposal before the solution has been properly developed.

- An 'offering led' proposal extols its virtues solely from the supplier's perspective. But that may not be how the client sees things. Don't alienate the client by failing to present the solution from his or her perspective or the benefits may not be fully appreciated.

- Be specific about your solution. Demonstrating an understanding of the client's requirement is valuable – but not at the expense of clearly describing the solution.

- Don't make wild promises. Winning at all costs isn't really winning.

- Think about the client's starting point. You may need to adopt a different bid strategy for a client who only knows what end result they want compared to one who knows both the end result and how it must be reached.

- Don't automatically assume the client knows what they are asking for. An innovative bid may open the client's eyes to different possibilities – and give you the edge.

- 'Connecting' with the client means three things: understanding their needs, demonstrating capability and establishing trust.

- Go the extra mile. If you can deliver more than the client expects (and still stay within the budget) you will have gained an advantage over your competitors.

6

Establishing the Project Framework

A good estimate is an estimate that provides a clear enough view of the project reality to allow the project leadership to make good decisions about how to control the project to hit its targets.

Steve McConnell,
Software Estimation: Demystifying the Black Art *(2006)*

A fundamental step in establishing the project framework depends on obtaining good estimates. The estimation process not only quantifies the amount of work or other resources needed, it forces the project manager to understand what needs to be done and how this work is organized. Get the estimates wrong at the bid stage and the project may never stand a chance.

It could be argued that an accurate estimate is a contradiction of terms. An estimate is produced precisely because there is a lack of definite or accurate information. By definition, an estimate has inherent uncertainty, i.e. there is always an associated margin of error.

Worse, talk of accurate estimates can be self-deluding for planning purposes. What we really mean is that there are good estimates, poor estimates and then everything in between. Since building a sound project framework fundamentally depends on good estimation, this chapter looks at what this means in practice.

The Role of Estimation in Bidding

Here is the problem: a client wants to see in your proposal not only *what* you will deliver but *when* (and how) it will be delivered. In other words, a credible bid must have a detailed delivery plan. But detailed planning at the bid stage is hard; you probably won't have all the answers until the project actually begins. So inevitably you must estimate some or all of the following:

- What tasks need to be done to achieve the project's objectives?

- What resources do these tasks need?

- What is the likelihood and impact of external factors on this plan?

However, the bidding process adds certain pressures:

- There may not be enough time to complete a thorough estimation.

- The objectives, component tasks or other aspects of the client's requirements may not be fully specified (and there may be constraints on elaborating the requirements during the bidding process itself).

- There may be limited access to those best placed to provide good estimates.

- Those producing the estimates may not be the ones who have to deliver the project.

Figure 6.1 shows how estimation drives the planning process. First comes the knowledge of the tasks to be carried out, broken down to a suitable level of detail (i.e. the work breakdown structure). Then an estimate is made of the skills, effort and elapsed time needed to generate the required outputs (i.e. deliverables). The next stage requires the project manager to apply judgement. Some tasks may be dependent on (or influenced by) external factors which cannot be controlled. It may be necessary to allow contingency in case these areas of uncertainty give rise to problems. Or there may be considerable uncertainty in the estimates themselves.

Having weighed up these factors, the project manager develops a plan informed by the estimates but not necessarily dependent on them. If the project manager has confidence in the estimates, they may plan on the basis that project events will run close to the estimates. On the other hand, in a high-risk project, a sensible course of action is to plan on the basis of the estimates plus a sizeable contingency (or error margin).

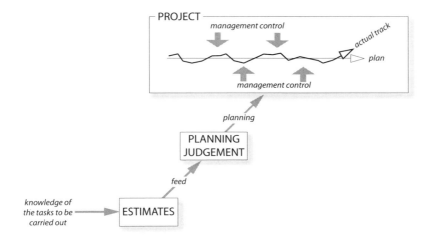

Figure 6.1 **Estimation underpins the entire planning process.** *Since estimates can never be a totally accurate prediction of real project events, the resulting gap between the plan and actuals must be small enough for management controls to keep the project on track*

The judgement of the project manager is a vital part of developing the high level plan, not least because it is a mistake to think that reality will stick to the plan. (Remember Field Marshal Helmuth von Moltke's famous quote: 'No plan survives contact with the enemy.') During the bid stage, the plan only needs to be good enough so that effective management during the project will keep the deviations within tolerance.

ESTABLISHING THE PROJECT FRAMEWORK IN FOUR STAGES

During a bid, the project framework is built in four logical stages (see Figure 6.2). Estimation is a vital part of this process.

Solution design must come first. This is where the project is designed. What is the technical solution? What are the pieces of the puzzle that must be fitted together? How do we go about producing the 'products' which will achieve the project objectives? Until the solution has been designed, the picture of what needs estimating is incomplete.

OBJECTIVE   STAGE   MINDSET

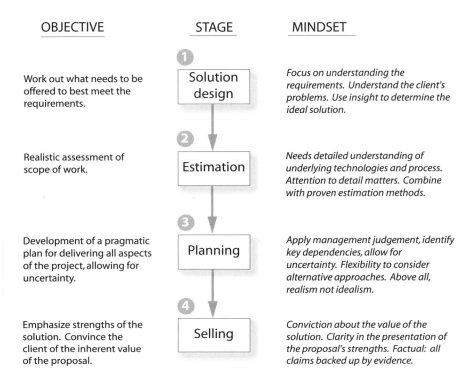

Work out what needs to be   **Solution**   Focus on understanding the
offered to best meet the   **design**   requirements. Understand the client's
requirements.   problems. Use insight to determine the
                                                     ideal solution.

Realistic assessment of   **Estimation**   Needs detailed understanding of
scope of work.   underlying technologies and process.
                                                     Attention to detail matters. Combine
                                                     with proven estimation methods.

Development of a pragmatic   **Planning**   Apply management judgement, identify
plan for delivering all aspects   key dependencies, allow for
of the project, allowing for   uncertainty. Flexibility to consider
uncertainty.   alternative approaches. Above all,
                                                     realism not idealism.

Emphasize strengths of the   **Selling**   Conviction about the value of the
solution. Convince the   solution. Clarity in the presentation of
client of the inherent value   the proposal's strengths. Factual: all
of the proposal.   claims backed up by evidence.

Figure 6.2   Estimation is one of four key stages in establishing the project framework. *A different mindset is needed at each stage. Using the wrong mindset is a common cause of poor estimation*

Estimation. This is process of making an informed judgement of the various items (usually effort, cost or materials) required to deliver all or part of the project objectives. Judgement is the vital word here. An estimate is not the same as an accurate forecast of these quantities.

A good estimate is one where a reliable and well-executed estimation process has been followed. (In contrast, a bad estimate will be based on insubstantial evidence or will have been produced without following any kind of rigorous estimation process.)

A good estimate will also have some kind of error range associated with it. However, the size of the error bars is not necessarily an indication of the quality of the estimate. A good estimate may have a large error range because there is insufficient information on which to estimate with any greater precision. It remains a good estimate because the error bars make this clear. All too often estimates with very small quoted margins of error (or worse, no uncertainty at all) are actually based on invalid assumptions and should not be believed.

Planning. This is the process of taking the estimates, making allowance for the error bars and translating this into a workable plan. Again, good judgement is required on the part of the project manager. Contingency planning may be called for, or 'slack' may need to be added to accommodate possible slips in meeting timescales. If maintaining the schedule is paramount (which is generally the case for most commercial projects), the plan will need to be based on the more pessimistic end of the error range for the estimates.

The most common cause of subsequent failure occurs when this planning step is missed out. The estimates become, de facto, the plan and so there is no opportunity to apply the judgement, wisdom and experience of the project manager.

It is an unwelcome fact of life that the estimation process, even when carried out with care and diligence, often produces results which are incompatible with the commercial goals laid out in the ITT. Perhaps the estimates show the project will take too long, or cost too much or require resources which cannot be found. However, an estimate should not be open to debate once created – at least, not if it is the product of a proven estimation process and the best available information. The only time an estimate should be challenged is if the estimation process is believed to inadequate or its assumptions can be shown to be faulty.

None of this prevents the project manager from choosing to plan either optimistically or pessimistically, as long as the error bars are respected (i.e. the project manager works with values falling somewhere within the estimate's error range). This choice determines whether the project will follow a high- or low-risk strategy.

Selling. The job of the selling stage is twofold. First, it must accurately communicate all the positive aspects of the solution – the benefits, the innovation, all the features which are superior to your competitors' – on the basis that the client doesn't know any of this (because they probably won't). There may be many people in the client organization who will need to evaluate your proposal (often in different ways, looking for different things) and they won't all be familiar with every aspect of your offering. So the positives need to be spelt out clearly, concisely and with appropriate enthusiasm that avoids tipping over into bragging.

Its second job is to explain the difficult choices that have had to be made. If the client has asked for goals to be reached in an impossible timescale, you must explain what makes it impossible and what you can offer instead. Better still, if you can improve on what the client has asked for (or deliver the same thing more efficiently) now is the time to lay out the details.

Explaining why some requirements cannot be met need not be detrimental. (It is certainly better than the alternative: agreeing to impossible requirements and letting the project worry about how to deliver them when the bid has been won.) Pointing out home truths to the client actually has two important benefits:

- It demonstrates that there is a sound basis for your estimates.

- It undermines competitors who promise to deliver the impossible.

Most clients would rather be told of impracticalities at the bid stage (particularly by a supplier who can then present feasible alternatives) than be misled and only discover the consequences much further downstream.

Each stage requires a different mindset. Using the wrong mindset will jeopardize the project, i.e. don't use a salesman's mindset when estimating, use an engineer's because precision and realism are needed. Here, the goal is to arrive at the best possible estimates – and you can't do this with one eye on what you know to be the client's budget. Similarly, don't have a 'planner' mindset when designing the solution. The solution must be driven by the things needed to deliver the client's business objectives. How these are best carried out (i.e. the project planning) comes later.

THE DANGERS OF TAKING ESTIMATES AT FACE VALUE

No matter what your role in the bid, there is a good chance that you will be dependent on others to estimate some key elements of the work. It is easy to feel powerless in this situation, especially if you lack the technical or specialist knowledge to carry out the estimation yourself. Yet, as Figure 6.1 shows, it is a step that you can't afford to get wrong. Good estimates underpin the whole planning process. For the project manager, this is an uncomfortable position:

the validity of the entire plan depends on estimates which may sit outside their control.

Faced with this situation (and working under the inevitable time pressures of a bid) many managers accept estimates at face value. This is the point at which subsequent project failure is introduced. Let's examine this further.

Recall the three key bid-writing principles of Chapter 1 (see Figure 1.3). What are the implications of accepting face-value estimates on each of these principles?

For the *client*, there is no immediate problem. Since poor estimates often turn out to be underestimates, this translates into lower costs and therefore a cheaper price to the client. This can make a bid appear more attractive, consequently increasing the chances of the proposal being selected. However, in the long run, a project working to an inadequate budget will eventually encounter difficulties: corners will need to be cut and quality may suffer. The supplier may attempt to renegotiate the project or use more devious ways to increase the budget through change control. Sooner or later the client will suffer the consequences of the poor estimation. This may range from the inconvenience of being forced to 'get tough' with the supplier, holding them to their contractual commitments, through to the embarrassment of a project failing because it was never viable in the first place.

The consequences for *bid production* may even appear beneficial. Taking estimates at face value means more time available for other bid activities. However, this is clearly a misguided view. What we are really saying is, it leaves more time to bid for work which it may not be viable to deliver: a fool's task if ever there was one.

The whole concept of developing the *project framework* during the bid is concerned with protecting the long-term prospects of the project. If, through lack of due diligence in the bid stage, poor estimates become the planning basis for the project, the project is flawed from the outset. This may not be picked up during the bid stage at all, but there will be no hiding from it when the project is underway.

The bid manager's best defence against these problems is to build awareness amongst the bid team of what constitutes a good estimate. You may be able to work alongside the experts providing technical estimates and make sure they are following best practice. If not, you will need to recognize the signs of poor estimating and seek alternatives while there is still time left in the bidding process.

What Needs Estimating?

For most kinds of projects, you will almost certainly need to estimate some (perhaps all) of the following:

- *Task durations* (i.e. how much elapsed or calendar time will a given task take?).

- *Work time* (i.e. how much effort will a task need?).

- *Cost* (i.e. what is the cost to you the supplier? Note: this is not the same as the price the client is charged).

- *Physical resources* (i.e. materials, goods, services, etc.).

- *Throughput* (i.e. how quickly can the project utilize resources?).

More specialized projects may demand other types of estimates.

These items are often closely related. Suppose you estimate a task will take a week to complete, providing three members of staff work on it simultaneously. That is a task duration of 5 days but a working time of 15 days. Let's say this depends on having sufficient materials available at the start (i.e. an estimate of physical resources). We not only have to worry about estimating quantities but also the dependencies: if there are insufficient materials (or too few staff) the task can no longer be completed in a week. Furthermore, all these things will have an associated cost – not just a basic cost such as a day-rate for the team or the purchase cost of materials – but a dependency cost: the cost for storing materials, hiring staff who are not already on the payroll, etc. Very quickly, the estimation process can become complicated, particularly if you are trying to plan for contingencies as well.

CONVERTING ESTIMATES TO COSTS

Ultimately, you will need to assign a cost to each of the elements being estimated. This is the purpose of the cost model – more on this in Chapter 8. However, cost is not the only product of good estimation. It is just as important to estimate how long things will take and understand the sequence and dependencies of key tasks.

At an early stage in the bid, it is a good idea to have a list of what kinds of things need to be estimated. Despite what you may think, these aren't always obvious. Don't rely on the client's ITT to identify all the cost model elements – after all, cost is the supplier's problem.

Naturally you can't estimate all aspects of the solution until you properly understand what the solution entails. Problems often arise late in the bid because important items are missed out of the costing model. For example, the cost of providing support while training users might have been overlooked, or the cost of setting up a helpdesk, or the renewal of annual licences, etc. These are obvious in hindsight, but because they are consequential activities arising from other elements of the solution, they may be implied requirements rather than explicitly identified, and hence easy to miss.

This brings us to another important point which we will return to in Chapter 8: *set up your cost model as early as possible in the bid*. Bid costing should not be left to the end of the bid. The cost model needs to evolve as the solution is developed, ideally keeping the two in step along the way.

KEEP THE ESTIMATION PROCESS SIMPLE

Unless you are producing estimates for a highly specialized task, it is best to keep the estimation process as simple as possible. If there are a lot of complex factors to estimate, it becomes easier to make mistakes. It can also lead to a false sense of security: more factors in the estimation process don't automatically make for more accurate estimates.

The best advice is to stay focused on what you most need to know. What are the key questions to be answered?

1.   How long until … ?

2.   On what date will this be delivered?

3.   How many of these will we need?

4.   What size team will we need?

Such questions dictate at a fundamental level what needs to be estimated.

DURATION AND TIMING

Questions 1 and 2 require an estimate of the work needed to complete a series of tasks and the number of people available (with the right skills) to work on these tasks. Taken together, this will provide an estimate of the total elapsed time (or duration) of the work. Knowing these facts will allow a forecast to be made of when key project events will occur.

QUANTITIES

Question 3 requires an estimate of resources which in turn means understanding the dependencies (i.e. what things determine when these resources are available?) and the project processes (i.e. how quickly does the project consume these resources?). At its simplest, estimation may be a case of counting objects, but this will depend on project circumstances. For example, a quantity surveyor needs to estimate how much raw material to order for the construction of a building, but to do so requires a detailed understanding of the plans, the design of the building, plus experience of the build process, e.g. how much material is likely to be wasted through spoilage or accidents (and when it actually needs to arrive on site).

HOW MANY/HOW MUCH?

The answer to Question 4 is often derived from other estimates. Once task durations have been estimated, it is a simple calculation to work out how many people are needed for a given task to ensure it is delivered in a certain time period. However, the calculation needs to take account of variables such as differences in individual productivity and dependencies on other tasks which could delay progress.

Figure 6.3 **The time–cost–quality triangle.** *These three elements are interdependent for a given scope of work. Changing one element must have an effect on at least one other element, assuming the scope of work is unchanged*

THE 'TIME–COST–QUALITY' TRIANGLE

Project estimates will need to take account of the time–cost–quality triangle (see Figure 6.3). In essence, this says that for a given scope of work, the sum of time, cost and quality considerations is fixed. Reducing one parameter (say, time to complete) usually means a corresponding increase in costs (perhaps from the inefficiency of bringing more staff on to the project late on), or reduction in quality (perhaps because tasks are rushed) and vice versa.

Figure 6.4 shows another way of looking at this relationship. Each axis shows increasing negative attributes (more cost, more time, lower quality). Suppose a given task scores 5 on each of these axes. A measure of the scope of the work is the volume of the cube. We can adjust time, cost or quality within certain limits, but the volume (scope) is fixed. Thus, we could perhaps reduce the cost of the task by extending the time taken or, more likely, by accepting a lower standard of quality. However, we cannot reduce all three elements simultaneously. The volume must remain constant unless the scope of work is changed. The only justification for reducing time, cost or quality independently is if the scope of the work is reduced.

This leads to the following working principles for bid estimation:

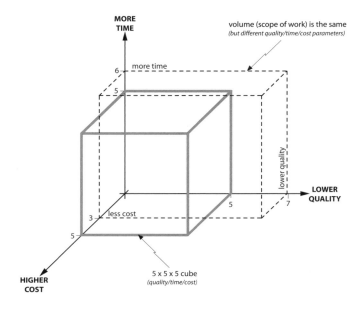

Figure 6.4   An alternative representation of the time–cost–quality relationship. *The volume (scope of work) remains constant when time, cost or quality is varied*

- Doing things more quickly generally costs more.

- Producing work to a higher standard will either cost more or take longer (or both).

- Cutting costs means things will take longer or will be produced to a lower standard.

INGENUITY: THE FOURTH DIMENSION

It is not uncommon for an ITT to attempt to fix the time, cost and quality parameters. The client's requirements specify the expected quality of the work, the delivery timescales are mandated and the available budget is capped at a specified figure. What then?

Bear in mind that the time–cost–quality relationship holds true for a given *scope of work*. A solution has an inherent scope of work associated with it, but not all solutions have the same scope of work, even though they may all satisfy the same set of requirements. Put simply, there are easy ways and hard ways to achieve the same goals.

As we saw in Chapter 4, by analysing the requirements in detail we often find that there are several possible solutions, all of which are capable of satisfying the requirements. By using ingenuity to find a solution which not only fulfils the requirements but can also be delivered or implemented more efficiently, we can establish a project which, in effect, has a smaller scope of work than the alternatives. Consequently, it often pays to look beyond the obvious solution.

Prerequisites for Good Estimation

WHY ESTIMATES, TARGETS AND COMMITMENTS ARE DIFFERENT

The process of estimating also means establishing the relationship between three crucial pieces of information (see Figure 6.5):

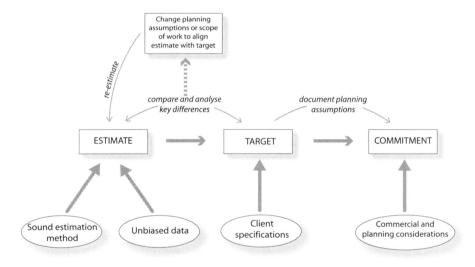

Figure 6.5 **Estimates, targets and commitments.** *The target is independently set by the client. The commitment is the commercial agreement on project delivery. The estimate is the objective assessment of what is achievable. Don't expect all three to be equivalent. Work may be needed to change scope, planning assumptions or delivery methods in order to align these quantities*

- the *estimate* (the output from the estimation process)

- the *target* (the 'ideal' answer, often specified by the client in the ITT)

- the *commitment* (what the project signs up to)

Only very rarely (*very* rarely) are these three quantities the same. Confusing them can be disastrous later on for the project.

Let's look at how things can go awry. Usually target dates are set by the client in the ITT (or are easily deducible from the requirements). However, once the requirements are properly understood, the bid team must make their own estimate of delivery dates. Suppose the team's estimates contradict the client's delivery targets (i.e. it doesn't seem feasible to meet the target dates)?

Often what happens next is that the estimates are 'manipulated' until they lie close enough to the target to enable a commercial commitment to be made. 'Manipulation' almost certainly means bringing pressure to bear on the estimators to revise their estimates until they indicate delivery by the target date is possible. In reality, all that is happening is that the estimates are being fiddled until the desired result is obtained. (Sound familiar?)

At this point the estimate is transformed into a commitment. From a sales perspective, the bid arrives at a stage where the estimates are apparently showing that the project will be able to deliver what the client wants, i.e. the estimates support the commitment that is made when the bid is submitted.

Clearly this manipulation of the estimate is highly dangerous – it is altering the outcome to reflect the answer being sought. Is that useful? Not in the slightest. It builds up false levels of confidence that the desired outcome can be achieved. If the project is complex, it may take a long time to uncover the truth of how the estimates have been fiddled – or more likely, the truth reveals itself as the project heads further into difficulty and the meaningless nature of the estimates is revealed in hindsight.

It is down to the bid manager to prevent this self-deception. As we have seen, it may mean working harder to find more ingenious ways of altering the scope, thereby bringing estimates and targets into alignment, or it may mean confronting the client with the implausible timescales and offering a workable alternative.

THE ROLE OF THE MANAGER IN BID ESTIMATION

When a bid is prepared, experts will often be drafted in to provide estimates for key elements of the solution. Even if you have no direct input into the estimates, there are several ways to ensure you are working with good estimates.

Before the estimates are done:

- Prepare the ground for the estimators. Helping them to understand the context of the estimate will get the estimator into the right mindset. Some estimators are naturally conservative, perhaps seeing problems which don't actually exist or don't have a good grasp of what needs to be done.

- Make sure the high-level project objectives are understood by the estimators.

- Provide sufficient background material to put what is being estimated into context. In a large or complex bid, it may be necessary to create a summary or briefing pack for the estimators containing the pertinent information.

- Ensure that the scope of work to be estimated is well defined and that any dependencies on other parts of the solution are clearly addressed. This will avoid 'double-counting' of boundary issues.

- Make sure any questions raised by the estimators can be answered quickly.

- Assess the estimator's mindset and character. (Cautious or over-confident? A details person or big-picture wizard?)

After the estimates are done:

Perform due diligence on the estimates you get back – that is, check that good estimation processes have been followed. You may not have the technical background to judge if the estimates appear reasonable but you can recognize the warning signs that the estimates don't have a sound basis. We will look at this further in Chapter 7 after first discussing the principles of good and bad estimating.

UNDERSTANDING THE SOURCES OF ERROR

Poor estimates usually arise in one of two ways:

- either the process of estimation is flawed (Chapter 7 describes a number of tried and tested estimation methods), or

- the inputs to the estimation process are deficient. Table 6.1 summarizes the most significant sources of error.

Table 6.1   Sources of estimation error

Sources of error	Consequences
Insufficient information about the subject of the estimate	• Misunderstandings about what is being estimated. • Double-counting where the boundaries between estimates are unclear. • Key tasks omitted because end-to-end processes have not been thought through. • Errors due to lack of relevant knowledge or previous experience of real issues. • Faulty assumptions.
Insufficient information about the context (e.g. how does the task being estimated align with the goals of the project?)	• Misunderstanding how quality objectives influence the work to be done. • No allowance for learning lessons from similar experiences. • Misinterpreted scope of work. • Missed opportunities for more creative approaches.
Insufficient information about the organization's delivery capabilities (e.g. will the project team have the right skills?)	• Faulty assumptions about the capabilities of the organization and/or the project team. • Unrealistic expectations concerning productivity.
Unrealistic expectations of the accuracy of the estimation method	• Insufficient attention paid to understanding the error bars. • Propagating false expectations of the accuracy of the estimate into key parts of the proposal.
Confusion over where to allow for risk (i.e. contingency in the estimates)	• Unduly pessimistic estimates. • No clear visibility of assumptions and hence inability to decouple core estimates from provisions made against key risks.

Table 6.1   *Concluded*

Optimism	• Bias towards low-end estimates. • Omission of crucial tasks (e.g. planning for a 'right-first-time' approach instead of allowing for re-work). • Optimism is generally a good thing during the bid stage but if this is allowed to unduly influence the estimates, it will store up trouble for the project later on.

If you are relying on others to provide estimates for the bid, make sure you are not being given 'off the cuff' estimates. Ask to see the working behind the numbers. A good estimate will be based on some kind of analysis, otherwise the figures are no more than guesses. If necessary, challenge the estimator to justify the figures and try to understand how much thinking has gone into them.

Once a project is up and running, there is a third factor which leads to a project failing to live up to its estimates. In this case, the estimates are not primarily at fault, it is the project itself. If the project is poorly managed (for example, best practice is ignored or management controls are weak, or the project is simply allowed to descend into chaos) then the estimates will be wrong, no matter how good the estimation process. In short, poor management will always invalidate the estimation assumptions.

You might think that this is not really an issue for estimation during the bid stage; the solution to the problem is more effective project management. This is true up to a point, but the estimation process should take into account the expected management style and competence levels. It is pointless estimating and planning a project on the basis of a fully skilled team if in reality the team will be under-staffed with novices.

Most formal estimation processes make an allowance for the skill and experience levels of those likely to be engaged on the project. Even with the crudest estimation process, if you know key members of the team lack experience or ability, it is important to make allowances. If your estimates are based on deploying the A team, then you had better be certain that the A team will actually be the ones executing the project.

CHARACTERISTICS OF A GOOD ESTIMATE

What then are the hallmarks of a good estimate?

- It should be possible to state the method (or methods) used to produce the estimate. (Be very wary of the 'expert judgement' method – Chapter 7 will explain why.)

- Two or more different (and objective) estimation methods have been used.

- More than one person has independently estimated the tasks.

- The estimators have demonstrated a good grasp of what is to be estimated and understand the context.

- Estimates have not been produced too quickly (indicative of guesswork or lack of detailed thinking).

- Estimates are accompanied by detailed assumptions.

- The estimates have been assigned confidence levels (or error bars).

- Metrics used in the estimates have been referenced (although not all estimation methods will depend on metrics).

Good estimates may not tick all of these boxes depending on circumstances, but a poor estimate will typically meet only a small number of these criteria.

TRACKING REQUIREMENTS

There is a fundamental relationship between a project's requirements and its estimates. Part of the secret of good estimation is building the link between the two and then maintaining it. Requirements are often unstable during the bidding stage (despite what the client may say). Sometimes this is because the business analysis of the problem hasn't been thorough enough, leading to confusing, contradictory requirements, or requirements which have been overlooked or are merely implied. It may also be true that the client doesn't yet know in sufficient detail what their requirements are. In both cases, expect the requirements to change, either during the bid stage or more likely, during the early stages of the project.

Is this a problem? Not if you have established a mapping between the requirements (even in their incomplete state) and the estimates. Once you have built this model, even though the requirements change, you can see the impact on the estimates and adjust them accordingly. The estimates will track any changes in the requirements.

Figure 6.6 shows the relationship between the project's requirements and the estimation model. Although there is a hierarchy (in the sense that the requirements are a detailed statement of how the project objectives will be achieved which in turn will – we hope – lead to business benefits), really it is the requirements which sit at the heart of the bid process. Every time the requirements change, the estimation must track these changes and take into account their implications.

We can think of the requirements as a detailed expression of the project's objectives. Satisfying these requirements should mean the goals of the project are reached. If goals are met, then we should expect business benefits to be achieved

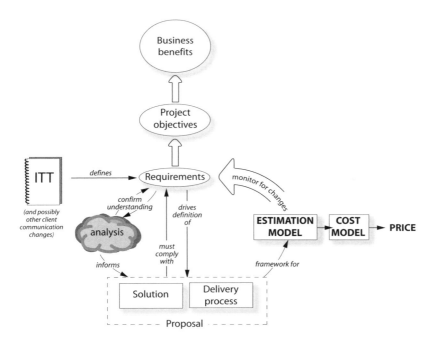

Figure 6.6   **The estimation model tracks any changes in the requirements.**
Very few projects have truly stable requirements. If (when) the requirements evolve, unless the estimation model is also adjusted, the project is likely to hit difficulties

– always supposing that the business case has been properly developed. Whilst these are ultimately the *raison d'être* for the project, we need the detail provided by the requirements to undertake both planning and estimation. You can't plan a project solely on the basis of its objectives or its expected business benefits: requirements are key.

It is the job of the solution to satisfy the requirements. However, the boundary between requirements and solution is often blurred. Too many ITTs contain 'requirements' which are actually the solution in disguise. This is a difficult situation because suppliers are then beholden to meet those requirements, even though better solutions may be available. Furthermore, the client is limiting the breadth of solutions offered by the bidders, often for no good reason except that someone holds a 'vision' of what the solution should look like.[1]

What we are left with is a simple cycle: the requirements drive the creation of a solution. How that solution is actually delivered is down to project planning (and the combination of solution and delivery approach is the *offering* we looked at in Chapter 2). The job of the estimation model is to quantify as best we can what is needed. The estimates have to take into account what the solution requires and the way in which it will be delivered. If the solution is the *what*, and the project delivery is the *how*, then the estimation model says *when* and *how much*.

Any change to the requirements will change either the solution or the delivery approach, or both. Even though small changes to requirements may not have any meaningful effect on the estimates, (i.e. they may be absorbed within existing error bars or there is no tangible impact on time, cost or quality) it is important to check. Requirements have a habit of evolving slowly. Small changes accumulate and if the estimation process is not tracking these changes, the project may suddenly find that the solution being bid is not what has been estimated.

---

1   A smart bidder will recognize this and challenge requirements which are not actually requirements at all but a representation of what the client expects the solution to look like. If done in the right way, not only does it open up more beneficial and cost-effective solutions, it allows the bidder to gain an advantage over competitors. Those who remain locked in to responding to 'pseudo-requirements' lose out on the opportunity to propose a more innovative solution.

Summary: Establishing the Project Framework

- *The estimation process fundamentally drives the development of the project framework.* To give the project the best chance of success, estimation must be done thoroughly.

- *Don't take 'expert' estimates at face value.* Check that a good estimation process has been followed and don't be afraid to challenge estimates which cannot be substantiated.

- Good estimates always have some kind of *associated error range.* An estimate is not the same as a *planning fact* so it is important to understand how much uncertainty attaches to each estimate.

- *Don't offer to deliver the impossible.* It is better to point out unfeasible requirements to the client than commit to something that cannot be delivered. The client may be impressed by the thoroughness of your analysis, particularly if you can suggest better alternatives.

- *Keep the estimation process simple.* Focus on estimating only those things that you most need to know.

- If the scope of work is fixed, *the sum of time, cost and quality considerations is also fixed.* Increasing one parameter means adjusting the others to compensate. Try to find more ingenious solutions which have a smaller scope of work.

- *Estimates, targets and commitments are different* and serve different purposes. Confusing these items can lead to serious problems later on.

- There are *three main sources of estimation error:* (a) a poor estimation process, (b) poor inputs to the process (e.g. poor data, invalid metrics), (c) misunderstood assumptions about how the project will be executed.

- An *estimation model captures the outputs of the estimation process* and relates them to the requirements. This model needs to be maintained during the bid: if the requirements change, so too must the estimates.

- Start building the estimation model as soon as possible.

7

Estimation Methods

I never guess. It is a capital mistake to theorize before one has data. Insensibly one begins to twist facts to suit theories, instead of theories to suit facts.

Sherlock Holmes in Arthur Conan Doyle's The Sign of Four

Now that we have seen the importance of estimation in the bid process, this chapter examines a number of tried and tested estimation methods. You will need to decide which methods to use (either independently or in combination) based on the scope of the project being bid, how much time there is to prepare the estimates, the availability (or otherwise) of experts in the relevant areas, the risk levels inherent in the project – and quite possibly a whole host of other factors.

Over the years certain industries have developed specialized estimation techniques which are tailored to their particular challenges and constraints. However, it is beyond the scope of this book to study domain-specific techniques. Instead, we will look at generic estimation methods. These can be used in most situations, irrespective of the nature of the project. These are worthy of consideration if you don't already have your own estimation methods.

All that really matters is that an appropriate level of rigour is used in the estimation, because the alternative is really no better than guesswork. Guesses may be enough to convince the client to award the contract, and so outwardly all may seem well. However, sooner or later, the guesses will be revealed for what they are. The project – and most likely, the project manager – will then find themselves in serious trouble.

Ground Rules For Estimation

Before choosing an estimation method, we first need to cover some basics which apply to all the estimation methods under discussion.

GRANULARITY

The *granularity* of an estimate refers to the smallest units (or objects) that form the basis of the estimate. A common unit is the 'work-day' but depending on the nature of your project, there may be better alternatives. Note that it is preferable to avoid estimating in terms of cost (at least initially) as this will confuse the process of converting the estimate into a cost and a price later on. (See Chapter 8.)

Suppose you are estimating tasks in terms of work-days. This is the number of days' effort required to complete a given task, not the elapsed time (which could be shorter if two or more people work on it full-time). On a large project, it generally doesn't make sense to estimate in anything less than whole numbers of days because the estimates rarely contain sufficient precision to justify it. In this case the granularity of the estimate is one work-day. Smaller projects may wish to estimate in hours, but in most cases a work-day (or possibly a half-day) is good enough.

DECOMPOSITION

Most estimation methods depend on breaking down (or 'decomposing') large tasks into smaller ones which are inherently easier to understand and quantify. The general rule is to keep decomposing the scope of work until you have tasks that are just above the chosen limit of granularity. Often this means identifying tasks which fall in a range between one to five work-days of effort. Don't settle for a mix of large and small tasks; there may be hidden complexity in the larger task that needs to be drawn out. For example, if you estimate a task at 20 work-days, it probably needs breaking down into sub-tasks. (See Figure 7.1.)

The decomposition of a project through many layers – workstream, product group, activity, task, sub-task, etc. – is a valuable part of the estimation process because it reveals details that might otherwise be missed. For example, take a simple job such as the production of a report. Suppose we base our estimate on previous experience where we recall spending two or three days writing a similar report. So four days sounds like a reasonable estimate in the circumstances.

However, this changes when we think more carefully about what actually needs to be done. What about the time to research key facts, put the first draft out for review, update the report based on feedback, print and bind copies for distribution, etc.? These tasks weren't readily apparent in the original task description. Without thinking through what the job actually entails, these steps could easily be missed out of the estimate. Four days to write a *draft* may be a reasonable estimate for that part of the task, but the actual scope of work is much broader. A better estimate might be closer to six or seven days – nearly double what we initially thought.

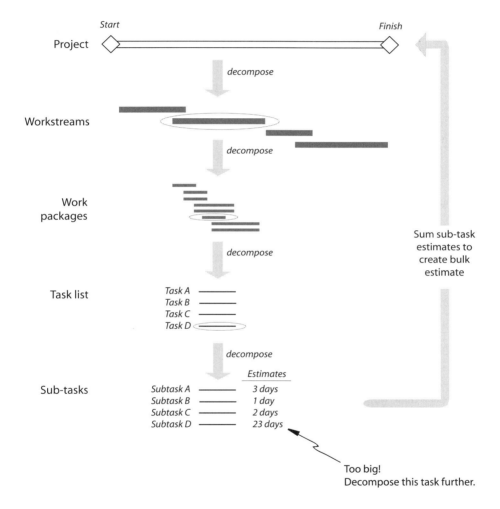

Figure 7.1   **Task decomposition is the first (and crucial) step in estimation.** *The project is broken down until sub-task estimates approach the chosen granularity for estimation (in this example, one work-day). Summing the estimates for each sub-task builds up an estimate for the entire project*

RANGE, PRECISION AND RELEVANCE

A good estimate embodies a range of possible outcomes, not a single value. Suppose your boss asks when you will have that feasibility analysis report ready. It is 1.04 p.m. You do a quick calculation and estimate there is another three-and-a-half hours of work left. 'It will be on your desk at 4.34 p.m. this afternoon,' you reply.

Full marks for a snappy and competent-sounding answer, but let's see what trouble you may be storing up.

- There is no *range* associated with the estimate. How late might you be? Hours? Days? Is it even possible you might beat that deadline?

- The *precision* of the answer sets false expectations. You can't possibly know that you will deliver at precisely this time (unless you finish early and stage-manage the delivery).

- The answer may not be providing the right information (i.e. is the answer *relevant*?). What you meant to say is that this is the time you think you are *most likely* to deliver the report, but your boss may be more concerned with when delivery can be guaranteed to his line manager.

RANGE

If we simulated carrying out the report-writing task enough times, we might end up with a graph like that shown in Figure 7.2. Each point on the curve represents a possible completion time, with the vertical scale showing how likely that outcome is.[1] The peak of the curve corresponds to the most likely completion time (4.34 p.m.) But even though this is the most likely, there is still only about an 8 per cent chance of actually achieving this, and a less than 50 per cent chance of completing on or earlier than this time. Lots of things could go wrong: you may be distracted by a phone call, or the printer jams, or your computer crashes, or … equally, everything might go swimmingly well and you could finish *before* the most likely time.

---

1   This is similar to the Monte Carlo statistical method where an activity is simulated many times and each outcome is plotted. The resulting graph typically has a distended bell shape.

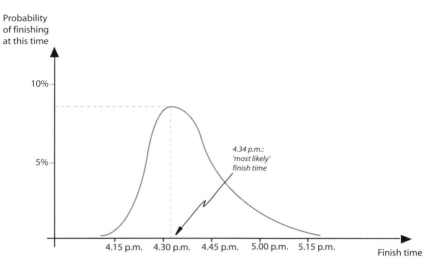

Figure 7.2   **The theoretical spread of possible outcomes.** *An estimate tries to establish the 'most likely' result but also needs to express the possible range of outcomes*

What the graph shows is that it is almost impossible (i.e. less than 0.5 per cent likely) to finish before 4.15 p.m. It also shows that even if all the risk factors actually materialize, the work should be finished by 5.15 p.m. These mark the end points of the range, the points at which the likelihood of such an outcome is so small (typically less than 0.5 per cent) that it can reasonably be ignored.

PRECISION

The apparent precision of the answer is likely to set false expectations. It implies you can estimate to the nearest minute when this work will be complete, which is ridiculous: 4.34 p.m. is only the *most likely* time to complete the report; the actual range of possibilities is much broader.

RELEVANCE

The answer given might have misjudged what the other person is really looking for. Your boss may not be interested in the most likely estimated delivery time at all. Perhaps they need a *worst-case* estimate, the time by which the report is virtually guaranteed to be ready. Giving a single-value answer doesn't address this. You don't want your boss to assume you are guaranteeing completion by 4.34 p.m. when in fact there is a greater probability of finishing after this time.

So a better answer might have been, 'The report should be ready sometime between 4 and 5.15 p.m. I'm aiming for about 4.30 p.m. but even if there are problems, it should be done no later than 5.30pm.'

ERROR BARS

Figure 7.2 is all very well, but particularly during a bid you are unlikely to have the results from multiple simulations available to plot in this way. Instead you might need to express the inherent uncertainty of an estimate more simply with an error bar.

Error bars show the range of possibilities from worst case to best case, usually with an assessment of the most likely result (which may not necessarily be the middle of the range). Figure 7.3 shows the estimated number of days needed to complete five project deliverables using error bars.

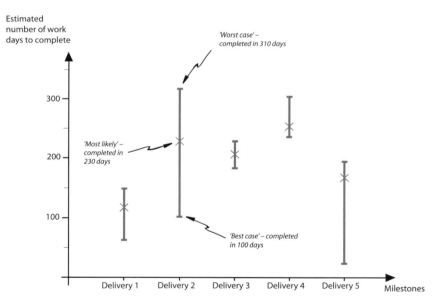

Figure 7.3   Using error bars to show the estimation range and confidence level. *An estimate should always be expressed as a range not a point value. This provides valuable context for assessing and making use of the estimate*

Notice how much more information is contained in Figure 7.3 than simply listing the five *most likely* work estimates for the deliverables. For instance, we can tell that there are relatively high levels of uncertainty associated with Delivery 2 because the error bar is much larger. Delivery 3 appears much more predictable as it has the smallest errors bars of any of the deliverables.

Deliveries 4 and 5 have 'most likely' values which are skewed away from the mid-range point. It is likely that Delivery 4 can be completed close to the 'best case' date but there may be some risks which could significantly extend the duration. Conversely, there may be an opportunity to achieve Delivery 5 much earlier than otherwise expected, but the likelihood is not great.

CONSTRAINED BY THE CONE OF UNCERTAINTY

You may already be familiar with the cone of uncertainty. This is a common-sense model that simply states the further ahead we try to predict, the more uncertainty there is (see Figure 7.4).

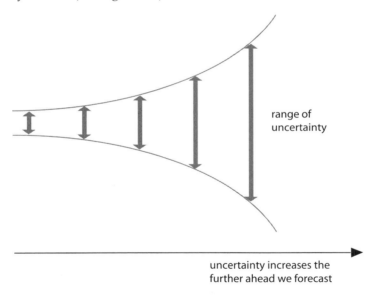

range of uncertainty

uncertainty increases the further ahead we forecast

Figure 7.4   **The cone of uncertainty.** *Uncertainty increases the further ahead we forecast, undermining estimation precision*

The accuracy of any forecast (which is all an estimate is, after all) generally worsens the further ahead we try to look. For impending events, we are more likely to have better information, a clearer understanding of what is involved and can therefore estimate with greater precision. Conversely, estimating activities which will occur months or even years in advance attract much wider margins of error. This has nothing to do with how good the estimation process is; it is a fundamental limit on the precision of the estimates.

This has important implications for estimation during the bid because estimates will be used to determine firm delivery commitments which sit far out in the cone of uncertainty. A bid manager's best defence is to pay careful attention to the error bars implicit in the bid-stage estimates.

SIZE MATTERS

A 10 per cent margin of error on a very small (say 50 work-day) project may be acceptable at the bid stage. The same margin on a 5,000 work-day project may not. So the size of the project will almost certainly influence the choice of estimation method and the diligence and care with which it is applied. This is tempered by the effort and cost of the estimation process and the constant pressure from limited time and resources during the bid.

HOW MUCH ESTIMATION CAN YOU AFFORD?

How good do the estimates need to be? It is worth asking this question because there is no point committing large amounts of bid effort to create estimates with very narrow error margins when less precision will suffice.

It is really a question of risk. What are the consequences of basing the project plan on relatively imprecise estimates? What tolerances are being set on the project? Is there scope to avoid making firm commitments until better information is available, e.g. once the project has started? These questions can only be answered once the project risks are better understood.

ESTIMATION ASSUMPTIONS

Estimates are only suitable for planning purposes if:

   •   the scope of what has been estimated is clearly defined

- the underlying assumptions are documented.

Whilst the first is usually covered, the latter is frequently overlooked. Assumptions are usually obvious to the estimator at the time, but if not written down, are quickly forgotten when someone else is asked to review or re-estimate.

CHANGING ASSUMPTIONS

If you are already familiar with the submission process for large-scale commercial proposals, you will know that there is invariably an adjustment period late in the bidding cycle. Perhaps the client wishes to 'play off' shortlisted bidders to see who can provide the most attractive solution or price (the 'best and final offer' or BAFO stage). Sometimes the client realizes late in the day that the requirements need to be modified. Or they may have been intrigued by a particular supplier's proposal and want to see if the others can match or better it.

Whatever the reason, there is often a change to the requirements which needs to be reflected in the solution, the estimates, the cost model and ultimately the price. (And usually very little time in which to make these changes.) A change to the requirements therefore ripples down through various constituents of the bid as Figure 7.5 shows.

The supplier who has all these elements assembled, documented and linked together (or at least understands how they influence each other), clearly has an advantage. They are quickly able to assess the impact of the changed requirements on the solution and delivery approach, and ultimately how this will affect the price. The supplier who doesn't have these things in place has a choice: work very hard to manually compute the impact of the changes – or guess. (No prizes for spotting which is the most common choice.)

To be well-placed to handle BAFO-type situations requires well-documented assumptions. These, together with the agreed scope, are the foundations on which the estimates are based. If these foundations change, it is much easier to see how this affects the estimates.

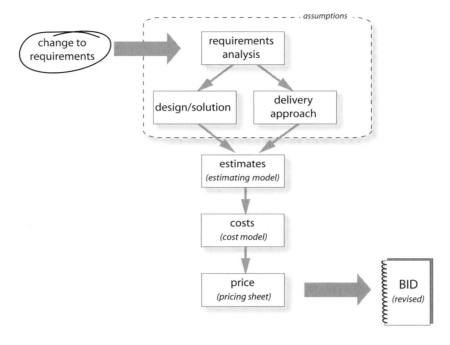

Figure 7.5   The ripple-down effect caused by a last-minute change to the requirements. *A supplier needs to be able to assess quickly the impact at each stage in the process, much of which depends on understanding the underlying assumptions for the estimates*

DOCUMENTING ASSUMPTIONS

There are really only two criteria for recording estimation assumptions:

- A list of all the things that must be true in order for the estimate to remain valid.

- A list (but almost certainly not a comprehensive one) of things which must be avoided for the estimate to remain valid.

Returning to the earlier example of estimating the time needed to produce a report, Table 7.1 shows some examples of estimation assumptions.

Table 7.1   Estimation assumptions for producing a report (example)

Things that must exist, or remain true or unchanged	Things which must not happen
The scope of the report.	Assignment to higher priority work.
Agreement on the content and structure of the report.	Lack of access to IT equipment (computer, printer, etc.).
A template for the report.	Inability to work (e.g. illness).
Knowledge of the intended audience and what they are expecting.	
Access to the necessary research materials.	

It is true that assumptions can be rephrased so that they appear in both columns. However, it is best to think of the left-hand column as a closed list: what are the vital things in order to fulfil the task? The right-hand column is an open list. Avoid restating the negative version of left-hand column items and instead look further afield for risks which could disrupt the task. Bear in mind that the right-hand list can never be exhaustive, so focus only on the things which represent the greatest threat to the basis of the estimate.

ESTIMATE BIAS AND SECOND-GUESSING

An estimate must be honest. It must be free from bias or influence. The estimator must ignore preconceptions of the expected result, or pressure applied by others as to what the answer *ought* to be. Providing the estimation method is valid, properly applied and draws on objective data, there is no justification for refuting the estimate, no matter how unpalatable the answer may be. Resist any attempts to 'refine' or 'tweak' or 'fine-tune' the estimates. Recognize them for what they are – attempts to move the estimate closer to a more desirable outcome.

BIAS

Biasing the estimates – that is, allowing preconceived notions to influence how much work particular tasks *ought* to take – is an inherent weakness of estimation methods which rely on judgement. Since judgement – even that of recognized experts – is often flawed by all kinds of bias, it is a reason to avoid this estimation method if there are suitable alternatives. An estimator may catch themselves thinking, 'Oh, that's a lot more than I expected. Perhaps I've made a mistake. Let me run the figures again.' However, the best estimate is almost always the first estimate. Unless you realize that a factor in the estimation process has been omitted or wrongly interpreted, the temptation to re-estimate should be resisted.

SECOND GUESSING

'Second guessing' is a variant of the estimation bias problem. It is common among less experienced estimators who, sometimes unconsciously, aim to come up with results they believe will satisfy their bosses. Subtle psychological factors are often at work. An estimator may be reluctant to present their manager with an unexpected answer. Perhaps they feel under pressure to provide results which conform to expectations. Unfortunately, second-guessing the 'right' outcome helps no one. Although a larger than expected estimate may cause immediate problems, it is far better to tackle these head-on in the bid stage than win a project which must then try to meet impossible goals.

Simple precautions to reduce bias include:

- give estimators 'permission' to estimate honestly

- avoid preconceptions of the 'expected' answer

- estimate individual parts in isolation (this prevents cumulative totals from biasing the remaining estimates)

- resist the temptation to re-estimate (assuming the method has been diligently carried out).

Case Study: Task Estimation

James is summoned to Sophie's office. 'I have an important task for you,' she says. 'The company wants to announce the launch of a new product at the shareholders' meeting next month. Before then, I'll need to run a feasibility study. I need you to work out how long the feasibility study will take and provide me with the planning data so that I can schedule the resources. Talk to Peter; he organized the last one for me.' As James is about to leave, Sophie says, 'Oh – and James. You won't let me down like Peter did, will you? This launch is a vital one for the company.'

James gets straight on to it. He speaks to Peter who gives him a copy of the estimates he produced for his earlier study. When James reviews them, he notices that this was a smaller-scale study in a different market sector. No matter – he can reuse the work breakdown. Using this as a template, James spends the afternoon developing his estimates.

The answer dismays him. The numbers are coming out about 50 per cent higher than they did for Peter's study. Worse, they show that it may not be possible to complete the feasibility study in time for the shareholders, meeting. Clearly, Sophie will not find that acceptable.

James takes a hard look at his estimates. There are a few areas where he feels his judgement may have been too cautious. He goes through his figures again, trimming where he feels able. The results are better, but still on the high side. A third pass enables him to really pare some of the estimates to the bone. Now his figures are comparable to Peter's – and that tells him he must be in the right zone.

Fast forward several weeks. The feasibility study has turned into a shambles. It has become apparent several important tasks have been forgotten in the estimates. Why? Because they didn't feature in Peter's smaller study and James didn't think to look beyond this. Worse, James' figures are proving to be systematically underestimated. There is no possibility of completing the feasibility study in time. Had this been known at the start, it might have been possible to defer the shareholders' meeting but now it is too late. Sophie is fuming because the event is going to be an embarrassing fiasco.

Did you spot where things went wrong?

Estimation bias. From the outset there was an expectation (by Sophie) that the study could be completed in time for the shareholders' meeting, but there was no basis to believe this. This acted as a strong bias on James' estimates. Added to this was the pressure 'not to let her down like Peter'. This sent a clear message that Sophie was not expecting to be told that the feasibility study could not be done in time.

Invalid comparison. There was merit in looking at the comparable elements of the work previously done by Peter. However, James failed to look beyond this for other tasks which needed to be included. What looked to be a comparable piece of work at first sight actually turned out to be only partially comparable.

Confusing estimates with commitments. The commitment to complete the work by the time of the shareholders' meeting went unchallenged. It was assumed that the estimate would back this up. In fact, James' first estimate refuted this. He rejected this important fact because he knew it didn't fit Sophie's preconceptions.

Invalid adjustments to the original estimate. James didn't like the first answer he got. This was due in part to second-guessing Sophie's assumption about the shareholders' meeting. By refining the estimates twice more, all objectivity in the original estimate was lost. In fact, James only stopped at this point because he had arrived at the answer that everyone was hoping for. The estimate was reverse-engineered to fit with the known commitment.

Ignorance of actual data. James looked at Peter's estimates but did he think to look at how long it actually took Peter to complete the earlier study? Judging by Sophie's remarks, Peter's estimates had also proved to be poor. James was merely compounding this error. Had he based his estimates on 'actuals' he would have avoided making the same mistakes that Peter did.

Commonly Used Estimation Methods

Some estimation methods are better suited to certain situations than others. Table 7.2 introduces some commonly used methods and provides guidance on their selection. The following sections will then explain how to apply each method.

Table 7.2   The suitability of different estimation methods

Estimation method	Best suited to ...
Expert judgement	Although commonly used, this method delivers relatively poor precision. It is, however, a quick method and may be suitable for: • Small to medium projects (typically less than 1,000 work days.) • Projects with well-defined areas of specialist work. However, if different experts are estimating different parts of the project, boundaries need to be clearly delineated. • Bids with very short response times.
Consensus expert judgement	This is a variant of 'expert judgement' which aims to achieve better precision by aggregating several expert judgements. Following the old adage of two heads are better than one, it is reasonable to expect some improvement in precision. However, if the experts share a similar background and mindset, it risks propagating systemic errors. It is suitable for: • Medium to large projects (greater than 1,000 work days). • Complex projects with many internal or external dependencies. • Projects with a clearly defined scope and stable requirements. • Long lead-time bids.

Table 7.2   *Concluded*

Estimation method	Best suited to ...
Count and calibrate	This simple but highly effective method can be used in virtually any situation. The key is to identify suitably representative elements to count. It is suitable for: • Any scale of project. • Projects with a clearly defined scope. • Projects where good historical data exist (i.e. metrics). • Projects with a recognizable (and quantifiable) attribute, e.g. production units, function points, discrete requirements, etc.
Comparison method	Comparisons are often misleading because projects that appear similar at first glance frequently turn out to have very different factors at work. It is suitable for: • Truly repeatable projects. • Projects where good historical data exist (i.e. metrics). • Projects which can draw on previous lessons learned. • Small to medium projects (typically less than 1,000 work days).
Industry or proprietary methods (i.e. specialist methods)	Use existing methods if they are established and well understood by your organization. These can be supplemented by the generic methods above to verify (and over time, fine-tune) the specialist methods.

EXPERT JUDGEMENT

Estimation via expert judgement is a simple concept: take an expert in the relevant field, harness their knowledge, wisdom and expertise (collectively, their 'expert judgement') and apply it to the task of quantifying individual elements comprising the task or work package.

Of course, different areas of the project may require different experts. (Be sure that the boundaries are clearly defined so that you avoid double-counting.) Collate the results. You now have a detailed set of estimates built upon expert judgement.

Obviously, the choice of expert is important and they should meet two criteria:

• The expert must have the breadth of knowledge to grasp the issues and break the work down into suitable tasks and sub-tasks for estimation. They must understand what jobs need to be done, how they interact, where problems are likely to occur, etc. – and be able to factor all these things into the estimate.

- The expert must have experience (and preferably hard data in the form of metrics) for how much time, resource or cost these activities will take. This incorporates lessons learned from comparable work, adjusted for the specifics of the new situation.

Arguably, expert judgement is the most commonly used form of estimation. It is relatively quick and straightforward – and there is sufficient ambiguity in what constitutes an 'expert' so that the method can be adapted to available resources.

However, it is often forgotten that being an expert in a given field does not automatically equate to being good at *estimating* in that field. The judgement required for good estimation is entirely different to the skills an expert undoubtedly has in their chosen field. There are no hard and fast rules: prior to formal training, some people are just inherently better at estimating than others. The only universal truth is that almost everyone is significantly worse at estimating than they think they are. It is the main reason why this method delivers relatively poor results.

Table 7.3   Getting the best from expert judgement

Try to ensure:	Avoid:
The expert has extensive experience of estimation, ideally through feedback on the precision of their estimates once the work has been completed.	Experts with a known track record of being poor estimators.
A 'blame-free' environment where there is no such thing as an unacceptable estimate.	Experts with a point to prove or a pet theory to be supported. This can lead to biased estimates.
The expert is prepared with a thorough background brief – a clearly defined scope of work, constraints, dependencies, issues to be considered, key assumptions and the overall goals of the project.	Placing pressure on the estimates to conform to preconceptions (either implicitly or explicitly).
All working assumptions are documented. These should be independently reviewed.	Revealing interim results of the estimation. These may bias the remaining estimates.
Estimates are based on established metrics where available. These should be as 'local' as possible, i.e. industry metrics are generally less useful than an organization's own metrics.	Re-estimating. The first answer will be the best answer unless the scope of work or underlying assumptions change.
	Making comparisons with other projects which are not borne out under scrutiny.

It is dangerous to be too prescriptive without knowing the context of the estimate, but the following process (see Figure 7.6) may be useful.

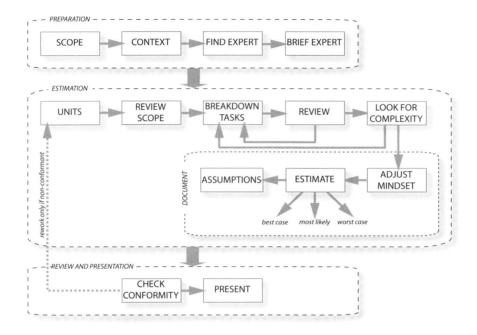

Figure 7.6   **Estimation using expert judgement.** *This shows a simplified process flow for estimation, broken down into three distinct stages*

PREPARATION

- *Scope.* Identify clearly what needs to be estimated (scope of work, where the boundaries lie, etc.).

- *Context.* Identify the context for the estimate (important constraints, key assumptions, particular factors to consider).

- *Find an expert.* This must be someone who has experience of this kind of work, understands potential problems and inherent complexities and, ideally, has a good track record in estimating such jobs.

- *Brief the expert.* Provide only the facts relating to the scope and context of the estimate. Don't bias the expert or give an indication of what answer is expected. Set a deadline for the estimation and any other ground rules to be followed (e.g. how it should be documented).

ESTIMATION

- *Units.* Decide on the estimation units. Are you estimating in work-days, or cost, or volume of material required, number of functions to be implemented, etc.? (See also the 'count and calibrate' method).

- *Review scope.* Review the scope and context of the estimate. Are there valid comparisons with previous jobs, preferably where good metrics are available?

- *Break down tasks.* Break the work down into smaller tasks.

- *Review tasks.* Review the work breakdown, remembering to avoid the assumption that work is done right first time.

- *Look for complexity.* Are there high scoring risks that need to be taken into account?

- *Adjust mindset.* Adjust your mindset to be as objective as possible (neither optimistic nor pessimistic about the tasks to be accomplished).

- *Estimate.* Generate three estimates for each element:

  1. A *worst-case* estimate. What if the key risks materialize? What if nothing goes according to plan? How long – assuming you have chosen to estimate duration – will the work take? Obviously there is no limit to the number of things that could theoretically delay the work, so a certain amount of pragmatism is needed. Suppose you had to give a guarantee of completing the work (say to 99 per cent confidence). How long would you want to allow in order to *guarantee* to have the job done?

2. A *best-case* estimate. Suppose nothing unexpected happens, work is done perfectly first time, and no problems or complications emerge? Another way of thinking of this is to ask, what is quickest this job could feasibly take, even if the chance of this happening is very small?

3. A *most-likely* estimate. This is your subjective view, taking into account all the known factors, weighing up your experience of this kind of job and your judgement about what kind of risks and difficulties are likely to emerge. This is the estimate that, in your judgement, is the most likely outcome.

4. Record estimates for each item at the lowest level of the work breakdown. A single pass is sufficient – don't be tempted to revise the initial estimates unless there is clearly a good reason for doing so.

- *Assumptions*. Document underlying assumptions and indicate how the estimates are likely to be affected should key assumptions change.

REVIEW AND PRESENTATION

- *Check method conformity*. Check that the estimates (particularly those prepared by others) conform to basic requirements: e.g. estimates have a range not just a point value, assumptions are documented, etc.

- *Present*. Decide how to present the estimates, typically either graphically (such as in Figure 7.3) or in a table.

CONSENSUS EXPERT JUDGEMENT

As the name suggests, this method is a variant of the expert judgement approach. The main difference is that two or more experts are asked to estimate the same thing independently. These estimates are then jointly evaluated by the group and the process repeated as many times as necessary until all the experts are able to agree on a single set of estimates.

Responsibility for reaching a consensus falls solely on the group of experts, not the 'owner' of the estimate (such as the bid manager or project manager). The owner may have a vested interest in a certain outcome (e.g. a low estimate to make the bid price look attractive) which could unwittingly bias the consensus outcome.

SECOND OPINIONS

Seeking a second opinion is not the same as a consensus approach. The danger is that if the second estimate is close to the original, this is often assumed to validate the original estimate. In fact, it may only be confirming that both estimates suffer from systemic error or the same bias.

Significant differences naturally indicate that further analysis is needed, but even so, with only two points of reference it is impossible to tell whether they define the error range or merely lie within it. (It is also common for discrepancies to be post-rationalized, as in: *Obviously expert B didn't have the same grasp of the problem because his estimate is wildly different, so we'll ignore it and go with the first estimate.*)

The process for consensus expert judgement uses many of the steps shown in Figure 7.6. For convenience, Figure 7.7 has collapsed these to highlight only the consensus part of the method.

Although better than relying on the judgement of a single expert, this method still has drawbacks. One problem is that the estimates may still contain systemic errors. If the experts share similar backgrounds, or work for the same organization or have been involved in the same projects, they may be subject to the same kinds of bias. Consequently, agreement amongst the group of experts is no guarantee of precision; it may only indicate that all members of the group share the same preconceptions.

The group of experts may also be subject to more subtle psychological factors. One such problem occurs when no true consensus emerges. If different opinions are strongly held, and some members of the group are unable to be reconciled, the will of the strongest personalities (or most senior staff) may well dominate. But those who shout loudest don't necessarily have a claim to better judgement. It is worth bearing in mind that more junior staff who are not yet indoctrinated into the systemic views of the organization can sometimes bring a fresh perspective to the estimation discussions. They may see problems and issues (or solutions and opportunities) which are missed by the greybeards.

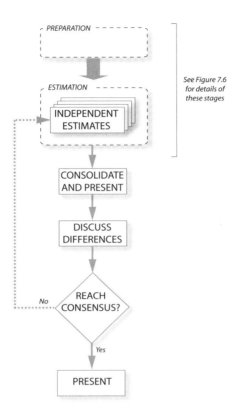

Figure 7.7   **Estimation using consensus expert judgement.** *The preparation and estimation stages are identical to the expert judgement approach of Figure 7.6. The process repeats until all experts can agree on a single set of estimates (including error ranges)*

Although the consensus expert judgement method is relatively sophisticated (and scores over the single expert method) it can also be quite labour intensive and potentially time-consuming depending on how many iterations are needed. Neither aspect particularly suits it to a bid activity where typically time and resources are both in short supply. However, if it is a high-stakes bid, such effort will more than pay for itself in a project which is set up with a realistic schedule and properly costed budget.

COUNT AND CALIBRATE

The count and calibrate method is deceptively simple but can be highly effective. It relies on finding some representative aspects of the work (sometimes called *proxies*), counting them and then converting that count into time or cost or some other chosen unit.

Remember the earlier example of trying to estimate the work in producing a report? Suppose we first work out what key sections and subsections are needed (i.e. break the work down into its components). We could then count how many subheadings appear in these sections and how many graphs or tables are needed. Let us say we count a total of twelve subheadings and five tables/graphs. Using metrics gleaned from similar reports, perhaps we know that a subheading section typically runs to around 750 words. The metrics also tell us that taking into account time for researching, drafting, review and revision, a technical author can, most likely, produce on average 500 words of finished text per day and that a table or graph typically takes a half day to produce.

Using this information we can convert the count of sub-sections into a word count (12 subsections × 750 words = a 9,000 word report). At an average of 500 words a day, the text will take 18 working days. With five tables/graphs planned, an additional 2.5 working days are needed – but since we only work in units of whole days, we will round this up to three. So altogether, we estimate the report will need 21 days of effort. This is our 'most likely' estimate. We then repeat the process using worst-case and best-case metrics to arrive at the full range of the estimate.

The validity and precision of this method depends on three things:

- Choosing representative aspects of the work to count. (This needs to be something tangible at the bid stage, not an artefact of the output of the task. Couldn't we have used page count metrics? Possibly, but the number of pages in the report would depend on layout, font size etc. – issues which have no real bearing on how long it would take to produce that page.)

- Accommodating different aspects of the work. (It was important to recognize that tables and graphs required different amounts of effort and needed to be counted separately.)

- Access to good metrics. (Unless we already knew from analysis of previous reports what the average production times for text and graphics were, we would have been reduced to guessing. Remember also, it is not the estimates from previous plans but the *actual* task durations that are important.)

The goal of this method is to eliminate judgement as far as possible. Counting is objective. Converting the counts into estimation units (e.g. workdays) using metrics is also objective. In so doing, we are removing the risk of human bias, although now a lot depends on the accuracy of the metrics. (This is why the continuous collection of project metrics is so important for future estimation.)

If possible, choose to count something where there will be actual data from the project early on. It will then be possible to calibrate the estimates early in the project. If this reveals systemic errors in the estimates, there may still be time to replan and work around this problem if caught early enough.

Figure 7.8 shows the main steps in the process.

COMPARISON METHOD

If you have previously managed a similar project and have access to actual task durations or other types of metric, then perhaps you can estimate using the comparison method.

There are obvious drawbacks. Strong similarities may exist at a high level but no two projects are ever quite the same. If you are using the comparison method for an entire project, there are bound to be important differences. The comparison will have some gaps and these will need to be filled by other estimation methods.

For ease of reference, let's call the historical project (or a subset of tasks in a historical project) the *reference* project. The thing we are trying to estimate is the *target* project.

A reference project that is more than about three years old probably isn't suitable for comparison estimation. Too many things change in that time: delivery processes are improved, key staff move on, technology advances, clients develop different expectations, etc. Also be wary of comparing projects

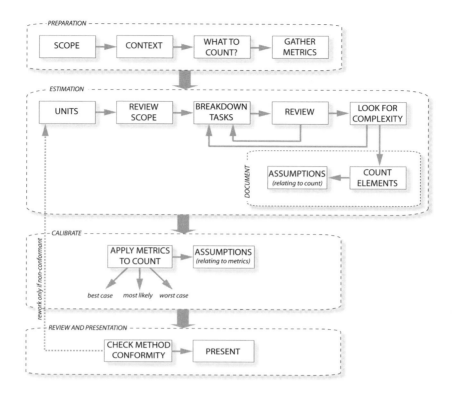

Figure 7.8   Estimation using count and calibrate. *The aim is to reduce the dependency on subjective judgement. By counting tangible elements of the work and calibrating using proven metrics, much greater precision is achieved*

of differing sizes. Bigger projects will have 'overhead' factors: they will take longer to get going (i.e. inertia), will require more effort to maintain good communication across the team, and may suffer from lower productivity and general inefficiencies.

Three key questions will determine the suitability of the comparison method:

- *What are the differences between the reference and the target?* How significant are they? How will you estimate their impact if there is no direct comparison in the reference project? It is often easy to spot similarities, but these can blind you to the differences. Such differences may have a large effect on the estimates, and may even invalidate the comparison method.

- *Do you have accurate data for the things you are comparing?* The data must quantify what actually happened in the reference project. It is no use going back to the *estimates* for the reference project; if these were inaccurate last time, you will simply be repeating the same errors in the estimates this time round. You should also review any lessons learned from the reference project. Note that not all organizations will have good enough data to support the comparison method.

- *Are the similarities superficial?* Many projects will appear similar at first glance. Peel away the superficial layers and look closely at the details. How similar is the work break down structure? Will the client behave differently? How different are the delivery timescales? Are there different external dependencies? Will the same staff be working on the project? If not, will the team have the same skills and experience? There are many such questions. Before using the comparison method, make sure there really are enough similarities to make a meaningful comparison.

Figure 7.9 shows the main steps in the comparison method.

PREPARATION

- *Identify the reference project.* Examine the reference project carefully. Are the similarities just superficial? Is there enough data on the reference project to use in the comparison?

- *Scope.* Check that the scope of work in the reference and the target are broadly equivalent.

- *Context.* Are there key differences in the context of the project which might invalidate the method? For example, are timescales shorter? Is the client harder to please?

- *Gather history.* There needs to be access to good data on the project (i.e. what *actually* happened, not just what was planned) for any meaningful comparison.

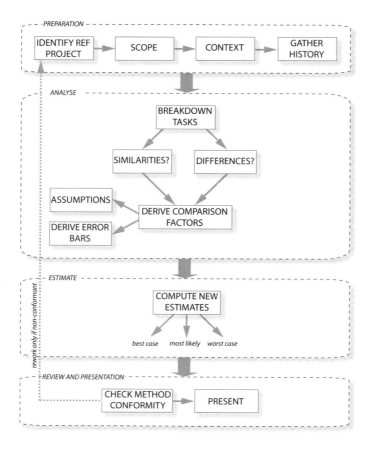

Figure 7.9   Estimation using comparison. *The validity of the method depends on how well the similarities and differences can be factored into the reference estimates*

ANALYSE

- *Break down tasks.* Work out what sub-tasks are needed. How does this structure match the sub-tasks in the reference project? Get as close as possible to the chosen granularity of the estimate, i.e. aim for sub-tasks with durations of less than 10 days.

- *Similarities?* At the most detailed level, how similar are the tasks? What percentage of the sub-tasks are similar?

- *Differences?* What are the key differences? Any aspects of the work not present in the reference project will need to be estimated using a different method.

- *Derive comparison factors.* Determine how the reference data will be used. For example: is the work comparable but requires twice as much effort due to size differences? Then a comparison factor of two is used on the reference data.

- *Derive error bars.* Capture any uncertainty in the comparison factors, for example: target estimate = reference data × 1.5 (comparison factor) +/– 25 per cent (error range).

- *Assumptions.* Document any assumptions made when deriving comparison factors.

ESTIMATE

- *Compute new estimates.* Apply the comparison factors to the 'actuals' data from the reference to arrive at the estimate for the target project. As with other estimates, it should be possible to calculate best, worst and most likely estimates using the error bars set in the previous step.

REVIEW AND PRESENTATION

- *Check method conformity.* Check that the estimates (particularly those prepared by others) conform to basic requirements: e.g. estimates have a range not just a point value, assumptions are documented, etc.

- *Present.* Decide how to present the estimates, typically either graphically (such as in Figure 7.3) or in a table.

Due Diligence on Estimates

A manager working on a bid of a reasonable size (say, anything in excess of a few hundred work-days) will most likely need to rely on others to provide estimates for at least part of the work. It is therefore useful to be able to recognize the warning signs of poorly executed estimation.

RECOGNIZING THE WARNING SIGNS

Generally, most problems arise either from a poor choice of estimation method, a method applied with insufficient rigour or a failure to take proper account of margins of error. Table 7.4 shows some of the warning signs to look for.

Table 7.4   How good is the estimate? A checklist

Warning sign	Indicates:
A quick response	Quick estimates may have been made subjectively. Good objective estimation takes time (for example: to fully understand the scope, analyse the sub-tasks, etc.) and requires access to historical data. A quick answer may well suit the needs of the bid manager, but make sure you are not being given a 'guesstimate' instead of a properly developed estimate.
Lack of detail	A well-developed estimate will have detail: estimates against a detailed work breakdown, well-documented assumptions, confidence levels, etc. Single value estimates have not been produced by a rigorous estimation method.
Emphasis on judgement (or instinct)	Too much emphasis may have been placed on expert judgement. All expert judgement is subjective and may be open to bias. A certain amount of judgement is unavoidable in producing most estimates, but it should be treated with caution nonetheless.
Poorly documented (or missing) assumptions	Either not enough thought has gone into the analysis or assumptions have been made but not recorded. In the latter case, the precision of the estimates may not be jeopardized, but last-minute changes to requirements will be very difficult to factor into revised estimates.
No error bars (i.e. single value estimates)	A lack of rigour during estimation. Single value estimates say nothing about inherent uncertainty. Very often they belie a confusion between 'best case' and 'most likely' and set incorrect expectations.
Preoccupation with a target result	Bias may creep into the estimation process if the estimator has an expected result in mind. For this reason it is best to avoid cumulative totals during the estimation process; there is always a temptation to adjust the remaining estimates to steer towards a particular target.

Table 7.4   *Concluded*

Warning sign	Indicates:
Too much faith in comparable projects	A failure to analyse the similarities and differences with sufficient rigour. This leads to key elements of the work being overlooked in the estimation process or incorrect factors being applied.
Poor mindset	Do you recognize the estimator as a natural risk-taker or are they overtly cautious? Will they let this mindset cloud their judgement? Where this risk exists, it is best to avoid methods which rely too much on judgement.

OPTIONS FOR DEALING WITH POOR ESTIMATES

Suppose we recognize some of these danger signs in the estimates we have been provided with. What to do?

The chances are that the pressures of the bid schedule and/or lack of expert resources leave little room for manoeuvre. However, you may be able to do at least one of the following:

- *Arrange to re-estimate* – using different people (with different mindsets, skills or experience) or different methods. You will also need a strategy for reconciling the different estimates (a consensus judgement method might work, if time permitted).

- *Increase error bars to reflect uncertainty in the estimates* – but without close involvement yourself in the estimation process, you may lack the information to properly quantify these.

- *Add contingency* – this is similar to arbitrarily increasing error bars. Since the goal of estimation is to provide objective data, any allowance for uncertainty should ideally be made later in the process. Adding contingency at the estimation stage can confuse matters. This is entering the realm of judgement factors which are applied to convert objective costs into a price (see Chapter 8 for details). If you reach a position where you have little or no confidence in the estimates, the whole process becomes subjective and degenerates into guesswork.

- *Document any concerns for possible rework later* – this approach accepts that there are flaws in the estimates but that the planning must proceed anyway. Although unsatisfactory, it will at least provide the project manager with early warning of possible problems. For instance, it may prompt the project manager to validate estimates during early stages of the project and be prepared to replan accordingly.

- *Play for time* – you may have an option to ask the client for more time to prepare the bid. If so, this may allow re-estimation to take place using better estimation methods.

- *Avoid commitment* – what scope do you have to avoid making firm commitments to the client if you suspect the estimates to be poor? The options are probably limited if this is a commercial bid. However, consider the commercial dangers of any contractual commitments. One way might be to propose a replanning activity not long after the start of the project. This will allow the project manager to factor in new information on requirements, timescales, etc. once initial discussions have been held with the client. It can be presented to the client as a way of keeping the project flexible, i.e. the schedule is not fixed in stone until after this planning meeting, so the project can be refined once underway. (Remember the discussion around the cone of uncertainty.) Naturally, it will also allow time for the project team to produce more thorough estimates and therefore plan on the basis of more realistic data.

Summary: Estimation Methods

- *Strive for an even breakdown of work* where the most detailed task is typically only a few days' effort. Large tasks may be concealing unexplored complexity which won't be properly factored into the estimates.

- *An estimate always has an uncertainty range (or error bars) associated with it.* The simplest way to quantify this is to estimate best-case, worst-case and most-likely case values.

- *Avoid estimating with meaningless precision*. The precision of an estimate can set false expectations. If your estimate has an error bar of several days, it is pointless specifying a most-likely delivery time in hours and minutes.

- *Uncertainty increases the further ahead we try to forecast*. If possible, look for ways to avoid estimating for activities far into the future, e.g. by providing indicative estimates for future phases and then replanning/re-estimating nearer the time.

- *Document the assumptions which underpin the estimate*. The estimate may need to be modified (possibly by someone else). It is vital to understand the basis on which the original estimate was made.

- *Avoid estimation on the basis of judgement*. Judgement is often flawed. Those who are experts in doing something are not necessarily experts in estimating those tasks. It is much better to use objective estimation methods, e.g. count and calibrate.

- *Be sensitive to things that might bias estimates*. Don't specify what the expected answer is ahead of estimating. Steer clear of running totals during the estimation. Avoid putting pressure on estimators, and don't automatically dismiss estimates which are very different to what is expected – there may be important messages here! Above all, don't be tempted to re-estimate solely because the first estimate is unpalatable.

- Check for the warning signs of poor estimation (see Table 7.4).

8

Realistic Costing and Pricing

Get your facts first, then you can distort them as you please.
Mark Twain, American author and humourist, 1835–1910

Having produced the best estimates we can, given the circumstances of the bid, it is time to convert these estimates into financial figures. The price quoted to the client is obviously a vital part of the bid and – all other things being equal – could be the deciding factor which determines whether your bid is successful or not.

But before we can propose a price to the client (bearing in mind that the price offered is a subjective, sales-influenced decision) the bid team must develop (and maintain) an underlying cost model. The role of the cost model and its relationship to the bid price are addressed in this chapter.

Price Versus Cost

Don't confuse price with cost. These are two very different aspects of the bid and need to be dealt with separately:

- *Price* – this is what the client pays. It represents the value of what you deliver to the client (which may be hugely different to what it costs your organization to deliver). You may choose to present the price as a single number or break it down into any number of components. (Usually the client will tell you how the price should be presented: make sure you follow these instructions to the letter.) Regardless of this, the price is a judgement call. Someone in your organization will need to decide what is a commercially acceptable price, taking into account many variables such as competitiveness, risk, market positioning and the strategic importance of the contract.

- *Cost* – this is what it will cost your organization to deliver the solution in full. The cost will encompass all aspects of the work – not just the cost of buying things such as hardware and software, but 'people costs' associated with developing, installing, configuring, delivering, managing and supporting the project. Your costs will also make allowance for risks, e.g. by setting a contingency budget, allowing for inflationary price rises, banking costs associated with late payments – and many other possible factors.

Table 8.1   The vital differences between cost and price

Cost	Price
… is what it will cost you as the supplier to deliver everything described in your proposal.	… is what the client pays.
… is objective. Costs are real – they are what your business will end up paying. Every part of the solution that goes into the bid has a cost, although it may be hard to figure it out accurately.	… is subjective. The price is often a judgement of what you feel will be acceptable to the client, or is competitive in the marketplace.
… is purely for internal purposes and is not usually disclosed to the client.	… is the only pricing information the client sees, i.e. the bid price.
… is calculated according to well-understood internal accounting practices. For example, your organization will have determined how manpower is costed to recover the overheads of your business.	… *may* be linked to the predicted costs (e.g. cost plus desired profit margin) or may be set at an arbitrary figure, e.g. one that is calculated to win the work.
… is never discounted. It is simply the cost of doing the work.	… may be discounted at the discretion of the supplier.
… reflects only the actual cost of doing the work, not profitability.	… includes a margin for profit or, conversely, may be discounted below the cost if deemed a strategic sale.

Your goal during most of the bid life cycle should be to focus on cost alone. Get the costs right and the pricing will be a straightforward job (see Pricing Review). To avoid confusion, keep costing and pricing entirely separate, e.g. don't add profit into your cost model. The cost model should state as accurately as possible what it will cost to do the work (and no more). What you then charge the client is a separate decision.

Cost Principles

Everything that goes into your solution has a cost, and you need to know what it is. As each element of the solution is developed, it makes sense to determine the associated costs and begin to build up a comprehensive cost model. Table 8.2 lists some key principles to bear in mind.

Table 8.2   Cost principles

Key principle	The benefits
Every factual statement in the bid has a cost	… even though you may not be able to accurately say what it is. So either estimate, or satisfy yourself this cost is covered elsewhere in the cost model. A requirement that has no cost associated with it can mean only one of three things: • you are prepared to do the work for free; • the requirement adds no real value for the client (i.e. it is either meaningless or is already covered by other requirements); • there is genuinely no cost associated with delivering this requirement. The last option is exceedingly rare.
Build your cost model bottom-up	A complex proposal usually requires costs to be assigned to low-level tasks which are then grouped together and summed, sometimes through several levels of hierarchy. This is 'bottom-up' costing, (i.e. summing individual costs up through the task hierarchy) as opposed to 'top-down' costing where you determine a total cost and then see how this is allocated across tasks.
Choose the right level of detail	The level of granularity in your cost model is an important decision. Too coarse, and you will have an inflexible cost model and probably an inaccurate total cost on which to price your solution. Too fine, and you may be setting yourself an impossible task to calculate and track costs. If costs are directly based on estimates of other quantities (e.g. a work-day which has a fixed cost), then the level of detail will be determined by the granularity of the underlying estimates.
Honesty	The cost model is worthless unless you are completely honest about the costs. If you estimate cost on a best case/worst case basis, use the median value in the first iteration of your model. (The time for tightening comes later – see Cost Scrubbing.) Remember, costing must be as objective and accurate as you can make it.
Make the cost model flexible	Costs may change during the bid. They may well evolve throughout the bid process as your solution grows and is refined. Every decision you make during the writing of the proposal has the potential to affect the cost model. And it doesn't end once the proposal is submitted. You may be called to negotiate with the client. Requirements may be dropped or redefined and you will need to know how this changes your costs and ultimately, the price.

Table 8.2   *Concluded*

Key principle	The benefits
Look for warning signs	A key benefit of the cost model is that it should warn you if you are likely to exceed budget. The sooner you know this, the sooner you can do something about it – i.e. by descoping some part of the solution or choosing a cheaper alternative. The cost model is a vital tool during bidding. It keeps track of how price-competitive you are. Make good use of it.
Be alert for opportunities	Challenge costs. Look for alternatives. Be alert to ways of achieving the same outcome for less, perhaps by combining elements that are usually done separately. Are there synergies with other projects? Can you be innovative in how the project is delivered? Can you negotiate a better deal from your suppliers?

Building the Cost Model

The cost model can take pretty much any form you choose. Your organization may have a standard cost model, but think carefully whether this is designed to best serve the needs of the bid team. It may be constructed in such a way as to feed the right information through to the accounts department or the sales director but be less suitable for your needs as bid manager. You may be better off building a separate bid manager's cost model and linking the key elements to other internal models. This allows you to tailor the cost model to the bid and keep control of its structure. You may also need to do something like this if asked by the client to provide a price breakdown. Table 8.3 shows what you need from your cost model.

Table 8.3   **Key aspects of your cost model**

The cost model	Why is this needed?
Is it complete and comprehensive?	Don't miss vital cost elements. It is easy to assign cost to obvious aspects of the solution such as hardware and software but make sure you've costed for *all* the client's requirements. If the client requires training, have you budgeted for materials and hire of facilities? If you need to travel to the client site frequently, make sure travel and accommodation are included. It is worth mapping each requirement to a matching cost in the model to be sure nothing has been missed.
Does it contain the right level of detail?	Break the costs down to an informative and manageable level. This is a judgement call: too high a level and you are not seeing the full picture and may be glossing over risks and uncertainties; too detailed and you will be wasting time on trivial things. If you have to crudely estimate a particular task, it may indicate that you need to break it down further to a point where you can more accurately estimate the cost.

Table 8.3   *Concluded*

The cost model	Why is this needed?
Can it be changed easily?	There are many reasons why the cost model may need to change – a change to the solution to bring the cost down, last minute additions of items that have been overlooked, etc. The client may want to negotiate with you on your price, i.e. trade off functionality against price, and will expect you to be able to rapidly come up with revised figures. Avoid 'hard-wiring' your cost model spreadsheet. By building in a little bit of flexibility at the start, it will save you considerable time in the latter stages of bidding.
Can you track those changes?	Several months into the project, the project manager won't thank you if you can't recall the reasoning behind the cost model. Because cost models are frequently adjusted – often at the last minute – you need to document why these changes were made. This can be done in two ways: • Major changes to the cost model should trigger version control, i.e. archive your old cost model and create a new version (suitably labelled) with the changes. • Annotate changes within the cost model spreadsheet. A simple notes field can save immense frustration later on. That revision to a licence cost may make perfect sense now, but could be meaningless to you in a couple of months when the reasons for making the change have been forgotten.
Does it directly map to the client's pricing structure?	Some clients request pricing information to be broken down into particularly awkward categories. Notwithstanding this, it makes sense to make it as easy as possible to calculate and produce the price breakdown directly from the cost model. This way, when costs are amended, the revised price is easily calculated. But the conversion process should be a separate step that takes you from the cost model to the pricing sheet. Ideally, you will be able to pick up subtotals from your costing model and convert these to their priced equivalents on a separate spreadsheet.
Are estimates based on quantifiable sources?	Can you justify the estimates in the cost model? Have you done similar work before? Do you have accurate metrics on what it took to complete (not just the estimates at the bid stage, or you may find you are simply repeating estimation errors from last time). If you are forced to make rough estimates, have you identified the risks which could affect their accuracy?
Can you independently verify the numbers?	Spreadsheets are wonderful things. Their flexibility means that you can lay out your cost model any way you want. It also means you can design all manner of errors into the model which, if you don't have a way of independently validating the model, can prove disastrous. Never entirely trust what the model tells you unless you can cross-check that the figures are accurate.

It is important to be scrupulously honest with yourself when putting the numbers into the cost model. If you are worried the bid is going to exceed the client's budget, don't be tempted to shave the cost estimates. The cost model has to be an accurate statement of anticipated cost – or at least, as accurate as you can make it in the circumstances. If there are problems with the price, then there are steps you can take: remove functionality (and therefore cost), look for more cost-effective ways of delivering the solution, discount the price. But first you have to have a firm and accurate cost model to work from.

MAINTAINING THE COST MODEL

Having set the cost model up, keep it up to date. Usually this job falls to the bid manager but on a large bid ownership of the cost model may be allocated to someone else, or even a small team. Each part of the proposal should have a corresponding section in the cost model. As a section is written, someone must check that the solution described in the text matches the costs in the model.

There are five key questions to be answered:

1.   Which part of the cost model does this section of the proposal correspond to? *(Has it been properly costed?)*

2.   Do the costs in the model match the scope of what is being described in the text? *(If the text is being rewritten, has the scope changed which implies a change in the cost model?)*

3.   Could the solution be interpreted in a different, more expansive way by the client which might therefore have a much higher cost implication? (*Consider rewriting the text to remove ambiguity.*)

4.   Does the cost model account for this part of the solution in more than one place (i.e. is there a risk that the cost has been double-counted?)

5.   Are there costs in the model which don't map back to a section in the proposal? *(Why not? Can these costs be removed, or is there a missing section in the proposal?)*

Key Stages of Financial Review

You will almost certainly need to be developing a good awareness of cost right from the start of the bidding process. The further you progress through the bid, the better your understanding of cost drivers and component costs. However, there are key stages where cost plays a particularly important role. (Refer to Figure 3.2 in Chapter 3 for a summary of the generic bid process.) These are summarized in Figure 8.1.

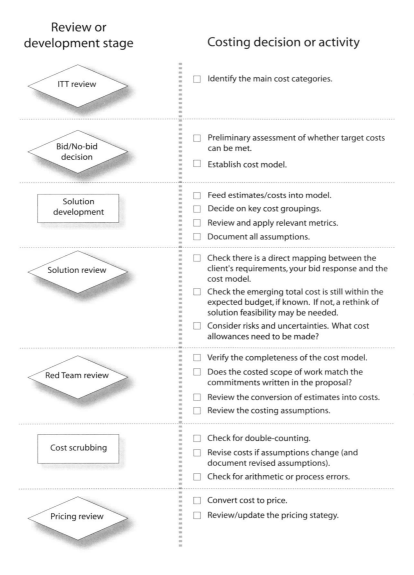

Review or development stage	Costing decision or activity
ITT review	☐ Identify the main cost categories.
Bid/No-bid decision	☐ Preliminary assessment of whether target costs can be met. ☐ Establish cost model.
Solution development	☐ Feed estimates/costs into model. ☐ Decide on key cost groupings. ☐ Review and apply relevant metrics. ☐ Document all assumptions.
Solution review	☐ Check there is a direct mapping between the client's requirements, your bid response and the cost model. ☐ Check the emerging total cost is still within the expected budget, if known. If not, a rethink of solution feasibility may be needed. ☐ Consider risks and uncertainties. What cost allowances need to be made?
Red Team review	☐ Verify the completeness of the cost model. ☐ Does the costed scope of work match the commitments written in the proposal? ☐ Review the conversion of estimates into costs. ☐ Review the costing assumptions.
Cost scrubbing	☐ Check for double-counting. ☐ Revise costs if assumptions change (and document revised assumptions). ☐ Check for arithmetic or process errors.
Pricing review	☐ Convert cost to price. ☐ Review/update the pricing stategy.

Figure 8.1   Key stages of costing activity in the bid process

BID/NO-BID

Can you price the work within the client's budget? To answer this question, you need to know two things:

- the approximate solution cost;

- your pricing strategy.

At this stage, your solution cost will be a rough estimate. Think about the components of the solution, how it will be delivered, maintenance costs, etc. and consider the full project life cycle from kick-off to contract end. Are there figures from similar projects which will serve as a guide? How risky is this work – what contingency costs will you need to allow for?

You may not have all the answers, but it is important to ask the questions. You need to establish if your price is likely to be in the right ballpark. If you can see major cost obstacles, perhaps you shouldn't bid. Far better to realize this now before resources have been committed.

Although cost and price are related, as we have seen, the total project cost should be arrived at objectively, whereas your pricing strategy will be dictated by internal policy or sales strategy. For instance, if senior management have decided that all projects must achieve a certain profit margin, you need to understand the pricing implications, and whether it will price you out of the competitive running. You may need extra time to discuss specific pricing strategies with senior management before a decision can be made on whether to proceed with the bid.

Many organizations have different procedures depending on the size of the bid in financial terms. It is important to know if your proposal will cross a threshold which requires you to follow a different internal sign-off process. On large bids this can sometimes be lengthy and bureaucratic, and you will need to allow time for this in the plan.

ITT REVIEW/SOLUTION DEVELOPMENT

As your understanding of the requirements develops, the main cost drivers will become apparent. Key points to look for are:

- Do you understand all the components of the solution, including how it will be developed, delivered and maintained?

- Are there difficulties, for example: parts of the solution which you lack experience in, untried technologies, or requirements which have no obvious solution?

- Are there synergies with other projects or products, i.e. opportunities to save money by interpreting the requirements creatively?

- Are there requirements with hidden depths? These are requirements which look deceptively simple but prove to be fiendishly hard (and therefore expensive) to fully address. (You will probably want to keep a separate list: these can be the subject of a trade-off analysis. You may be able to offer the client a significantly cheaper solution if they are willing to relax or waive certain requirements.)

Each of the above will drive the cost – either up or down. Keep a list of these factors, particularly areas where there is uncertainty over costs.

SOLUTION REVIEW

You will be reviewing your solution at regular intervals, checking for the five Cs:

- *Conformant* – is it delivering what the requirements asked for?

- *Comprehensive* – are all the requirements covered? (Are there issues to address which the client hasn't specifically mentioned in the ITT?)

- *Coherent* – has the solution been clearly described?

- *Consistent* – are there any contradictions in the solution?

- *Cost-effective* – does the proposed solution represent value for money? Is it innovative?

- You will need to add detail to your cost model throughout the solution development stage, assigning cost against each component. When you review the solution, review the costs at the same time, even though there may be more work to come.

- What areas are difficult to cost? (What needs to be done to fix this?)

- How close are you to the target cost? (If it looks like you may overshoot significantly, you may need to change your solution or adopt a different pricing strategy.)

- What are the assumptions on which your costs are based?

- How can you validate your costs? (Are there other cost models you can compare against? Can you involve independent reviewers?)

- What are the risk areas that will need to have a contingency cost attached?

RED TEAM REVIEW

There is more detail on the 'Red Team' in Chapter 12, but the point of the Red Team review is to assess the completeness of the proposal and assess (from the client's perspective) how well it has addressed the ITT. It is important that this is always done within the context of pricing. The review team will need to form a view on the suitability of the solution but also its affordability (and value for money) to the client.

By this stage, the cost model should be mature. It will have been broken down to an appropriate level of detail and all costs will have been entered (or estimated).

The Red Team reviewers will want to satisfy themselves of the following:

- Does the cost model reflect all aspects of the solution? (Is there anything missing from the cost model?)

- How accurate are the costs? (Have steps been taken to independently verify estimates or cross-check with other cost models?)

- What are the key risk areas and what provision has been made in the costs?

- What are the cost drivers? (Can an alternative, more creative approach result in significantly lower costs?)

- Are the cost assumptions valid?

This is the last chance to make significant changes to the solution. It is vital that changes arising from review comments are then reflected in the cost model. Keeping the cost model in step with the proposal is demanding (and may be resource-intensive on a large bid) but is crucial nonetheless.

COST SCRUBBING

Cost scrubbing typically happens during the final scrutiny of the cost model just before the pricing section is finalized. After this stage, there should be no major changes to the costs. However, there is always scope for errors in the cost model or refinements. Cost scrubbing is the process of examining each element in the cost model and spotting errors or double-accounting.

As we have seen, there may be pressure to cut costs to achieve a desired price, but costs should never be reduced arbitrarily. To reduce cost, you must reduce functionality. The golden rule is:

Only reduce cost if there is a clear and justifiable reason for doing so.

Points to bear in mind when cost scrubbing:

- Check for the same cost appearing in two different places (usually under different guises).

- Check that the cost model is complete, i.e. it reflects all aspects of the requirements and the proposed solution.

- Check for arithmetical errors in the spreadsheets (a very common problem!) (Use checksums and different subtotals to catch discrepancies.)

- Document the reasons for any cost changes to provide an audit trail for future use.

- Challenge the basis for each cost. (Are the assumptions valid?)

PRICING REVIEW

The pricing review has a different focus to costing activities, although pricing and costing are often addressed at the same time. In any pricing discussion it must be recognized that the costs are fixed. If the price that emerges is too high, it is the pricing strategy that needs to be changed, NOT the cost model. If the costs have already been 'scrubbed' there is no more scope to cut costs – at least, not without significant risk of the project subsequently failing.

Of course, the reality is rarely so black and white. This is why it is a good idea to separate the cost scrubbing from the pricing review. It distinguishes between two distinct processes. The first enables a best and final estimate of costs, based as much as possible on objective estimation. The second process sets the price, based on cost but taking into account a number of more subjective factors.

Nevertheless, what are the options if the price is too high?

- Change the pricing strategy – reduce the profitability or discount the work.

- Modify the allowance for risk – reduce the contingency set aside to cover risk areas (but think very carefully about how this reduces the likelihood of the project's success).

- Change the scope of the solution – i.e. by removing elements (or finding cheaper ways of implementing them) it is legitimate to modify the cost model accordingly.

In any of the above, make sure there is full discussion of the consequences and that the decisions are carefully documented.

Factors Affecting the Price

Whereas costing takes place throughout the bid, pricing decisions can be made relatively late on – but make sure unusual pricing strategies have been considered at the bid/no-bid stage. There is nothing more demoralizing than realizing just before the submission deadline that you cannot meet your client's budget.

Your organization will most likely already have a pricing model which determines the optimum price based on your known costs. In the simplest case, it will take your total cost, add an appropriate profit margin and this will set the price quoted to the client. But there are many other factors you may need to consider:

- Is it a fixed price contract or time and materials? The price may need to include additional contingency to reflect your risk as the supplier.

- What is the value of your solution, as perceived by the client? The client may be prepared to pay more for this perceived value.

- How much uncertainty is there in the cost model? Does the price need to include higher than normal levels of contingency?

- Do you know the 'price-to-win', i.e. the price in the marketplace which will undercut your competitors?

- Are you prepared to offer discounts on your usual pricing model to improve your chances of winning the work? This may be a strategically important sale that perhaps justifies making a loss on the work.

- What price is the client expecting? Is the client's budget capped? There is little point in submitting a price that the client can't afford.

Summary: Realistic Costing and Pricing

- Keep *the difference between price and cost* firmly in mind at all times. Costs are objectively·estimated and stay fixed. Pricing is a strategic decision, depending on what profit levels are desired.

- Every element of the solution should map to a requirement and will have an associated cost.

- *Build and maintain a cost model* throughout the bidding process to keep track of costs.

- Where costs are likely to evolve or change during the bid, consider *linking the pricing model to the cost model*. This way, when the cost changes, it is automatically reflected in the price.

- Keep the cost model as simple as possible otherwise errors may creep in.

- Every time the cost model is adjusted, *keep notes* about why the change was made. What assumptions have changed?

- Use the cost model to *check that the solution is within budget*. If not, don't fiddle with the costs, look for ways to reduce the scope of work or provide a more creative (and cost-effective) solution.

- Review costs against the five Cs of the solution: conformant, complete, coherent, consistent, cost-effective.

- Only reduce cost if there is a clear and justifiable reason for doing so.

- *Modifying the price is a sales decision*. This may squeeze profit margins because the costs are still fixed.

9

A Structured Approach to Writing the Bid

Any intelligent fool can make things bigger, more complex and more violent. It takes a touch of genius – and a lot of courage – to move in the opposite direction.

E.F. Schumacher, economist, 1911–1977

Back in the 1970s the British comedians Morecombe and Wise performed a much-loved comedy sketch with the famous conductor and pianist André Previn. After the first few bars, Previn is appalled at Eric's excruciatingly bad piano recital which is most definitely not Grieg's piano concerto in A minor. 'You're playing all the wrong notes!' Previn exclaims. There follows a few moments of shocked silence, then Eric grabs Previn firmly by the lapels and says, 'I'm playing all the *right* notes, but not necessarily in the right order.'

If you don't have the right structure for your proposal, you will end up sending the right messages but not necessarily in the right order – and that matters. You need the proposal to flow, just like a piece of music. Structure is vital for getting your messages across clearly: it orients the reader, putting each idea within the proper context. If you don't have structure, your proposal becomes a formless mess of ideas, facts and sales messages. This chapter will look at how to avoid that.

However, before you can present these ideas in a logically consistent structure, you must have a well-developed bid solution (Chapters 4 and 5) and a project framework (Chapters 6, 7 and 8). Once the structure of the bid is defined, the final stage is the presentation and choice of writing style (see Chapter 10). These things will have a major influence on the persuasiveness of the proposal.

Why Structure Matters

The bigger and more complex the proposal, the greater the importance of choosing the right structure. Various aspects of the structure will often be dictated by the client and your starting point must always be the instructions given in the ITT. But there is usually some leeway – how you break a chapter into subsections, the order in which topics are addressed, and the logical flow of your arguments from paragraph to paragraph.

Establishing a structure before you begin writing has a number of benefits:

- It is easier to see what sections need writing if these are mapped against an outline for the proposal.

- The structure defines the scope of what needs to be addressed – it avoids the problems of including too much or too little. A good structure will ensure that your proposal covers all the right topics, and doesn't wander off into irrelevant areas.

- A good structure enables better planning of bid resources. Progress can then be measured against this plan.

- Writing and reviewing assignments can be allocated according to the bid structure.

- Repetition is avoided. If the bid is logically structured, information need only be written up once. The client will be able to quickly find the relevant information without needing to search through the entire proposal.

Choosing the Right Structure

The structure of your proposal should meet the following criteria:

- *Informative* – it must be clear what information is contained in each section by using meaningful titles and subtitles.

- *Logical* – the sequence of sections must make sense. The client shouldn't need to read the sections out of order to understand the proposal.

- *Comprehensive* – don't miss out any important sections just because the client hasn't explicitly asked for them.

- *Hierarchical* – important components of your solution should appear more prominently in the structure than less important topics. As you descend the hierarchy into the subsections, the client will expect to see greater detail which expands on the themes in the top-level headings.

- *Emphasis* – the proposal structure will reflect areas you wish to emphasize. An important topic may be addressed over a large number of pages (although most likely broken down into carefully chosen subsections). Less important issues need only be covered briefly.

- *Relevant* – are you adding sections which aren't needed merely because you think they will impress, or because you already have material to hand?

A TYPICAL PROPOSAL STRUCTURE

Most proposals will need to address the following types of information in one form or another. (Note: this is not intended to be a complete list. More complex bids are likely to require many more additional sections.)

- *Executive summary* – a high-level view of the salient points of the bid.

- *Business context* – demonstrating an awareness of why this work is important to the client, and the constraints and assumptions which act upon it.

- How the *client's goals and objectives* will be met – what does the client hope to achieve from this project? If you can't state this clearly, you can't make a persuasive argument for choosing your solution. (Note: this section must not simply repeat what the client tells you in the ITT. It should begin to outline the key parts of your solution and show how these will satisfy the objectives. By doing so, you also demonstrate you understand the client's goals and underlying problems.)

- *Technical solution* – the 'what' and the 'how' of your solution.

- *Management solution* – how will you implement the project? When will the components be delivered? How will the project be managed? (More on this in Chapter 11.)

- *Your qualifications for doing the job* – why should the client pick you as the supplier? Can you demonstrate the right skills and experience?

- *The price for executing the project* – what will it cost the client? How is this price broken down? Are there options and other variables?

- *Compliance* – demonstrate by cross-references that the proposal addresses all of the requirements and issues raised in the ITT.

Differently worded headings could be used and sections may be combined or split up according to the complexity of the proposal. But what remains is a list of essential information that needs to be included *somewhere* in your proposal.

CUSTOM-BUILT

Your proposal must appear to be custom-built for the client even if, in reality, you have been fortunate enough to reuse some material from previous bids. This is true for the structure as well: what worked for an earlier client is not necessarily the right structure this time round. You may need to change the emphasis of the bid by reordering sections, or 'beef up' a section because it has special relevance to your prospective client.

There is often a temptation to throw everything you have into the structure, particularly if you have a rich archive of proposals to consult. For example, suppose a client requests specific details of service delivery levels. Resist the temptation to add many pages of pre-written material on generic service management principles from a previous bid. The client is interested in specifics, not an essay on service management.

A certain amount of reuse may be a good thing, if it genuinely adds value to the bid. You may be able to suggest new elements of the solution that the client hasn't thought of. However, your proposal structure can quickly grow convoluted if you add in irrelevant subsections. These won't be of interest to the client and will damage your efforts to show that you understand what the client needs. Think carefully about whether recycled material is strictly relevant. Setting yourself page limits against major section headings can help prevent the proposal becoming bloated and unfocused.

Keep generic materials such as sales brochures, product specifications or other types of promotional literature out of the main part of the proposal structure. Since these are not tailored to the client, you don't want to appear to be 'padding out' the bid. Background material can go in an appendix – and even then it is in your interests to keep it to a minimum.

SETTING PAGE LIMITS

Size does matter. Working without page limits often leads to inflated, poorly structured proposals. The temptation is to include everything you can think of, no matter that it may be of little or no relevance.

Most clients appreciate brevity. They have better things to do with their time than read unnecessarily wordy bids. Don't skimp on the important issues, but you will make a more favourable impression on the client if the proposal is concise and keeps to the point.

Take a close look at the bid structure and decide how many pages you will allow for each section or subsection. Aim for a consistent approach. For example, important sections might need five or six pages each, less important ones perhaps only half a page. Obviously, if the client has imposed page limits in the ITT these must be followed – although you might need to break these down further to make sure you don't exceed the page budget.

Once the page limits have been set, do everything you can to stay within them. If you don't keep to the page budget, the brevity of the proposal will suffer. Words are cheap and paper isn't rationed, so proposals can quickly grow to unwieldy lengths, particularly if no one is coordinating inputs from a team of writers.

Page limits will also keep the writing process honest. It forces you to edit judiciously, pruning away irrelevant material, polishing it for succinctness. By limiting each section to a set number of pages, suddenly your sentences and paragraphs are precious commodities: you can only afford to put your best material down on the page.

ACTIVE VERSUS PASSIVE HEADINGS

The words you choose for each section heading perform an important job: they signal what information will be found in the following section. Don't miss the opportunity to use the section headings to make an impact.

Each heading should be a signpost: this is what you can expect to find in this section of the document. Try not to use a title that only makes sense *after* you have read the text. If you use a misleading or obscure form of words, you may confuse the reader from the outset, or signal to the reader that you were confused when you wrote the section.

One-word titles are very common but generally unhelpful because it is difficult to convey much meaning in a single word. At best, the one-word title will state the subject, but it says nothing further about the topic or the conclusions reached.

Take the title 'Risk'. It is a safe bet that the section will contain some pertinent information about project risks, but will this section identify specific risks or does it merely acknowledge that there will be some? Does it describe the risk-management process? We have no way of knowing until we read the section. As a pointer to (or a reminder of) the content of the section, it is relatively unhelpful. If instead the title read 'Use of Contingency Planning to Avoid Risk', we would immediately understand the context of what followed. (Yes, this title is more unwieldy, but the additional information it conveys makes up for this.)

A good way to find a communicative title is to use active sentence fragments. As the name suggests, an active sentence conveys the impression of something actually happening instead of being reported in a passive style. Table 9.1 shows some examples to give you an idea.

In some cases, these titles almost become mini-themes (see Chapter 4 on key themes). This is the goal. By using a more meaningful title you are reinforcing the themes that are the backbone of your proposal.

The downside is that active headings are generally longer, and it is equally important not to end up with long and unwieldy sentences for titles. Use discretion.

Table 9.1   **Using active headings to communicate with the reader**

Unhelpful heading ...	Active heading ...
Management Approach	Our Standards-Based Approach to Management
Track Record	Our Experience and Capabilities in this Market Sector
Objectives	Fulfilling the Goals of Your Long-Term Business Plan
Communication	Establishing Clear Lines of Reporting
Quality	Applying Our Independently-Audited Quality Standards

Another tool at your disposal is the direct form of address. Direct address recognizes that there is a dialogue going on between you (the supplier) and your reader (the client). Here is an example of a direct form of address:

> **Our** *proposal describes how* **we** *will implement the application on* **your** *live server.*

The highlighted words speak directly to the reader. Contrast this with an indirect form:

> *The proposal describes how Company X will implement the application on the client's live server.*

It is plainer English to use 'our' and 'your' rather than the more formal organization names (as long as you have established who the relevant parties are at the very start). Modern business writing tends towards the use of formal modes of address, but this often results in dull, convoluted sentences which send the reader to sleep.

Direct forms of address are associated with plain-speaking. There is much less room for confusion, and meanings are obvious. Although there is a time and a place for formal writing, bear in mind that we all respond better to people who say what they mean, clearly and directly – and your clients will be no exception.

DON'T SAVE THE BEST UNTIL LAST

Assume yours readers are fickle: they may not make it right to the end of your masterpiece. Perhaps they will dip into the proposal, read a section here or there that seems relevant, and then grow bored towards the end. So don't save your best material to the end of the proposal, because it may not get read by everyone. Aim to get your key themes across early on. After all, you are not writing a novel; the client won't be expecting you to build up the suspense and unmask the killer in the final section.

The first few pages in a proposal (and to some extent, in each section) are the critical ones. These are the most-read pages, and this is where you need to summarize your arguments as concisely as possible. This is why the Executive Summary (or Introduction) is a vital section: it is the one part of the proposal you can be certain everyone will look at. You have a captive audience, so seize the opportunity to tell them what they need to know. (See Chapter 11 for more on how to write the Executive Summary.)

How to Develop the Proposal Structure

Before you can really begin to develop the proposal structure, you need to have completed the detailed analysis of the ITT and worked out the key elements of your solution. Your analysis of the ITT will, amongst other things, guide your decisions on which are the important sections and what needs to be emphasized. You can then begin to develop a structure which promotes all the benefits of your solution against these requirements.

TOP-DOWN AND BOTTOM-UP

A top-down approach means starting with the highest level section headings and breaking these down into subsections via several passes through the document. The top level may be specified in the ITT or you can start with your organization's generic proposal structure. On the first pass through, take a section heading, think about what material it should contain and how this is ordered, and create the subsections which group and present the material in a logical sequence. On the next pass, repeat the process, taking each subsection in turn and breaking that down even further. Keep repeating until you have reached the point where a subsection will be a manageable length, typically no more than a page or two, and not less than a paragraph. Aim for a logical, hierarchical structure where all the sections at a given level will contain material of similar detail and overall importance.

Although this top-down approach is an excellent start, it is not perfect. Sometimes, important parts of the solution are missed out in the top-down decomposition, or aren't given the emphasis they deserve. To counter this, you can add to the structure bottom-up.

As you carry out your analysis of the ITT and then begin developing the solution, keep a note of important issues. Check this list against the top-down structure. If the corresponding subsections are missing, slot them into the right place. If an important issue sits too far down in the hierarchy, you may need to promote one or more subsections to a higher level to give it the recognition it needs.

By balancing the top-down and bottom-up approaches, your proposal structure is set up to present the right information to the client at the appropriate level of detail.

OUTLINING TOOLS

There are plenty of other ways to develop your proposal's structure if you don't want to start working directly in the proposal template. There are many different commercial outlining tools which will let you create and expand topics (i.e. proposal sections) into ever greater levels of detail, which is ideal for developing a proposal structure. But if you use a software tool, make sure it is compatible with your word processing software – remember, you will need to transfer all the sections and subsections you create into the master proposal at some stage.

For the visually oriented, *mind maps* are a great way to develop the structure. The main topic sits in the centre of the mind map (like a spider in its web). Top-level section headings form a set of branches radiating from the centre. Each branch in turn has sub-branches, and so on until the lowest level of detail has been covered. Relationships between branches are shown with lines linking between two ideas. The whole thing is topped off with annotations, pictures, and diagrams which help to make the mind map unique, distinctive and memorable (see Figure 9.1).

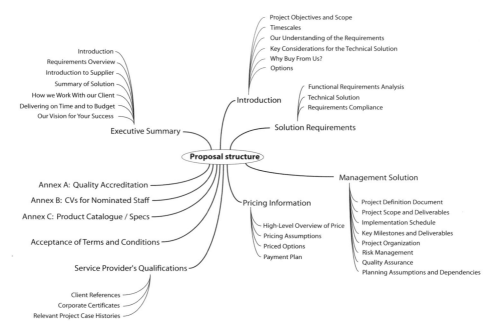

Figure 9.1   An example proposal structure captured in mind-map form

Mind maps have some great features:

- They are concise. Sometimes you can fit the entire structure of a complex proposal onto a single sheet of paper. That is very useful for gaining an overview of the bid.

- You can promote or demote entire branches very simply. This is helpful when trying to make sure that sections of equal importance are given equal prominence in the structure.

- Flexibility – changing the running order of sections is easy.

- The depth of branching is obvious, showing where the proposal descends into details.

- You can collapse or expand the mind map to focus in on a particular area of detail.

Creating and ordering your proposal's section headings only goes part way towards defining the structure. You also need to plan what will be written into each subsection.

The subject matter should be obvious from the section title if you have used meaningful headings (see Table 9.1). But which key themes do you need to emphasize? Which other sections need to be cross-referenced to avoid duplication? Is there a compelling argument to put forward in the introductory paragraph? To answer these questions before committing time and energy in writing the section, you need to *storyboard* your proposal.

STORYBOARDS

'Storyboarding' is an old term borrowed from the movie industry. A film plot is broken down into different scenes. A rough sketch of the action or a few words of dialogue is enough to convey the important elements of the story. Sometimes these story elements are pasted on to boards and switched round until the right sequence is found. It quickly becomes apparent where the story is weak, where a scene can be cut or a flashback inserted to increase the pace. Once the sequence is agreed, various teams can begin work – carpenters to build the sets, lighting crews to figure out the best way to light them, special effects guys to plan their visual trickery – all before a single frame of film has been shot. Good storyboarding means good planning – without this crucial process, everything would take much longer and costs would rocket.

The purpose of a proposal storyboard is to capture the essence of a bid segment without investing all the time and energy in writing it first. Why? Because it is much more efficient to refine your thinking at the storyboard stage. You can cut and paste the written proposal to some extent, but unless you take great pains, the 'joins' (in terms of writing style, continuity and context) will be visible. However, at the storyboarding stage, it is easy to change the order, adjust the emphasis, spot the missing items, remove duplication and, what is more, communicate all this to the rest of the bid team.

In case you are not convinced, here are all the things that storyboards let you do:

- *Agree the scope of writing tasks* – an author can be confident of not overlapping with other authors, providing they stick to the topics within the storyboard.

- *Manage the boundaries between sections* – gaps and overlaps are much easier to identify (and avoid) at the storyboarding stage.

- *Invite comments from external reviewers at an early stage.* The earlier ideas are fed into the writing stage, the better. Reviewing storyboards gives a useful (albeit high level) view of how the proposal is going to be tackled, which allows reviewers to feed in suggestions at an early stage.

- *Allocate workshare* – each storyboard should have a lead author assigned.

- *Size and resource the bid.* Storyboarding the proposal gives you much better information with which to estimate page budgets and the amount of writing effort required.

- *Fine-tune the proposal structure.* When you can see the high-level structure of the proposal laid out as a set of storyboards, it becomes easier to see the best (and most logical) order to present information. It is worth taking some time shuffling the order of storyboards to get a logical 'flow' to the information you are presenting.

THE STORYBOARD TEMPLATE

If you are outlining with storyboards, you will need a storyboard template. How much detail you choose to include in the storyboards is entirely up to you, but the best advice is to keep it simple. If you load your template with too many topics, it becomes onerous and self-defeating.

Figure 9.2 shows an example of a storyboard. Each of the headings are explained below. The storyboard distils the essence of what needs to go into each section. This covers more than just content and how to organize the information, it is a record of where to place emphasis, what underlying messages need to be communicated and the practicalities (length, who is needed to work on it, presentation style, etc.)

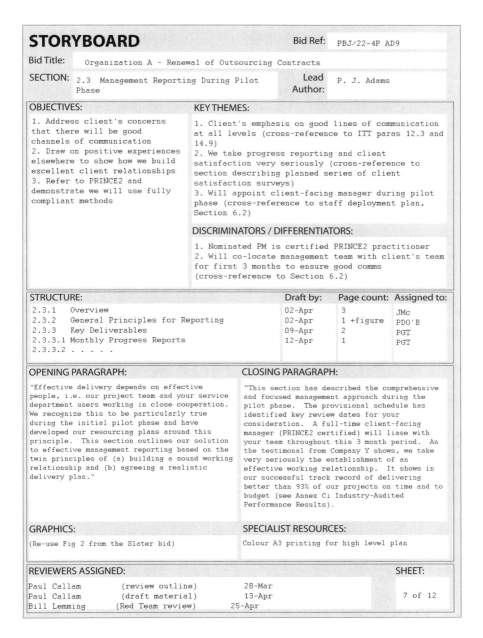

Figure 9.2   A page from an example storyboard. *This is a relatively detailed storyboard to illustrate the different elements it could contain. A real storyboard might well consist of a subset of these topics*

As with most things, a certain amount of discretion is required. You may not want to use all these headings on a small bid, or you may feel certain sections of a large bid won't benefit from, say, a draft of the opening and closing paragraphs. That is fine – the storyboard is there to help, not hinder. It should be helping you think about how each section of the proposal will be created, so don't let it become a task for its own sake.

Table 9.2   The main topics in a storyboard template

Storyboard topic	Used for
Section title	Use the headings and numbering scheme from your high level outline. If you reorder or rename, it is important to keep the storyboards and the proposal outline synchronized.
Owner/lead author	This is the person responsible for maintaining the storyboard and, in due course, producing the draft of this section. The job of writing specialist sections may be delegated to others, but the lead author is responsible for assembling the final draft.
Objectives	What is the purpose of this section of the proposal? This is not as silly as it sounds. It is important to understand what effect you want your text to have on the reader. Is it going to persuade the reader of something they may not agree with at the outset? *(If so, you will need to think carefully about how your arguments are structured.)* Will it inform them of some aspect of your solution they are not aware of? *(Make sure sufficient details are included and clear explanations given.)* Is it designed to pick holes in a competitor's solution? *(Evaluate the risks and benefits objectively, but lead inexorably to your conclusions.)*
Key themes	List the key themes you want emphasized in this section. Don't repeat the same statements word for word each time – this quickly gets monotonous and the reader becomes indifferent to the messages. Find alternative ways to subtly convey the key themes; use different phrasing or look at things from a different perspective. A note of caution: key themes should be stated sparingly, i.e. only in the appropriate sections. Is there a clear link between this topic and a key theme? If not, leave the discussion of the key theme to a section where it is relevant. Don't worry if this means there are some storyboards with no relevant key themes.
Discriminators	Refer to Chapter 4 for a description of the role and importance of differentiators and discriminators. The advice given for key themes applies here. Include only those that are directly relevant. Unnecessary repetition will bore the reader.
Evidence	Every time you discuss a key theme (particularly if it is also a discriminator or differentiator) you must provide evidence for your claim. This can take many different forms: project write-ups, market surveys, product specifications, client references, lab benchmarks, etc. By explicitly listing the evidence, the storyboard can help to ensure your persuasive arguments are backed up with hard facts that will convince the client.

Table 9.2   *Concluded*

Storyboard topic	Used for
Subsections/notes on content	Show how this section of the proposal is to be broken down (e.g. subsection titles or a document outline). It is often helpful to include some notes on scope, e.g. *'This section will list and define all of the computer room support procedures.'* If the storyboard is covering a big section, you may want to note down who is contributing to each subsection.
Illustrative graphic	Is there a diagram, picture, graph or chart which sums up what this section is about? Graphic elements catch the reader's eye and naturally draw them towards the explanatory text. Since most people have stronger visual memories, it is more likely to leave a greater impression with the client. If there is no obvious graphic, it is not necessary to invent one. Let the words speak for themselves.
Opening paragraph	If you are storyboarding a major section of the proposal, it is useful to create the opening paragraph in advance. This sets the tone for what follows. It should summarize (or allude to) the information to be presented and provide signposts so that the reader knows what to expect. The opening paragraph is often the most important part of the section. Getting it right sets the scene and prepares the client to listen out for your key messages. Drafting the opening paragraph at the storyboard stage has two powerful benefits: • it gives others in the bid team a chance to comment on and improve this critical piece of text; • it forces you to really think about what this section needs to achieve. It is the essence of what you are trying to capture on the storyboard.
Closing paragraph	Similarly, the closing paragraph needs to draw together all the threads of detail that the reader has just been exposed to. It needs to summarize and reinforce the central themes without overtly repeating those messages. This can be tough. Too much subtlety, and the client may fail to see the implications of your argument. Hammer the message too hard and you may sound patronizing. Early feedback from reviewers will help you get the right balance.
Page count	To keep the size of the proposal under control, set yourself a strict (but realistic) page budget. If the client has imposed a page limit, this takes priority.
Specialist resources needed	Do you need to arrange contributions from specialists? Is a graphic designer needed? Do you need a developer to produce simulated screenshots for the user interface?
Reviewers and dates	Make a note of the arrangements for reviewing the storyboards and the draft text. (If possible the same people should be involved in both reviews.) A key benefit of storyboarding is that you can review the essence of the proposal strategy at a sufficiently early stage so that major changes can be easily accommodated. Your options for change narrow as more of the proposal is completed in draft form.
Draft text completed by	When does the storyboard need to be converted into a proposal draft? This should correspond with the main bid plan.

WHAT NOT TO STORYBOARD

Save your storyboarding efforts for the most important parts of the proposal. These are the sections where you are showing ingenuity, marshalling arguments persuasively and demonstrating your capabilities and understanding.

For example, an appendix containing CVs doesn't need storyboarding: it just *is*. Similarly, any sections of the proposal which require boiler-plate information or stock material to be included won't need storyboarding. Examples include compliancy tables, details of product specifications and marketing collateral (i.e. 'glossies' and product brochures).

Your pricing section may very well not need storyboarding if it is mainly figures or tables, but large proposals will have a lengthy pricing section with many complicating factors (e.g. options, variations, different rates to be applied, caveats, discounts) in which case storyboarding may be essential.

Even for sections which don't need storyboarding, it may be useful to include 'place-holders' – often just the title of the section without any of the storyboard topics filled in. This allows you to lay out (or pin on the wall) the entire proposal, section by section in outline. This can be incredibly useful (particularly on larger bids) to get a sense of the whole document. Where do individual contributions fit? Which areas have been given particular emphasis?

PUTTING STORYBOARDS TO WORK

After the storyboards have been created, the next step is to review the emerging outline. Your completed storyboards give you an unparalleled view of how your finished proposal will look at both the macro level (i.e. section headings, logical order, depth of detail, etc.) and the micro level (what material to include, which areas to emphasize, how to phrase key messages) – so make good use of them to get the structure right. It is the closest you can come to seeing the finished proposal before you have actually written it.

Reviewing the Bid Structure

Gather the bid team and ask each member of the team to review the entire set of storyboards. This is important even though some individuals will only be involved in a certain part of the bid. It is always beneficial to gain an overview of the entire solution (and storyboards are the best way to do this), so don't underestimate the ability of others to spot things or make helpful suggestions that others have missed.

We will look at the bid review process in more detail in Chapter 12. However, if it is possible to involve any of the reviewers at this stage, then do so. Changing a storyboard is relatively easy. Changing the draft of the proposal at a later stage is much harder. Not only that, it will get the reviewers quickly up to speed on the bid and let them influence the sections they will be commenting on while there is still scope to make substantial modifications.

A REVIEW CHECKLIST

Ask your reviewers to comment on the following:

- Is the structure complete? (i.e. are there key sections missing?)

- Does the structure reflect what is asked for in the ITT?

- Is the bid the right length for the size of the opportunity?

- Are the right messages being put across in the right places?

- Is there too much/too little emphasis of the key themes?

- Are the key themes backed up by sufficient evidence to justify them?

- Is there a logical flow to the section headings at a given level?

- Is there unevenness in the level of detail between different sections?

- Do sections overlap or contain duplication?

- Is there a consistent tone throughout the bid (e.g. are some introductory paragraphs overtly formal/informal compared to the rest of the proposal?)

- Have the right people (with the right skills) been assigned to each section?

- Are the assignments realistic (e.g. is there an unfair or infeasible allocation of work to certain individuals)?

Summary: A Structured Approach to Writing the Bid

- *Work out what the structure of the proposal needs to be before beginning work on the detail.* Be prepared to change or develop this structure over several iterations before arriving at the optimum outline.

- *Don't rely on similar proposals for the structure.* Each bid is unique and the structure will need to be tailored to each client.

- Follow any instructions the client has given on bid structure very carefully.

- *Review the bid structure* with the following questions in mind – is each section informative, logical, comprehensive, hierarchical, relevant, and does it have the right emphasis?

- *Choose active phrases for headings* to convey as much meaning as possible.

- *Put the right information in the right place.* Don't expect everyone evaluating the proposal to read every word. Make it easy for them to go straight to the information they are looking for.

- *Choose an outlining method* that you are comfortable with (e.g. structured headings, mind maps, storyboards, etc.).

- *Outline the most important parts of the bid first.* There may be some sections which won't benefit from outlining, although it is often useful just to be able to see the entire bid at a glance.

10

Getting the Message Across

The single biggest problem in communication is the illusion that it has taken place.

George Bernard Shaw, Irish playwright and author, 1856–1950

Sometimes facts will speak for themselves, but mostly they don't. It takes a well-crafted paragraph or two to communicate an essential idea clearly or to marshal a compelling argument. Style, word choice, pace, formality of tone, sentence length – many factors must be combined to deliver 'strong' writing. Without it, a proposal can easily appear confused, disjointed or lacklustre.

Strong writing is important not only in terms of winning the work but in avoiding misunderstandings later on. A clearly written proposal reduces the chance of the client forming the wrong impression of how the project will be executed or having different expectations about what will be delivered. Both bid manager and project manager have a vested interest in making sure the proposal is well-written and unambiguous.

At the Heart of Good Communication

The right solution – the *best* solution, even – is not guaranteed to be the one chosen by the client. The strength of the solution is not enough by itself; the right messages must be communicated effectively to the client. A hurriedly written bid, full of first draft material, is unlikely to contain strong writing. There is yet more work to be done to get the message across.

CONTENT OR PRESENTATION?

Many people will tell you that it really doesn't matter how ideas are conveyed, as long as they are the right ones. It is the principle of 'good will out in the end'. Unfortunately this is not the case. The way your messages are communicated to the client, the clarity and persuasiveness of your arguments – in short, the quality of writing in the proposal – is every bit as important.

Think of your client as a food critic about to visit your restaurant. Even though you are using the best ingredients, cooked with exquisite care to a recipe that is a closely guarded secret, the whole effect will be ruined if the fine food is unceremoniously dumped onto a plate. The presentation of the food is not only a question of making it visually appealing, it compels the diner to appreciate the subtleties of taste and hints at the care and creativity that have gone into its preparation.

The same holds true for a proposal. How you present your key ideas for the solution makes a big impact on the client. The harder you force your reader to work in order to understand all your key themes, the smaller the impact. Use strong writing to make it easy for the reader to understand your messages. (Table 10.1 lists some characteristics of strong writing.)

If your statements are turgid and confusing, if the material isn't organized into a logical sequence, if the text is littered with spelling mistakes and grammatical errors, the client may well wonder if this standard of workmanship will carry forward into the project itself.

The bottom line is that content and presentation are equally important.

STRONG WRITING

Strong writing is also persuasive. Strong writing convinces the reader that there is truth in the arguments being presented. It carries the reader through a logical sequence of ideas as effortlessly as possible. The reader should be gripped at the beginning and, all being well, allowed no opportunity to wander away from understanding the key messages. It is an effortless process where meanings are straightforward and conclusions obvious.

Conversely, weak writing forces the reader to work hard. Ideas have to be picked out of a formless, rambling block of text and then assembled into some kind of order. It is easy to be vague or imprecise, forcing the reader to work hard to extract the real meaning.

We have all been subjected to many examples of weak writing – dry technical reports that take ten pages to express what could be said as easily in one, paragraphs that wander at random from idea to idea, never quite reaching a conclusion or making a telling point. Can you rely on your client putting all this effort in to appreciate the true value of your solution? It needs to be spelt out clearly so that there can be no misunderstanding.

Table 10.1   The characteristics of strong writing

Topic	Turning this into strong writing means …
Macro structure (how the proposal is organized into volumes, chapters, subheadings, etc.)	Your proposal won't persuade the client if it is badly structured. Similarly themed material should be grouped. For example, the technical solution, the implementation plan, pricing details and corporate case studies logically belong in separate sections (unless the client has asked for their own structure to be followed). The reader should be able to tell where to find specific information on the basis of the chapter headings alone. See Chapter 9 for further details.
Micro structure	The micro structure is the organization at paragraph level. Ideas are linked in a logical fashion, either as part of a reasoned argument or broken down into greater levels of detail in successive paragraphs. The golden rule is: start a new paragraph for each new idea (or element which builds into an idea). Don't combine several ideas in a single paragraph or you risk confusing the reader.
Know what you want to say	Some people write a first draft as an exercise in understanding what they wish to say. The act of writing helps to clarify their own thought processes. This is fine – as long as you are prepared to discard your first draft. It is a rare skill to be able to write acceptable first-draft material. However, a few minutes planning and ordering your thoughts in advance can improve things enormously.
Say it simply and directly	Avoid the tendency to hide behind long words and grandiose phrases. Simplicity counts: simple words are easier to understand and there is less room for ambiguity. For example: *'Should the client wish to employ an alternative architectural design, we will be willing to discuss this and amend our proposed approach accordingly'* might be better phrased as: *'We're happy to discuss alternative approaches.'* Or: *'Further to our underlying corporate approach, we propose to adopt market-leading technology in order to ensure that navigation of the website is consistent with a wholly satisfactory user experience'* could be rewritten as: *'We will use market-leading technology to make sure that the website can be easily navigated.'*
Spelling, punctuation and grammar matter	It is true that you are unlikely to lose a bid just because there is room for improvement in your grammar, but it will leave a negative impression. You can't be certain that the client will laugh off poor grammar and erratic spelling, or regard it as an endearing trait. A slapdash, error-riddled proposal could be taken as symptomatic of a cavalier attitude to the project itself. For the relatively small investment of getting the grammar and spelling right, you can eliminate this risk.
Enthusiasm	Enthusiastic writing makes the subject matter come alive. Academic or technical reports are often heavy going because they are written in a deliberately dry and impersonal style. You shouldn't be afraid for a certain amount of 'personality' to creep in to your proposal. If the authorial tone veers too far towards the impersonal, your prospective client may feel remote and disinterested. Contrast this with an enthusiastic writer. Someone who is clearly passionate and committed to a topic makes for interesting (and memorable) reading. We naturally respond to someone who is enthused and knowledgeable about their subject.
Brevity	Less is more. The client will thank you for it.

Getting to the Point

Every paragraph needs a reason to exist. You are not writing the paragraph for fun and neither is the client reading it for pleasure, so it must have a purpose.

There is a good test to make sure a paragraph is pulling its weight. When you have finished drafting a section, go back and jot down in the margin the key phrase that best summarizes each paragraph. If it is difficult to find your summary phrase, check that the paragraph actually has something to say. It may be grammatically correct, but is it really making a fresh point? If not, delete it.

Then look at the summaries in the margin. Is there a logical sequence to these ideas? Does the argument flow through the section? If not, you may need to restructure to get your points across.

MAKING THE KEY THEMES EXPLICIT

Some bid writers choose to include key themes explicitly in the bid as notations in the margin (see Figure 10.1). They draw the reader's eye to the key points, acting as a reminder of important messages (or possibly as a crib sheet for those too lazy to read the text carefully). It doesn't suit every style of proposal, but is a technique worth considering.

FACTS AND THEMES

A typical bid is largely composed of two kinds of message:

- *Facts* – the bulk of the proposal. These are statements about the work to be done, how the project will be carried out, etc.

- *Themes* – the persuasive sales messages, key themes and discriminators that will hopefully impress the client sufficiently to award you the work.

> **Proposal to XYZ Investments plc**
>
> ### 3.1 The Benefits of Selecting AAA Global Services
>
> | | |
> |---|---|
> | Shared vision for business change | Here are some of the highlights of our proposal. Following extensive consultation with your investment team throughout the tendering stage, we have demonstrated that we understand your vision for business change and can supply the necessary services to achieve this. |
> | Industry-recognized track record for delivery | Annex A lists our extensive track record of working with similar clients within this industry. We are proud of our long track record in successful delivery, which is among the best in Europe today. |
> | Proven technology combined with effective change management | Our experience shows us that single-minded focus on the delivery of the technical solution is insufficient by itself to guarantee a successful outcome. Therefore, we are proposing a comprehensive change management programme which will complement the customized technology platform at the heart of our bid. |
> | A comprehensive and realistic approach to integrating legacy systems | Integration with legacy systems -- the joining of the old and the new -- is never a straightfoward process. There are balances to be struck: established infrastructure may not permit the luxury of 'green field' development, which will pose additional challenges for deployment. We might reasonably expect data migration and data cleansing tasks to be difficult and time-consuming in such circumstances, and have planned accordingly. |

Figure 10.1   Stating key themes explicitly as notations in the margin. *This approach makes sure the reader picks up on all the key points*

LET THE FACTS SPEAK FOR THEMSELVES

Factual writing needs very little adornment – indeed, the simpler and plainer the style the better when conveying factual information. A large part of the proposal will comprise factual statements as you typically answer the who, what, where and how questions posed by the ITT. There is no need to dress up these statements of fact. The plainer they are, the less likelihood of misunderstandings arising.

Here are a couple of examples of straightforward factual statements:

> *The Solartrex database management suite shipped in excess of 50,000 units in the last financial year.*

Installation of a turnkey system can be achieved in less than three months.

These are both simple and irrefutable statements (assuming the figures can be substantiated).

Patterns of Argument

Most people are familiar with the following guideline on giving a presentation (and it also holds true for many forms of business writing): 'First tell 'em what you're going to say, then tell 'em, then tell 'em what you said!'

We can represent this as a simple pattern or 'writing template' as shown in Figure 10.2. This pattern is very common – and for good reason, because it really does work. Think for a moment about how this pattern can be applied in the chapters or large subsections of your own proposal. The introduction should put the reader in a receptive frame of mind. It provides the context for what follows. Presenting a series of facts without being able to place them in the proper context can confuse the reader. The summary is your chance to restate the key messages (just in case there is any doubt in the reader's mind). It emphasizes the most important points and leaves them fresh in the memory, particularly if you have covered a lot of detail in the main section.

Winston Churchill used to place particular emphasis on the benefits of repetition. He said:

> *If you have an important point to make, don't try to be subtle or clever.*
> *Use a pile driver. Hit the point once. Then come back and hit it again.*
> *Then hit it a third time – a tremendous whack.*

The trick is to avoid the impression of labouring a point. Using the same form of words to introduce, describe and then summarize a key point can come across as tiresome repetition. Try to find different ways of expressing these ideas, and remember that the detail only needs to go in the body of the text. Keep the introduction and summary succinct.

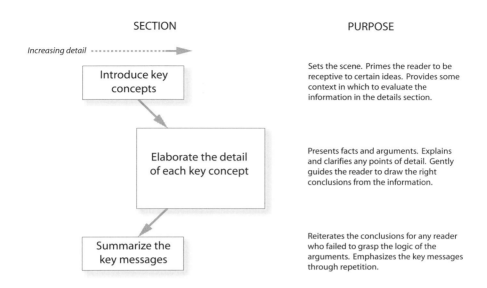

SECTION   PURPOSE

Increasing detail ⋯⋯⋯⋯⋯⋯⋯⋯⋯⋯▶

Introduce key concepts

> Sets the scene. Primes the reader to be receptive to certain ideas. Provides some context in which to evaluate the information in the details section.

Elaborate the detail of each key concept

> Presents facts and arguments. Explains and clarifies any points of detail. Gently guides the reader to draw the right conclusions from the information.

Summarize the key messages

> Reiterates the conclusions for any reader who failed to grasp the logic of the arguments. Emphasizes the key messages through repetition.

Figure 10.2   A pattern (or writing template) for a simple factual presentation. *Notice that the introduction and summary don't present any new material not already included in the body of the presentation. Instead, these stages are designed to first prime the reader to be receptive and secondly, reinforce the key messages that have been given*

INDUCTIVE AND DEDUCTIVE REASONING

Some parts of the bid may require a different approach. Perhaps you need to argue your case or persuade the client on a particular point, not just deliver a series of factual statements. One way to do this is through *deductive reasoning*. Suppose we write down two statements of fact, A and B. If A and B are linked in some way, we may be able to deduce some new fact C, as in:

Statement A: All mammals are warm-blooded.

Statement B: My cat is a mammal.

Therefore, via deductive reasoning:

Statement C: My cat is warm-blooded.

The corresponding writing pattern for this might look something like Figure 10.3.

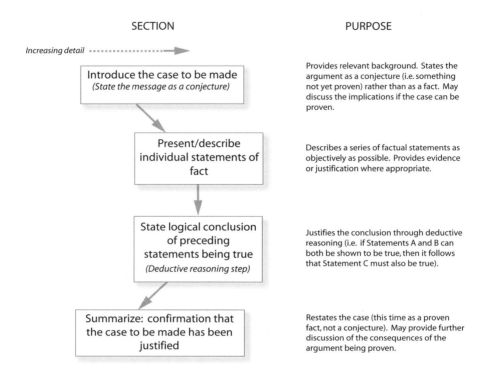

SECTION

PURPOSE

Increasing detail ······················►

Introduce the case to be made
(State the message as a conjecture)

Provides relevant background. States the argument as a conjecture (i.e. something not yet proven) rather than as a fact. May discuss the implications if the case can be proven.

Present/describe individual statements of fact

Describes a series of factual statements as objectively as possible. Provides evidence or justification where appropriate.

State logical conclusion of preceding statements being true
(Deductive reasoning step)

Justifies the conclusion through deductive reasoning (i.e. if Statements A and B can both be shown to be true, then it follows that Statement C must also be true).

Summarize: confirmation that the case to be made has been justified

Restates the case (this time as a proven fact, not a conjecture). May provide further discussion of the consequences of the argument being proven.

Figure 10.3   A writing pattern for an argument made by deductive reasoning

Another approach relies on *inductive reasoning*. Instead of a sequence of statements which logically implies some new statement of fact, inductive reasoning is more nebulous. It requires the mind to notice similarities between a number of facts and find a new statement which can account for all of them. Here is a simple example:

Statement A: There is a train due at 0734.

Statement B: There is a train due at 0804.

Statement C: There is a train due at 0834.

Through inductive reasoning:

Statement D: It is likely that trains run every half an hour from this station.

Presenting an argument using inductive reasoning, particularly if there is a lot of detail to take into consideration, requires skill. Although the temptation is to build the argument up logically, the reader may fail to see where the argument is heading and give up before the important conclusion is reached.

Instead, you may need to state the key message as a working hypothesis. Then you can persuade the reader of the conditions which must exist in order for the hypothesis to be true. Finally, you proceed to lay out the detailed facts which support these conditions. Figure 10.4 shows a pattern for this.

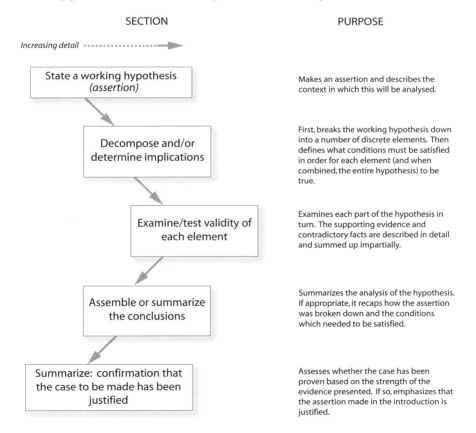

SECTION

PURPOSE

Increasing detail

State a working hypothesis
(assertion)

Makes an assertion and describes the context in which this will be analysed.

Decompose and/or determine implications

First, breaks the working hypothesis down into a number of discrete elements. Then defines what conditions must be satisfied in order for each element (and when combined, the entire hypothesis) to be true.

Examine/test validity of each element

Examines each part of the hypothesis in turn. The supporting evidence and contradictory facts are described in detail and summed up impartially.

Assemble or summarize the conclusions

Summarizes the analysis of the hypothesis. If appropriate, it recaps how the assertion was broken down and the conditions which needed to be satisfied.

Summarize: confirmation that the case to be made has been justified

Assesses whether the case has been proven based on the strength of the evidence presented. If so, emphasizes that the assertion made in the introduction is justified.

Figure 10.4   A writing pattern for presenting and justifying a working hypothesis

There are many such writing patterns to choose, from but none are intended to be used too slavishly. They provide a means to structure the writing of key sections of the bid and avoid rambling or confusing text that never quite reaches a conclusion.

ENDINGS

Whichever type of pattern you may have chosen, the concluding paragraph or sentence is vital. Once again, this is your chance to emphasize the key messages. It is the pay-off to the preceding argument, like the punchline to a joke.

If you have made a well-reasoned case, the client will readily agree with your arguments. However, don't rely on the body of those arguments alone. If the reader is in a hurry or hasn't understood your points as well as you would have liked, you need the concluding paragraphs to state explicitly what might otherwise be missed.

Assuming Too Much

An ever-present danger in bid writing is assuming the client knows more than they actually do. It tends to happen in the following situations:

- Making a statement, but not spelling out its implications.

- Referring to other work done by your company, but providing no details.

- Failing to describe the breadth of your organization's capabilities.

- Using unexplained acronyms.

- Failing to provide definitions of technical jargon.

It is often difficult to know exactly what the client understands about your business, your processes and your previous experience. Indeed, this will vary because different individuals involved in evaluating your proposal will have different levels of understanding.

The safest course of action is to spell everything out. Assume nothing: then at least you avoid the risk of leaving the client confused. This takes some skill: the tone needs to be business-like and concentrate on imparting the facts as concisely as possible. It must not sound condescending. If done well, the client will be grateful that you have made their job easier by explaining what they need to know. If you are telling them things they already know, they should be able to skip lightly through the explanations and definitions – and be impressed by your thorough approach. Table 10.2 provides some tips.

Table 10.2   Some tips on avoiding assumptions

Topic	Tips
Acronyms	Acronyms are a useful way to avoid tiresome repetition of key items or phrases but it must be easy to look up their meaning. Standard practice is to put the expanded definition in brackets immediately after the first use of the acronym, and include a list of acronyms either at the beginning of the proposal or in an appendix.
Make good use of cross-references	To keep your proposal succinct, you should provide all the relevant information (a) once, and (b) in the right place. Therefore, referencing material elsewhere in the proposal is important. If you don't make these references clear, your reader won't know where to find the details. By the time they stumble across that information later in the proposal (assuming they make it that far) the damage may be done.
Spell out the implications	A statement of fact will often carry an unspoken implication. Don't assume that the client will understand the implication as well as you. 'Last year, we supplied seven systems to central government departments.' Fine, but that may leave the reader saying, 'So what?' If the unwritten implication of this statement is that your firm outsold its competitors in the public sector domain, you need to say this explicitly.
Maintain a table of key assumptions	As you work on the proposal, keep a table of the most important assumptions. This can be included as an appendix to the proposal and saves you taking up valuable space in the bid explaining (or repeating) your assumptions. Key assumptions can be cross-referenced from the body of the bid in the normal way.
Document your understanding of the project's context	Many of your assumptions will relate to things on the client's side – the technical infrastructure, business needs, number of staff engaged in the project, etc. Describe as clearly as you can your understanding of the client's situation and the context in which the work will be done. This serves not only to demonstrate that you are on the client's wavelength, but lets the client spot if you have misunderstood any important points.
Independent review	An independent reviewer (or review team) will be especially useful in identifying where unwarranted assumptions have been made, because the reviewer won't necessarily share the same background and preconceptions of the bid team. See Chapter 12 for more details on review processes.

Objectivity

Objectivity is a vital part of the bid-writing process. If you can't (or refuse to) see anything other than the benefits of your solution, you are unlikely to counter potential criticisms of your approach. To win, your proposal will need to acknowledge its weaknesses – sometimes openly – and show the client that you have ways to deal with them.

Openness and honesty is generally appreciated by clients. A bid which deals solely in superlatives ('the best solution from the best supplier, guaranteed risk-free' etc.) is likely to be treated with suspicion. There are always going to be problems, risks, weaknesses or unproven elements of the solution. The bidder who acknowledges these (and shows how they will be overcome) can gain the client's trust far more readily.

Use the following questions to consider your solution objectively:

- Have you considered all the alternative solutions available to the client?

- Do you need to address the credible alternatives in your proposal? (Remember, you may have already carried out this analysis when you first studied the requirements.)

- Think about how the client will perceive these alternative solutions. What are the attractions from their perspective?

- What are the strengths of your solution?

- How do you rank alongside competitors' offerings?

- Is there compelling evidence to support your proposed solution?

- How will you address weaknesses in your solution?

- What is the industry perception of your products/services?

Bad Habits to Avoid

MAKE IT LOOK IMPORTANT

Some bids go too far in trying to impress. They are guilty of MILI: Make It Look Important. This happens when the bid loses focus on what actually matters (i.e. how the client's requirements are to be satisfied) and spends too much time trying to make the supplier look clever. If your bid truly addresses the client's requirements, it won't need dressing up in any other way.

MILI can strike in many forms, as Table 10.3 shows.

The good news is that MILI problems can be fixed during the editing and rewriting stage and are relatively easy to spot. However, time may be short at the review stage and this effort could be spent on improving other areas of the bid. Better to try to avoid MILI right from the start.

Table 10.3   The consequences of MILI: Make It Look Important

Verbosity	Verbose sentences make it harder for the client to understand your key messages.
Pomposity	'Show don't tell' is a useful principle. It is easy to make claims, but evidence to back them up is what counts.
Jargon	Jargon which isn't explained may irritate or confuse the reader.
Document length	Rarely does the length of the bid impress the client. Far more important is brevity, but with none of the important details missing.

LENGTH DOES NOT IMPLY QUALITY

Proposals have a tendency to grow by stealth. What starts out as a 50-page proposal at the planning stage creeps steadily upwards during drafting. Perhaps the page budgets for each section are exceeded by a few pages or someone realizes a new section is needed. Then CVs and company background material need to be added – and the 50-page proposal is now 100-plus pages.

'Padding' occurs when the author writes in a self-important way, uses an obscure style or doesn't pay sufficient attention to keeping it clear and simple. First versions of any document tend to suffer from padding as the author struggles to capture their thoughts in a logical sequence and then find the right words to convey them.

The author's mindset will be an important influence. Someone setting out to impress will write in a very different style compared to someone giving instructions in a life-or-death situation. Where possible, use short sentences, keep to a 'one idea per sentence' rule, and choose the simplest, commonest word where possible. Don't be tempted to think that the more you write, the better the quality of your proposal. The old saying is right: it is quality not quantity that counts.

Unfortunately, quality writing comes at a cost: time and effort are needed to polish your text to the required level of clarity, and these are always in short supply. So leave yourself some time in the plan for revision; a little is better than none at all.

DIFFERENT CLIENT, SAME BID?

Recycling an old proposal, i.e. lifting substantial sections and topping and tailing to pay lip service to the new requirements, is a risky business. It may be justified where the new client's requirements are remarkably similar to a previous situation, but this is rarely the case. Even if the client's requirements are identical, their business context, operating constraints and a whole host of other factors will be quite different. The perfect solution for client A may not be at all to the liking of client B.

This doesn't mean that some material from existing bids cannot be reused, only that this must be done with care. If you have honed a particular aspect of your standard offering, it makes sense to use this model answer – and save yourself time and effort in the process. But your goal must be to do so judiciously.

The larger the chunks of proposal that you are recycling, the greater the risk of failing to get your key messages across. Instead of addressing the real and specific needs of the client, your proposal will tend towards generalities or, worse, focus on issues that may have been relevant to a previous client but don't interest this one. From the client's perspective, the bid will appear superficial – at first sight it appears to be addressing their needs, but never quite gets to the point.

The motive behind proposal recycling is obvious: it is a huge time-saver. In the right circumstances, with care, it is a sensible course of action. The bad habit to avoid is always starting with a recycled proposal: better to begin with a blank template and add only the material that really counts.

Before you are tempted to recycle a proposal, check the following:

- What percentage of material is a direct match to your current requirements? If it is less than 75 per cent, your time will be better spent writing fresh material.

- Are there substantial sections of the recycled proposal which need to be cut out? If so, will there be consistency problems? Will the proposal still flow?

- Will you end up spending more time editing the recycled proposal than it would take to write new material?

- Are you using the recycled proposal 'because it's there' or are there genuinely useful or well-crafted elements?

- Was the recycled proposal a winning proposal? If not, do you risk repeating the same mistakes?

Summary: Getting the Message Across

- There is often a *small margin* between winning and losing a bid. Getting your key messages across to the client clearly and concisely plays an important role.

- *Strong writing is persuasive.* It makes it easy for the client to understand and appreciate the key messages.

- *Strong writing requires work*, but it is better to put the effort into the first draft than hope to fix the problems later in the review stage.

- A proposal is built up from two fundamental building blocks: *facts and persuasive arguments* (themes). These need to be woven throughout the bid.

- *The facts don't always speak for themselves*. You need to make sure the client is left in no doubt about the conclusions to be drawn. Remember Churchill's advice and be ready with your pile driver.

- Think about *different writing patterns* to ensure your arguments are well structured.

- Don't assume the client knows more than they actually do.

- Be on the lookout for *bad habits to avoid*: particularly MILI, excessive length and recycling old bids.

- *Stay objective*. Not everyone will share your view of your organization and its offerings and capabilities. If you think the client perceives weaknesses, it is better to confront the issues openly.

11

The Management Solution

Technology is dominated by two types of people: those who understand what they do not manage, and those who manage what they do not understand.

Putt's Law and the Successful Technocrat (1981),
Archibald Putt (pseudonym)

The mechanisms by which a project is controlled (the 'how') are just as important as the technical solution (the 'what'). Without careful planning, marshalling and coordination of resources, the delivery of the technical solution may turn into a logistical shambles – or worse still, prove to be impossible. It is common sense that all projects need proper management processes to be applied.

This is the job of the management section in the bid. It describes all aspects of how the project will be managed. Another way of looking at it is to view this section as the write-up of the project framework. It is worth noting that many clients give equal weighting in their evaluation to the technical and management parts of the bid.

This chapter looks at what you need to include in the management solution to convince the client of your ability to deliver, and how best to present this information.

Developing the Management Solution

Part of the job of the management solution is to describe how the balance is struck between quality, cost and time. By the end of this section of the proposal, the client must be left in no doubt as to how the solution will be implemented.

One of the challenges of writing the management solution is that it usually requires a first cut of the project plan to be presented in the bid. That can be hard. It may be too early to be able to commit resources, or not enough analysis will have been done to properly understand tasks at a detailed level, or dependencies on third parties (such as suppliers and contractors) are unquantified. Difficult though it may be, preliminary planning at an appropriate level must be carried out. This means that developing the management solution is a project-planning exercise in its own right.

Don't underestimate the work involved in this. Good planning is always time-consuming. You may be tempted to cut corners but oversights and false assumptions have a way of coming back to haunt a project manager who is guilty of insufficient attention to detail.

Many clients now ask for a draft set of planning documents to be submitted with the proposal. This can add considerably to the bid team's workload, bringing forward as it does many aspects of planning that might otherwise be done during the initial start-up phase of the project. The advantage to the bidder is that it provides a sound basis on which to plan and cost the work, i.e. fewer surprises downstream when the project is underway (which is clearly an advantage for the client as well). It is also another opportunity to evaluate the supplier: by reviewing the quality of the bidder's plans, the client gets a clearer idea of what to expect during the project.

There are obvious limits on how far management planning can feasibly go during bid preparation. Don't be too ambitious. Ensure you have enough time and resources for the intended level of planning activity.

Early planning is naturally prone to invalid assumptions and misunderstandings – hence the need to clearly document all assumptions. This provides the opportunity to recognize and deal with any misunderstandings early on.

These are the key objectives for the management solution:

- Showcase the professional standards and processes that will be used to manage the project.

- Reassure the client by providing details on effective project control.

- Be specific about what will be delivered and how this will be achieved (e.g. implementation schedules, communication plans, test and verification procedures, etc.).

- Open the client's eyes to the risks, but show how you plan to avoid or mitigate them.

- Describe contingency plans where they exist. No plan is foolproof and you will score points for taking a realistic approach.

PRELIMINARY PLANNING OUTPUTS

Let us suppose the ITT requires an initial set of planning documents to be submitted with the bid (e.g. a project schedule, product or deliverable definitions, a quality plan, a communications plan, definitions of acceptance criteria, etc.). Ask yourself why these have been requested. Is the client looking for early commitment from a supplier, or a demonstration of management competence? This kind of analysis will help decisions on where to place emphasis (or focus resources, if time is short).

It is also a great opportunity to showcase your organization's management capabilities. Early planning outputs give the client a taste of what can be expected when the contract is awarded.

Bear the following points in mind when providing early planning documents:

- Use existing material where possible but remember that it will need tailoring to create a bespoke plan. (Every bid has important differences, and therefore requires bespoke planning.)

- Be realistic about the time and effort needed. A half-baked, hurriedly constructed document may harm your bid more than doing nothing at all.

- Alternatively, consider including sample documents from other projects (suitably anonymized) as real examples of the kind of material and quality that the client can expect.

- Prioritize. The outline project plan is probably the key document. This needs specific details relating to the project under consideration. If resources are limited, concentrate your effort here.

- Consider providing document outlines rather than fully developed documents. An outline should contain the principle headings, subheadings and a paragraph or two describing what will be covered in each section. This should be enough to satisfy the client that all the relevant issues will be addressed when the final version of the document is issued during the project.

- If you have chosen not to provide a full set of draft planning documents, explain your reasoning to the client. For example, it may be too risky (a point in your favour if other bidders have taken a stab at doing this). You may feel it is more important to focus on getting the details of the schedule right than, say, documenting all the standard management processes which will be applied. Showing that you can be pragmatic is likely to be well received by the client. After all, it is in the client's interests (as well as yours) not to fudge the planning by cutting corners before the project has even started.

- Make sure the outline project plan clearly shows when full versions of other planning outputs will be provided.

WHY PLAN EARLY?

Why is it necessary to create a detailed project plan in the bid stage? You may have no choice if this is what the ITT requires. Even if this is not the case, it presents a great opportunity to distinguish your bid from the competition for the following reasons:

- An early detailed project plan demonstrates your depth of planning and your capabilities to execute the project professionally.

- It helps you understand the scope of the work, and therefore to cost it more accurately.

- Your planning will often reveal new layers of complexity that even the client may not have been aware of. By doing so, you are adding value and using your planning insights to distinguish yourself from the competition.

- The management approach will often reveal a lot about the culture of your organization – your values, priorities and the maturity of your management processes, for instance. How strongly does quality control feature in your planning? Is your planning standards-based? What importance do you assign to good communication channels?

- Early planning leaves you and the project team much better prepared once the work has been won, and helps to remove risk from the project.

Writing the Management Solution

Make full use of whatever planning resources are available to the project team. If you use a recognized management approach (e.g. PRINCE2) make sure the details are properly incorporated into the management section of the bid. Although the ITT may impose a structure on how the management solution is presented, you should be able to restructure the information to fit.

To some extent the structure of the management solution depends on which of the following approaches you choose:

- Focus on identifying activities which must be carried out (*task-based* planning).

- Identifying the outputs needed and working back from these (*product-based* planning).

Clearly, both aspects are needed to some extent in any plan, but usually one of these approaches dominates.

TASK-BASED PLANNING

Task-based planning gives consideration to what tasks are needed in order to achieve the desired results. This is often done in a top-down fashion, beginning with major streams of work and gradually breaking them down into lower-level tasks, identifying the appropriate sequence and any interdependencies. The approach is based on the premise that if the project team follow the task sequence, the project goals will be met.

However, it can sometimes lead to problems. If all tasks are deemed to be of equal importance, some less valuable (or even irrelevant) tasks are inevitably included. This may lead to inefficient planning, with the project team working on activities which superficially appear necessary but which actually make little or no direct contribution to the end goals.

PRODUCT-BASED PLANNING

Product-based planning places emphasis on identifying what needs to be produced (i.e. the project's deliverables). Some of these are obvious (i.e. they are already specified in the ITT) but some need to be derived, for example interim outputs which are necessary before the final products can be created.

Planning is centred on producing the required outputs and identifying the tasks which directly give rise to these products (and will satisfy the agreed quality levels). Working back from the end point (i.e. a delivery), only those tasks which make a positive contribution to the end goals are included in the plan.

WHAT GOES IN THE MANAGEMENT SOLUTION?

Use the following sections as a checklist for material to include in the management solution. Most ITTs will request this information and even for those that don't, you would be well advised to cover these sections in some form or other.

It may be worth presenting this information in the form of tables, charts or diagrams where appropriate. This relieves the monotony of long passages of text. Pictorial content tends to be more memorable and will make it easier for the client to quickly locate important planning facts. Although the details change from bid to bid (e.g. names, tasks, work packages) many of these diagrams can be relabelled or will require only minor modification to be reused.

The job of the management section is to answer the type of questions listed in Table 11.1.

Table 11.1   What questions does the Management Section address?

Question	Answered in section ...
What will the project produce?	Key Outputs (deliverables)
What work is needed?	Work Package Definitions
Who will carry out this work?	Roles and Responsibilities
How long will it take?	Project Schedule
What standards will be met?	Quality Plan
How will the client be kept informed of progress?	Reporting and Communication
What are the risks?	Risk Management and Mitigation
What is the basis for this plan?	Assumptions and Dependencies
How much will it cost?	Financial and Contractual Issues

The order in which you present this information and the choices of section heading will, of course, vary from proposal to proposal. A lot of this material will be perfunctory, factual and hence rather dry. The following sections show how you can add value to some of these topics and reinforce your key themes.

KEY OUTPUTS (DELIVERABLES)

A clear statement of what the project team will deliver lies at the heart of the proposal. The ground rules are simple. Make sure that (a) it is easy for the client to find and (b) the list is comprehensive. Many of the key outputs are obvious (not least because they will be specified in the ITT) but don't overlook interim deliverables – the plans, prototypes, working reports, drafts, etc. – that precede the final outputs.

In fully defining your management solution, you may well find your list of deliverables is longer and more comprehensive than the client has envisaged. Make the most of this by showing the client that you have carefully thought through what will be needed.

Outputs need not just comprise the physical items: transfer of knowledge, provision of training, consultancy or other support services may also be important outputs. It may help to group the key outputs under different headings, for example:

- Software and bespoke systems

- Hardware and ancillary equipment

- Infrastructure elements (e.g. accommodation, office equipment, etc.)

- Documents

- Data

- Services (e.g. change management, training, support arrangements)

- Capabilities (e.g. knowledge transfer or consultancy-type activities)

- Consider whether any of the following suggestions can add value to this section:

  - Link deliverables to the project schedule. Make sure the client knows when to expect each output.
  - Can outputs be grouped together? It may make life easier for you and the client by reducing the management overhead associated with having deliverables scattered throughout the project.
  - What will the delivery comprise? Defining the delivery is important because it will ensure the client expects what is actually produced. For example, if delivering a document, provide a draft table of contents and notes on what each section will contain.
  - What quantities will be provided? For example, how many copies of a report or what data volumes will be delivered?
  - What are the key dependencies on making this delivery?
  - What is the delivery mechanism? Should the client expect a bound, paper copy of a design strategy or an electronic file? If so, what format?
  - What is the client expected to do with the deliverable? Draft documents will probably need a formal review. How long is the review process planned to take? Do you require the client to sign off the deliverable before the next stage of work can begin? Make sure the client understands what is needed from them.

    – Is there a payment or other contractual significance riding on this delivery?

PROJECT SCHEDULE

The project schedule shows not only what needs to happen (i.e. the tasks which make up the project) but when they must take place, expressed either in terms of calendar dates or weeks/months/years elapsed from the start of the project. The latter can be useful if there is any doubt over start dates. This way you can avoid a milestone being tied to a specific calendar date which becomes difficult to achieve if the project is late starting for any reason.

Showing dependencies between tasks is vital, i.e. which tasks must run in sequence and which in parallel? As a result of these dependencies it is possible to see where there is slack, i.e. tasks which can overrun without affecting delivery milestones. You may be asked to show the *critical path* on the schedule. This is the set of tasks which cannot slip without causing a key delivery date to extend by a corresponding amount. This is valuable information because it identifies the tasks which need to be given highest priority if the schedule is to be achieved.

If the ITT identifies particular milestones which are important to the client, be sure to show these clearly on your schedule. You may want to show more detailed tasks to demonstrate your understanding of what needs to be done, but make sure these align with milestones or key events that the client will recognize.

It is important that the project schedule provides a complete picture of the project, not just one particular aspect. For instance, if you are bidding as part of a consortium or have key subcontractors, you need to include all parts of the project on an outline schedule.

The project schedule is also a good place to identify external dependencies – things which you (the supplier) may not be able to control but which can nevertheless affect progress. Leave no doubt in the client's mind about any aspects which depend on their participation in the project. It is important the client understands their obligations in making the project a success.

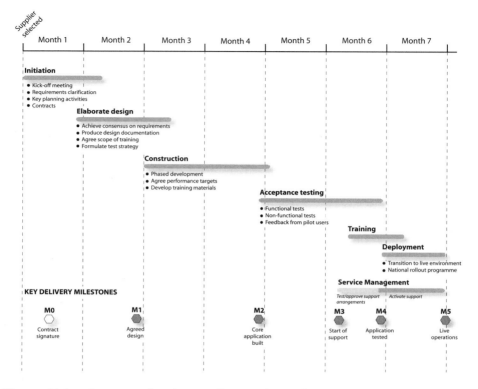

Figure 11.1 **An example of an outline project schedule.** *There is little actual detail on this schedule, but it provides a summary of all the key elements of the project. These would most likely be expanded to a much lower level of detail in a more conventional project schedule where, for example, task dependencies can be shown*

How much detail you choose to include in your project schedule will depend on the complexity of the project and what messages you want to convey to the client. For instance, on a complex project, you might want to provide a high-level schedule (see Figure 11.1) which only shows the key stages of work and then provide separate, more detailed schedules for each of the high-level work packages (see Figure 11.2).

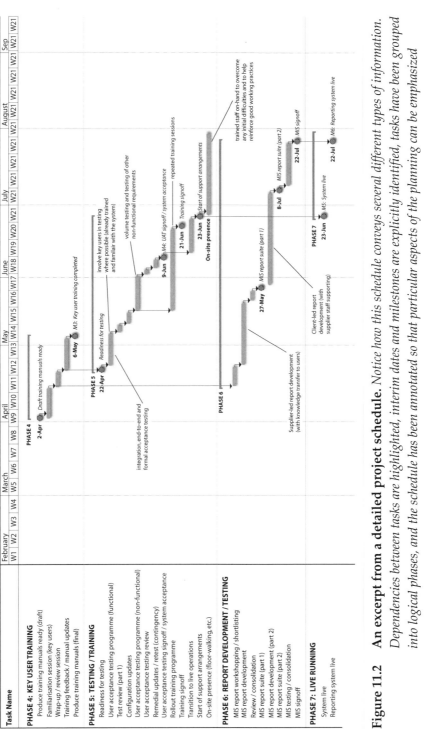

Figure 11.2   An excerpt from a detailed project schedule. *Notice how this schedule conveys several different types of information. Dependencies between tasks are highlighted, interim dates and milestones are explicitly identified, tasks have been grouped into logical phases, and the schedule has been annotated so that particular aspects of the planning can be emphasized*

Table 11.2   Guidelines for presenting the project schedule in the bid

What to include?	Notes
Key milestones	Include key milestones which the client has already identified, using the terminology from the ITT. This will help the client understand and relate to your project schedule.
Highlight things of importance to the client	What particular aspects of the schedule are important to the client? Include these as well as the supplier's milestones and tasks. For instance, if you know the client is concerned about reliability, it may be worth providing more detail on the testing regime.
Give a holistic view	Include all aspects which fall within the scope of the project. Project schedules sometimes focus too heavily on the 'obvious' aspects of the work and ignore supporting activities. Don't forget to include tasks relating to subcontractors and any partner organizations.
Structure the schedule	Structure the project schedule into logical phases and, where appropriate, show that there are clear start and end points for these phases. If you are using a project management methodology such as PRINCE2, there may be an expectation that the next phase won't start until the previous phase has been properly completed.
Put in the right amount of detail	You don't necessarily need a fully detailed implementation plan at the bid stage (but you will need to produce one quickly once the project starts). Provide enough detail to convince the client that you know how to plan professionally and maintain firm control of the project. Project schedules can quickly become overly complex if too much detail is included. If the client can't readily understand the schedule, they may conclude that you are over-complicating the situation.
Use different views for different information	Unless your project is very straightforward, don't overload your schedule with different types of information. Instead, provide different views of the schedule: for example, one which shows key tasks and their dependencies, another for payment milestones, a third for project deliverables, etc. Needless to say, each view must align to the same dates and be based on the same elapsed time periods.
Show dependencies	Dependencies are an important feature of your project schedule. They are points where a problem with one task (e.g. an over-running activity) may affect other tasks. Your schedule will have two types of dependency: internal (the sequence of tasks which you have control over) and external dependencies (tasks which affect the project but are not under your direct control). Identifying external dependencies lets the client know where there is an obligation to provide key inputs to your team, or where there is a risk which you cannot fully control.
Annotation	By annotating the schedule you can highlight specific features of your planning and guide the client through less obvious aspects of the project.

ASSUMPTIONS

In the course of preparing the proposal it is likely that many questions will arise concerning the requirements, or how the project is conducted, or what the client expects to be delivered. Some of these can be directly addressed by seeking clarification (see Chapter 4) and receiving a (hopefully) enlightening response from the client.

However, it may not be possible (or appropriate) to get answers to all your questions. For example:

- By asking leading questions of the client, you may risk disclosing a discriminator or some unique aspect of your bid strategy to your competitors.

- There may not be enough time left to get answers.

- There are too many uncertainties and you risk annoying the client by bombarding them with questions.

- The client does not know the answers.

Consequently you must include a list of assumptions in your bid for any such unanswered questions. If you don't list your assumptions, the client may not understand why you have made certain decisions. Remember those maths exams where you were told to always show your working? Sometimes, even though you got the wrong answer, if your working showed you were taking the right approach, you would still get some marks. Take the same approach in the bid. Even if some of your assumptions turn out to be wrong, the client can at least see what your solution is based on, and there may be a chance to correct these misunderstandings and revise the solution during the negotiation stage.

Start your table of assumptions as soon as you make the decision to bid and keep it constantly updated as you begin to define and write up your solution. Most likely, there will be assumptions relating to each section of the bid, so it is important that all members of the team have a chance to contribute, e.g. to produce technical assumptions, business requirement assumptions, implementation assumptions, etc.

Table 11.3   Guidelines for documenting bid assumptions

Approach	Notes
Keep them in one place	Put all your assumptions in one place in the proposal. The client can easily see what assumptions you have made and spot any areas which need to be explored during contract negotiations. This is usually done either as a table or a numbered list.
Label assumptions	Assumptions need to be uniquely labelled so that they can be easily referenced in discussions.
Cross-reference within the bid	It is a good idea to reference an assumption in the relevant section of the bid each time it occurs. By cross-referencing from your assumptions table to the relevant section, the client can see which parts of your bid depend on a particular assumption.
Provide justification	Generally, it is not sufficient to simply state an assumption. You need to provide the justification, unless it will be obvious to the client. Ask yourself why you believe it is valid to make this assumption (and what evidence led you to this conclusion)? Why is there no definitive answer, i.e. what is forcing you to make this assumption?
Implications	Some assumptions will have more important consequences than others. For any assumption which substantially underpins your solution, you might like to indicate to the client what the implications are if this assumption proves to be unfounded. Are you able to easily adopt an alternative approach or are you locked in to this assumption? How flexible are you prepared to be if assumptions are wrong? Not all assumptions will require this consideration, but you will want to build in some manoeuvring space for discussions with the client, rather than have your bid ruled out on the grounds of one or two unacceptable assumptions.
Test of reasonableness	Generally, the more detailed and explicit you make your assumptions the better, as it shows how thorough you have been in creating the bid. However, don't go too far by caveating every aspect of the bid with assumptions. This creates an impression of an organization that will take a very inflexible interpretation of the requirements and be hard to work with. Don't use assumptions as get-out clauses or as a way of transferring all risk onto the client. Use the 'test of reasonableness'. If you were the client, would you consider this to be a reasonable assumption to make in the circumstances?

DEPENDENCIES

As we have seen, there are two main types of dependency:

- *internal project dependencies* – things which are under the project manager's direct control;

- *external dependencies* – things which are beyond the project manager's immediate control.

Internal dependencies signify critical activities in the project schedule, such as where the output from one or more tasks forms the input to the next task. The next task is dependent on the previous tasks being satisfactorily completed: if they are not, this may cause a significant deviation from the plan.

Highlighting internal dependencies signals to the client that you understand the complex relationships between the tasks and have taken this into account in the planning. Although there may be little planning flexibility around internal dependencies, it is often possible to adjust other parts of the plan to compensate.

External dependencies pose a greater threat. By definition, the project manager's ability to control external dependencies is diminished. The client may have to take responsibility for managing external dependencies or, if they are also beyond the client's control, they will need to form part of the risk management plan.

If the client has ownership of external dependencies, your schedule should clearly show each of these dependencies. This not only lets the client see what they are responsible for and how this will impact on other parts of the schedule, but helps protect you as the supplier. Very often client-owned external dependencies will have commercial significance and may be referred to in the contract. In simple terms, if the client fails to meet their obligations in managing external dependencies, you may be entitled to a waiver on those portions of the schedule which have a direct dependency.

Effort spent on listing these external dependencies is worthwhile. If you miss the opportunity in the bid, the client may conclude you are willing to take full responsibility for all aspects of timely delivery – even if some of these are outside your control.

The guidelines for documenting dependencies are really no different to those for assumptions (see Table 11.3) with two important additions:

- *Ownership* – state clearly who owns the dependency (i.e. is best placed to control it). If this is a third party completely outside the contractual scope of the project, it may fall to the client to liaise and/or take direct ownership of the dependency.

- *Implications* – you must spell out what effect the dependency may have on the project. The client needs to know the consequences of failing to manage an external dependency; for example, a delay in an interim or final delivery, an increase in price, etc. This will feed into the project's risk assessment if the implications are severe enough.

Executive Summary

The Executive Summary is also a critical part of the management solution because it encapsulates all the key messages (and hence the key themes) even though it is placed at the beginning of the proposal and therefore separated from the management sections.

It is sometimes called the *Management Summary* or *Proposal Highlights* and is a vital section because it is the one part of the proposal that everyone looks at. As the name suggests, it is aimed at the executive who needs to quickly understand the gist of the proposal without getting into the detail. It necessarily provides a high-level view, but also contains all of the discriminators and key themes. (Refer to Chapter 4 for more details on these.)

Summarizing your entire proposal in a few short pages is not a trivial task and will take some effort. If you only have resources to 'polish' one section of the proposal, this is the one to spend the time on.

Writing the Executive Summary is best tackled once the rest of the proposal has been written. A lot can change during the drafting: a change in emphasis, the realization that a different strategy is needed, etc. Therefore you risk a substantial rewrite of the Executive Summary if you complete this first, time that could be better spent elsewhere. However, once the proposal is drafted, you will have a detailed understanding of both the structure and composition of the material; distilling the essence of it into the Executive Summary should be a straightforward process.

That said, some bid writers do prefer to draft the Executive Summary at the beginning as a way of 'discovering' what the important elements of the bid are going to be. By writing this section first, they believe the key themes become clearer and it is easier to see the relationships between sections and where the emphasis needs to go. You may want to experiment to see which approach you feel most comfortable with.

The Executive Summary is usually a stand-alone section. It must make sense to someone who will not read the rest of the proposal. It is almost a mini-proposal in its own right – a taster for the detail contained in the rest of the document.

You should avoid making the Executive Summary a compilation of the best bits from the proposal (although in a large bid you may want to extract a concept diagram or key sections of text if they are particularly apt). Its job is to complement the body of the proposal, highlighting its key strengths, commenting on areas of originality and value. If you simply cut and paste text from elsewhere in the proposal, the Executive Summary becomes very disjointed. Add real value by using it to provide a unique perspective on the rest of the proposal.

Finally, it is worth remembering that the Executive Summary introduces your proposal. First impressions count, so it is worth making an effort to convey the professionalism, expertise and values that you want the client to associate with your solution.

Summary: The Management Solution

- *Equal weighting* in the bid evaluation is often given to the management and technical solutions. Make sure you have given as much thought to the planning and execution of the project as to the technical solution.

- The management solution is a *dress rehersal* for the detailed planning activity. The client will be looking at the professionalism and insights of your plan as an indicator of how good a job you will do if you win the work.

- Submitting *full drafts of management deliverables* can be a considerable burden so plan accordingly. It may be acceptable to provide examples from existing projects or detailed document outlines as alternatives.

- A *detailed management solution* will impress the client and give a sound basis for the proposal, e.g. by quantifying risk and modelling costs more accurately.

- Management plans tend to be either *task-based* (identifying the activities to be carried out) or *product-based* (building planning around what is delivered) although a good schedule will almost certainly show some aspects of both.

- *Keep consistency between the different parts of the plan.* Use the same task names throughout, ensure dates in the text and on the schedule match up and that the cost model follows the work package structure.

- *Choose an appropriate level of detail* to show on the project schedule. You may want to show the 'shape' of the project at a high level and provide a separate, more detailed schedule.

- *Honesty when discussing project risks is a good thing.* Risks are better brought out into the open than pushed to one side.

- Include *clear statements on any assumptions and dependencies* you can think of. It provides a context for your solution, and a basis from which to negotiate the final contract with the client.

- The *Executive Summary needs to be distinctive*, not a cut and paste from other sections of the proposal.

- *Write the Executive Summary from the client's perspective.* This will ensure your proposal appears relevant and offers real value to the client.

- Leave time to *polish the Executive Summary*. This is the most-read part of your proposal so it is worth the investment of time.

- Show an *understanding of the client's business*. You may need to research this. Look for opportunities where your organization's skills are highly relevant.

12

Quality Control

Quality means doing it right when no one is looking.
Henry Ford, founder of the Ford Motor Company, 1863–1947

First-draft proposals are usually easy to spot: poorly structured, badly written, hurriedly assembled and full of punctuation errors, inconsistencies and contradictions. Key messages are obscure and sentences ramble on without a clear direction. First draft proposals appear amateurish, frankly. Flaws which may seem inconsequential as you concentrate on just finishing the draft on time, inevitably create a slapdash and unprofessional appearance to the client who looks at it with fresh eyes.

You can be forgiven these first-draft transgressions only if you have a killer discriminator – something so irresistible that the client will be prepared to overlook poor workmanship on the bid. But this is rare. If you are competing on level terms with other suppliers, quality control on the bid will be an important factor in its ultimate success. So be sure to leave enough time in the schedule to rework your bid. Revision may seem like a chore, but it will make a significant difference to the quality of the proposal and therefore its chance of winning.

Reviewing the Bid

Before the bid can be revised, it needs to be comprehensively reviewed. Ideally, several reviews will already have taken place at regular intervals so that quality is 'built in' wherever possible as the proposal is written. This is always easier than trying to add quality right at the end of the bid life cycle.

TYPES OF REVIEW

The number and type of reviews will depend on the size and complexity of the bid, but each review should have two parts:

- A *gatekeeper* part – a check to see if the material conforms to the appropriate standards, is compliant with the requirements, and is proposing something acceptable to the client, etc. The feasibility of what is being proposed (i.e. will this constitute a viable project?) is also a function of this part of the review.

- An *advisory* part – suggestions on how to improve the material, which could include ideas for alternative approaches, suggestions for better wording, or areas where more detail is needed.

Reviews fall broadly into the categories shown in Table 12.1.

Table 12.1   Three different types of review

Type of review	Examples
Strategic reviews	*Examples: ITT evaluation, solution review, key-themes review, engineering review.* Strategy is all about understanding your direction before you set off, so it follows that a strategic review must be scheduled in the early stages of the bid. Problems often arise when these are left too late. Key stakeholders in your organization such as the CEO or technical director or other senior managers may wish to have an input to the bid strategy. Clearly, if they are first involved only when a full draft is nearing completion, it is too late to change the high-level approach. Although it is natural to want something substantial and tangible to show senior management, a good strategic reviewer will be able to understand and respond constructively to ideas, concepts and strategies when they are still at the whiteboard stage. This has the big advantage that any changes to the strategy do not then require rewriting an entire proposal.
Output reviews	*Examples: storyboard reviews, first draft review, executive summary review, implementation plan review, cost model review.* As their name suggests, output reviews focus on specific outputs from the bid activity. Their main purpose is to assess whether the output meets the quality criteria that have been set. For instance, a review of the cost model will need to establish if the costs are complete, if the solution remains affordable for the client, if there is sufficient contingency allocated and whether the work will be profitable. Reviewers should also be providing advice where possible, i.e. suggestions for improvements or highlighting areas where greater clarity is needed. It is important that this is constructive criticism. If a reviewer identifies a problem, it is helpful to suggest possible solutions too.
Approval reviews	*Examples: Bid/no-bid review, cost/price sign-off, submission approval.* Approval reviews cover the activities which satisfy an organization's quality and commercial processes. For example, since bids cost money to produce, an organization needs to be satisfied that there is sufficient return (and sufficient likelihood of winning) to cover the cost of bidding. Furthermore, if the bid will be contractually binding, the supplier must be satisfied that it is not agreeing to commercial terms that will be impossible to meet.

Different aspects of quality controls are needed at different stages of the bid, but for reasons of efficiency you may wish to cover several in a single review. Here are the most important types of quality controls:

- *Structural review*. Is the material being presented in a logical and consistent order, with the right level of detail?

- *Compliance*. Have you demonstrated that your solution complies with all the requirements (and includes appropriate material to justify the statement of compliance?)

- *Feasibility*. Is your solution technically feasible? Has this been checked with experts not directly involved with the bid?

- *Deliverability*. Is your organization confident it can deliver the solution in the manner described in the bid, e.g. to time, within budget and to the required standards?

- *Commercial*. Is your organization satisfied with the commercial terms laid out in the bid?

- *Affordability*. Does the price represent a sound business prospect for your organization, given the scope of the work?

- *Presentation*. Is the proposal presented in an appealing, professional format, free from obvious errors and inconsistencies?

KEEPING A SENSE OF PROPORTION

Because the bid team often works under considerable time pressure, it may not always be possible to follow an ideal review timetable. Keep a sense of proportion when planning reviews:

- What are the most important aspects to review?

- How will each review add value?

- Can several aspects be covered in a single review?

- What action will be taken following a review?

Clearly there is little point in gathering comprehensive review comments if you don't have time to do anything about them. Reviews must be conducted in a way that helps rather than hinders the progress of the bid team.

Inevitably, each review incurs a time overhead: time to conduct the review, and time to respond and incorporate the changes asked for. Reviews can be distracting for the bid team working under pressure, so limit the number of reviews without losing sight of the quality control objectives.

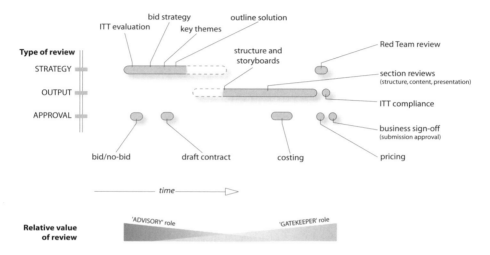

Figure 12.1   A typical mix of reviews during the creation of the bid.
Strategic reviews predominate in the early stages, providing advice and guidance to the bid team. Output reviews are generally more suited to the latter stages as a check that the agreed actions have been carried out

THE RED TEAM REVIEW

The term 'Red Team review' refers to a particular type of review that takes place towards the end of proposal development. It takes a holistic view of the bid, looking at all sorts of different aspects and forms a judgement on the completeness of the bid and whether there are still major flaws to be addressed. It is a 'first read-through' review of the proposal in its nearly completed state.

Different organizations have different names for the this kind of review, but 'Red Team' is a commonly used term. On a large bid, there may be several iterations of this review with colours to match: pink, red, silver, gold reviews, etc. Each occurs at a key stage when various aspects of the proposal (e.g. solution, costs, risks, price, etc.) are completed.

The Red Team review is often the first time the draft proposal is exposed to senior managers and careful thought is needed on the timing and the way the review is managed.

- If there are known problems or gaps, it is important to communicate this to the Red Team reviewers. There is no point in receiving feedback on problems which you are already aware of.

- Direct the reviewers to particular parts of the proposal which you feel will benefit from independent scrutiny.

- Provide the context for the review. Ideally, the Red Team should be properly read-in and conversant with the ITT before conducting the review, but this won't always be the case. You may even need to supply a briefing paper to provide context against which the proposal can be reviewed.

- The Red Team review will often focus on high level issues such as sales messages and key themes. It is always worth having a good, polished draft of the Executive Summary ready because this captures the essence of the bid.

- Since the Red Team review is a holistic review, make sure the reviewers have access to the full set of documentation: ITT, proposal, cost model, trade-off analyses, etc.

- Schedule the Red Team review late enough in the bid schedule that the proposal is in a substantially completed state, but leave enough time so that comments can be acted on and changes made.

Planning Your Reviews

The number of reviews and their timing will vary according to the nature of the bid. You will need to decide on your own review plan, taking into account your organization's business processes. Once the review plan has been formulated, check you are meeting the following conditions:

- There is at least one of each review type shown in Table 12.1, no matter how small the bid.

- The reviews are built in to the bid plan, including activities to prepare for the reviews and follow up once the reviews are completed. (See Planning the Bid in Chapter 3.)

- The timing of reviews is realistic. For instance, reviewers need sufficient time to conduct the review, which may include background reading (particularly of the ITT). The bid team will also need time to respond and incorporate changes into the bid. Finally, there will need to be a follow-up process whereby the reviewer approves the changes made and confirms all the comments have been dealt with appropriately.

TIMING OF REVIEWS

Generally, the earlier a review is carried out, the more useful it is. Although some reviews are late-stage events such as output reviews which check that specific targets and objectives have been met, other types of review are best carried out much earlier on because they will influence, guide and advise the bid team. This type of review can be scheduled even before any words have been committed to paper, i.e. before it becomes too difficult to change the shape of the bid.

Some reviewers fixate on the 'gatekeeper' part of the review (i.e. checking that the material meets the standard required) and overlook the opportunity to advise on ways to improve the bid. However, a review's influence on the quality of the bid decreases as the submission deadline approaches (see Figure 12.2), so the changes that have real benefits – and may therefore mean the difference between winning and losing the bid – are most likely to arise from advisory reviews done early on.

Involve reviewers as soon as practical after the decision to bid has been taken. It is much easier to adapt your bid strategy to take account of guidance you receive at this stage. Not only that, but you will have support and commitment from the reviewers if they can see that their comments are being acted on. Then when they return later to undertake the final reviews, those reviewers will be fully up to speed.

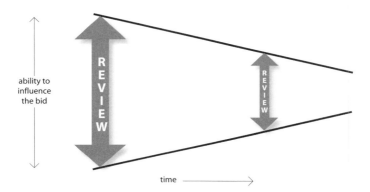

Figure 12.2   **The decreasing value of reviews.** *The ability to influence the proposal (in a positive way) decreases as the submission deadline approaches*

Managing the Review Process

It is worth spending time considering how to get the best from the review process. Table 12.2 provides some guidance.

Table 12.2   **Guidelines for managing the review process**

Review guideline	Notes
Use a fresh pair of eyes	Where possible, have someone other than a member of the bid team conduct the review. A fresh pair of eyes is always helpful.
Use specialists	Using unqualified reviewers won't produce useful feedback. Specialist sections of the proposal will need to be reviewed by a suitable expert – someone with the relevant background and experience to spot flaws and omissions. Book a slot in their diary early.
Work top-down	Review high-level issues (e.g. the proposal structure, key concepts, etc.) before concentrating on the detail. If there are problems at the high level, detailed sections may need a complete rewrite so there is little point in addressing minor spelling and grammatical issues at this stage.

Table 12.2   *Concluded*

Review guideline	Notes
Have a clear purpose	Be clear about the purpose of the review. Is it to assess the feasibility of the technical solution? To check the completeness of the proposal? To confirm whether key issues have been fully addressed? A review may be trying to assess the quality of the material on several different levels. It is sometimes useful to provide the reviewer with guidelines on where to focus, or a short briefing paper explaining both the background and nature of the review.
Keep the review focused	Be wary of arranging reviews which try to achieve everything in one go. It is often better to have several different passes with each focusing on a different aspect of the proposal.
Make review arrangements well in advance	Identify who you need to involve in the review. Confirm their availability and, if necessary, the willingness of reviewers to participate. If the reviewer is not personally known to you, check your assumptions about their skills and knowledge. Is this person really qualified to undertake the sort of review you need? Let the reviewer know what material will be provided (and when). If the schedule changes for any reason, make sure you keep the reviewer informed.
Set a review timescale	You cannot afford for the review date to slip. You will also need a quick turnaround to give the bid team plenty of time to take the comments onboard. Provide the reviewer with a clear timetable for their response.
Agree how comments are provided	How do you want to receive the output of the review? Verbal feedback is rarely good enough because it can lead to misunderstandings and leaves nothing to refer back to later on. Review comments can be embedded in an electronic copy of the bid, but bear in mind that consolidating several sets of comments can be quite a headache. Check that however the comments are provided, you will be able to process the information efficiently.
Agree the resolution process	A reviewer may request changes that you disagree with or feel are inappropriate. Who arbitrates? The bid manager should be empowered to make only changes which tangibly improve the bid. Do you need to confirm with the reviewer what action will be taken against each comment? It is good practice to have a sign-off process to verify that the feedback has been incorporated appropriately.

Polishing As You Go

Reworking the bid, particularly under severe time pressure, is never a pleasant prospect. Generally, the more you can spread this work throughout the bid, the better – and in particular, avoid leaving everything to the end.

You don't need to wait for review feedback to fix obvious problems with style, spelling, grammar, etc. Sections which don't have dependencies on other parts of the proposal should be 'polished' as they are produced, providing the high-level structure isn't likely to change. This is one of the many advantages of storyboarding – by establishing the broad themes and structures early on, you can fill in and rework the detail without worrying that structural changes will force major rewrites late in the day.

Polishing is not just a case of obeying basic rules of spelling and grammar (although that certainly helps). It also means:

- Checking that the meaning of each sentence is clear (and that this is what you meant to say).

- Cutting out verbosity – aiming to get the right messages across with the least number of words.

- Removing unnecessary repetition.

- Making the text readable and engaging, e.g. by using active rather than passive sentences.

- Adjusting the tone of writing to make it sufficiently interesting to hold the reader's attention.

- Polishing as you go has additional benefits, too:

  - It is a good opportunity for peer reviews (i.e. authors involved in the bid can review and polish each other's sections) which helps to achieve a uniform style throughout the proposal.
  - A bank of second-draft material builds up through the course of the bid, so the shape and content of the final proposal emerges earlier.
  - Important sections get the most attention. If you run out of time, it should be the least important sections that receive least attention.

PADDING

Plenty of proposals contain empty sentences. An empty sentence has no real meaning and therefore adds little value. Such sentences may give the appearance of saying something important, but when we look closer there are only clichés, jargon or important-sounding words.

This is often done to pad out a section, i.e. to make it seem longer, or more important-sounding or more complex than it really is. The bid writer may be trying to impress the reader (or perhaps concealing the fact that they cannot think of anything meaningful to say).

There is a simple test for identifying empty sentences. Take a page or so of text and try to imagine yourself reading this for the first time without any particular background knowledge. Summarize the gist of the material in note form. Now look to see which sentences or paragraphs those notes relate to. Very often, there are just one or two key sentences (or perhaps a paragraph) which contain the bulk of the information. Everything else acts either in a supporting role (e.g. scene-setting, preparing the logic of the argument, etc.) or doesn't make a contribution. Often this may be the author 'limbering up' or trying out a number of tangential approaches to the main message before hitting the nail on the head. When you find empty sentences, prune them back ruthlessly to the central idea or message.

WORD COUNT REDUCTION

Word count reduction is a really effective way to polish your text. It works as follows:

- Take a section of first draft proposal text and count the total number of words.

- Set yourself a target to reduce the word count: 10–15 per cent is a realistic goal.

- Work through the text, sentence by sentence, removing padding, finding ways to say the same thing in fewer words and ruthlessly cutting out anything which doesn't directly contribute to the point you are trying to make.

- When you have reduced the original word count by the required amount, the revision is complete.

You must retain all the ideas and messages in the original text, which means you can't simply delete whole paragraphs if they contain important messages. If your first draft material has been hurriedly written, cutting 10 per cent is comparatively easy. The writing will be sloppy, repetitive and often padded out with redundant phrases. These should be replaced with a more succinct alternative. More polished material will present a greater challenge to reduce, but it almost always results in sharper, more direct (and therefore, readable) text.

One of the reasons this approach works so well is that it forces the writer to think carefully about the messages in the bid. A lot of bid-writing slips unconsciously into trite phrases and jargon-speak. This may look good on the page at first sight, but when the superficiality is stripped away, often all that is left is a confusing mess. To get your message across in fewer words, you really have to know what you want to say. Simple and concise should be the bid writer's watchwords.

Summary: Quality Control

- Decide *when is the best time* to conduct each of the different types of bid review.

- *Early reviews* should focus on guiding and shaping the bid strategy.

- Reviews held *later in the bid stage* should confirm that all the components of the proposal are in place and meet the necessary standards.

- The ability of a review to *beneficially influence the proposal* decreases the closer you get to the submission deadline.

- Be sure to understand your organization's *approval process* and factor in the right reviews to get your proposal signed off by the right people at the right time.

- There are many possible reviews, so your review plan must be *relevant and proportionate,* i.e. enough to cover the ground but not so many that the bid team are swamped.

- Many minor issues picked up in reviews can be prevented by *polishing sections of the bid as they are written.*

- *Don't include first-draft material* in your submitted bid if you can help it, but revise according to the priority (i.e. importance) of each section. It is always worth spending extra effort on the Executive Summary.

- *Don't ignore issues which are uncovered in a review.* The job of a review is to both challenge and guide. In an extreme case where there are major problems, it may mean recommending that the bid is abandoned.

13

The Transition to a Project

Plans are only good intentions unless they immediately degenerate into hard work.

Peter F. Drucker, management consultant, 1909–2005

Congratulations! The end is in sight: the technical solution has been written, the delivery plans formulated, a cost model prepared, and any remaining proposal sections (paying particular attention to the Executive Summary) written, reviewed and revised. With the necessary sign-offs obtained on the final draft, the hard work has been done. All that remains is the final push – the production stage: printing, assembly and dispatch.

This chapter briefly discusses production tasks and the steps needed to get the proposal delivered on time. But it also looks at what happens next. If the client selects your proposal, some important steps are needed to transition from bid to project.

We began in Chapter 1 with the premise that what happens during the bid life cycle has a big influence on the success or failure of the project. This final stage – the transition from bid to project – is crucial. A lot of knowledge has been gained during the development of the project framework. This now needs to be transferred to the incoming project team.

Producing the Finished Proposal

KEEPING CONTROL

With the submission deadline looming, the pressure on the bid team has never been more intense. Many things can conceivably disrupt the final stages of the bid plan: 'day-job' distractions, illness, failures of equipment or infrastructure, etc. Now is the time when the bid planning will really pay off. Make good use of bid preparation checklists. These will guide the bid team through the final stages, making sure nothing gets forgotten and allowing you to keep control of the proposal production.

An example bid checklist is included in Appendix A. Although this covers all stages of the bid life cycle, the latter parts will be particularly useful as a final check during the production stage.

Preparing for the Next Stage

It's done! The final copies of the proposal have been dispatched, and the client has confirmed receipt. Now is obviously a good time to catch a breath and take a well-earned rest. Soon though it will be time to begin the post-submission work (see Table 13.1 for examples).

Table 13.1   Preparing for the next stage: after the bid submission

Down-selection	Major procurements often go through a shortlisting process called 'down-selection' which whittles away the number of credible bidders in stages. Two or more down-selection stages are not uncommon – for instance, pruning 30 initial responses down to a more manageable dozen in the first round, then twelve down to three in the second round, and finally selecting the winner in the third round. If you are at an early stage of down-selection, think ahead to the next submission. What can you improve upon? What ideas didn't you have time to explore? How do you expect the client to react to this submission?
Clarifications	If the client has questions about your proposal, you will be asked to provide clarification. Questions will arise from aspects of your bid which are poorly explained or perhaps from issues raised in a competitor's bid. Don't be dismissive of clarifications which don't appear to relate to previously documented requirements. Ask yourself why the client might be requesting this information. Are you being given a second chance? Have you missed a clue in the ITT? Are you being asked to respond to a competitor's bright idea? Since you can't predict what clarifications will be raised, it is important to have ready access to research materials and domain experts so that you can respond quickly. Your organization remains on show during any dealings with the client, so it is as important as ever to make a good impression. Give the same attention to detail in preparing the response to clarifications as you would to any other section of the proposal.
Negotiations	There can be many reasons why the client wants to negotiate on your proposal: • It may indicate that you are the preferred supplier and the client is looking to close a deal. • The client may be 'playing off' several potential suppliers and looking to achieve the best possible deal. • Some clients will negotiate simultaneously with all shortlisted candidates, either to shorten the procurement process or to keep their options open. The final stages of negotiation with the client can be a fraught, drawn-out process, but it is important to stay responsive and be as helpful as possible.

Table 13.1   *Concluded*

Presentation	The client may call on the shortlisted suppliers to present their solutions in person. This is an opportunity for the client to meet some of the potential project team and judge what sort of working relationship will be formed, and ask probing questions. The structure of the presentation should be guided by your understanding of the client's key concerns. The objective is to complement what is in the proposal, not just repeat key sections.
BAFO (Best And Final Offer)	A BAFO stage occurs at the very end of the negotiation period. This is your chance to take into account any recent changes, additions or concerns highlighted by the client during the negotiations, for example: waived requirements, functional trade-offs, final discounts to the price, etc. The BAFO will be your final submission ahead of contract award. The BAFO is a binding offer. If the client is pressing hard for discounts, make sure you understand where your limits are.

NEGOTIATING WITH THE CLIENT

Keep the feasibility of the project framework (particularly the assumptions and underlying risks) firmly in mind during any negotiations with the client.

There may be last-minute pressure to cut the price, add a few more features, squeeze the schedule, etc. If you are confident the client wants to award you the contract, providing 'extras' may not seem like too much to ask, particularly if it will swing the decision in your favour. However, care is needed. Having estimated as diligently as possible, remember that any extras will genuinely carry an additional cost. Whilst you can always choose to reduce the price (in other words, cut the profit margin) you can't reduce the cost (or ignore additional cost) arbitrarily. Be careful not to abandon assumptions or overlook risks in order to clinch the deal.

For every point you negotiate, ask yourself three things:

- Is this a change to the requirements?

- Does this alter any assumptions or impact the risk assessment?

- How should I modify the cost model to allow for this?

It isn't hard to see how planning and careful analysis in the preceding stages now begins to pay off, particularly the work that has gone into updating the cost model. Remember Figure 6.6 which shows how the estimation model needs to track any changes in requirements? This is when you put it to the test, feeding changes through the estimation model, flowing these into the cost model, and finally determining a revised price.

TRADE-OFFS AND CONVERGENCE

Trade-off discussions are designed to strike a balance between what is achievable and what is affordable. A trade-off is necessary when the client has, in effect, asked for the near-impossible: for example, a major operationally critical service to be run on a shoestring budget, or the seamless integration of new technology with unsupported legacy systems. (Admittedly, these are fairly extreme examples.)

Infeasible technical requirements (i.e. the truly impossible) will have been addressed back at the solution definition stage – either by seeking clarifications which reduce the scope of the requirements, deciding to bid a non-compliant solution or arriving at a no-bid decision. However, sometimes the impracticality of certain requirements doesn't become apparent until the proposals are being evaluated, particularly if the client has not indicated what their budget is. This can lead to the situation where there are several fully compliant bids but none which are affordable to the client.

Generally, the best option for a client in this situation is to forgo enough of the lower priority requirements to bring the price within range of what is affordable. This will need to be explored via trade-off discussions and will require you to be able to accurately specify the cost (and hence the price to the client) of each requirement under discussion. Again, the effort of maintaining good estimation and cost models will now bear fruit. Keep in mind the guidance given in Table 13.2.

The outcome of most trade-off negotiations is a re-priced bid. Therefore give some thought to how the revised price is ratified by your organization (and the timing of this), particularly if your internal sign-off procedures are long-winded.

Table 13.2   Guidelines for trade-off discussions with the client

Are you the preferred supplier?	It is important to understand if the client is discussing trade-offs with a number of competing suppliers or whether you have been singled out as the 'preferred supplier'. In the latter case, the client believes you offer the best solution, but certain aspects need to be modified (e.g. the price) before the bid can be accepted. In a competitive situation you will need to take account of your competitor's strategy. Will they significantly reduce their price? Are there features of their offering or product range which are differentiators? Can you counter these?
Keep a clear distinction between cost and price	Refer back to Chapter 8. Costs are objective and are based on your detailed model of the end-to-end solution. Each requirement in the ITT therefore has an implicit cost. The price offered is a commercial decision. Normally this would be based on the costs plus a profit margin, but you can set the price to be whatever you like – for example, the price might even be lower than the cost if there are strategic benefits in winning the bid (i.e. as a loss-leader).
Cost reduction equals waiving requirements	To reduce the cost of your proposal, some of the client's requirements will need to be relaxed or removed altogether. If the client expects you to reduce the *cost* of your bid (cf. reducing the price, which is a commercial decision for your organization), then there must inevitably be a trade-off discussion on requirements.
Be able to justify your position	At some point in the negotiation, the client may ask to see the details underpinning the trade-offs. 'If I waive *this* requirement, what effect will it have on the price? Or suppose I relax *that* requirement – will that save more money?' The benefits of having a linked estimation and cost model are clear. It provides the justification for the trade-off options. Don't pluck numbers out of the air: feed any changes into the estimation and cost models and trust the answers.
Use negotiations as a chance to show your mettle	How you handle the negotiation process is a good indicator of how the client–supplier relationship will develop after the contract is awarded. Don't be awkward or evasive or slow to respond during the negotiations. The client will be looking for a supplier who behaves with integrity, demonstrates a professional approach and a sound knowledge of their specialist domain. A key part of this challenge is your willingness to tailor the solution to fit the client's budget.

Learning Lessons

One of the secrets of good bid-writing is to recognize that each bid is different (even when they appear similar) and demands a unique approach. In addition, the business world is fast-moving and constantly changing. Today's winning proposal might easily be out-classed next time around. Consequently there are always lessons to be learned at the end of every bid. Take time to review these lessons so that you can keep your bid process sharp and up to date and improve your chances of success on the next bid.

- What could you have done differently? Are these things likely to crop up again or were they specific to this particular bid?

- Ask others involved in the bid the same question. Are there different points of view or suggestions to consider?

- What parts of the proposal might be useful for future bids? Using too much boiler-plate text lifted from another proposal should be avoided, but equally there are benefits in reusing well-polished, generic material where appropriate. Build up a library of bid components, e.g. diagrams, technical specifications, glossaries, model answers, etc. which can form the starting point for your next bid.

- Keep an archive of ITTs, submitted proposals and research material. You are unlikely to ever dust off an old proposal that exactly matches a new ITT, but it is always useful to mine them for ideas and see how previous proposals have addressed particular issues.

- Study your competition. You won't often get the chance to read a competitor's proposal but if it happens, grab the opportunity. Compare your bid section by section. How did they tackle the key issues? Where was the emphasis placed? Did they identify different key themes? Was more or less detail provided? What were the key differences in the solution offered? And yes, how did their price compare? Did they offer value for money? The differences won't necessarily mean your competitor produced a better proposal, but it is still a great opportunity to learn from someone else's approach.

ASKING FOR A DEBRIEF

Asking for a debrief – win or lose – ought to be standard practice in your bid process. Don't expect all clients to oblige, but make the most of those that do. The fact of winning or losing the bid tells you little, but a client's honest feedback provides invaluable detail on what you did right and where there are lessons to learn for next time. Without the client's perspective, you have no way to judge the pros and cons of your submission.

Let the client know why you would like feedback (i.e. to improve your bid process and strategy for future bids). Particularly if you have not been successful, try to avoid giving the impression that you are gathering evidence against the client or want them to justify their decision.

If you have lost, accept it gracefully and remain professional. After all, you may soon have the opportunity to submit a new bid to this client. Legal challenges to the award of a contract are not unheard of, but it is questionable whether they really bring lasting benefit to the supplier making the challenge. If you have lost this time, you may be more fortunate next time – particularly if your proposal made a favourable impression. Avoid anything that might alienate the client (e.g. by being an awkward loser) or you may lose the client for good.

It can seem strange to ask for a debrief if you win the work, but it is just as important to know why the client selected your proposal so that you can incorporate these features into the next bid. In this case, a formal debrief may not be necessary; you may be able to gather the information during regular project meetings with the client or find opportunities to discuss the bid informally.

Here are some simple guidelines for the debrief:

- *State your purpose.* Make sure the client understands that a debrief will help your organization to provide a better response to future ITTs. Ultimately, this is in the client's best interests too.

- *Seek unstructured feedback,* i.e. avoid a questionnaire or form-based response. The client will naturally recall key factors in your proposal which influenced the evaluation – things they liked, things they didn't like. This is the information you are after. If you put questions to the client, make sure they are open ones. What aspects were most appealing? In which areas would you have liked to see more detail? Where did you feel there were weaknesses in the solution?

- *Analyse the feedback very carefully.* Some clients may feel uncomfortable offering direct criticism of your proposal (though many won't!), so be alert to the subtleties of their comments. Are there hidden messages? Are there common themes in the feedback? Does the feedback hint that you came close to being selected (or was the bid wide of the mark)?

- *Don't make a nuisance of yourself.* It is pointless to challenge or dispute any client feedback, although it is not unreasonable to ask for clarification if the feedback is confusing. The bid is either won or lost and there is nothing to be done to alter this. Remember that the client isn't under any obligation to help you by providing feedback. If after asking politely two or three times, no feedback is forthcoming, retire with good grace.

- *Debrief even when successful.* If the your proposal has won, try to find out where it scored more highly over competitors' bids. Were there still weak areas? What changes to the bid process would strengthen these next time?

- *Review the feedback with the bid team.* Be as objective as possible. Involving others will give different perspectives. Don't hold an inquest or look for scapegoats: remember, the purpose is to learn lessons and work out what can be improved next time.

- *Plan how you will incorporate lessons learned into future bids.* This step is often overlooked. Decide what it is that needs to be changed. Is it the bid process, better training for the bid team, better support from the organization – or is it tacit knowledge, e.g. things to be aware of or do differently next time?

TRANSLATE INTO ACTION

Too many lessons-learned reviews arrive at a consensus on things that went wrong but don't then translate them into actions for improvement. Suppose the bid team agrees there were critical weaknesses in the bid, but nothing is written down and no corrective actions are set. They return to their day jobs and gradually forget about their experiences. Consequently, six months down the line, the same mistake is repeated in the next bid.

At the very least, write up a list of the problems identified and what changes need to be made. Assign actions which will lead to improvements. You may not be able to effect dramatic changes overnight, but a plan to improve the bid process or increase project-planning and bid-writing expertise can be developed. Distribute the lessons-learned review and the actions plan as widely as possible in the organization. Other people need to be aware of the lessons if they are going to benefit from them.

Final Steps

The final steps in transitioning from bid to project are obvious ones, but vital all the same. They centre on knowledge transfer and communication. The proposal is the product of a large amount of knowledge gained about the client, the requirements, your organization's solution and delivery capabilities and the circumstances in which the project will be executed. The incoming project manager therefore needs to understand the context in which the bid has been developed and quickly get to grips with all the assumptions, dependencies and risks which underpin it.

- *Preserve continuity* during the transition from bid to project. Keep key members of the bid team available during the early stages of project start-up. Consult with them frequently. Explore ways to transfer their bid knowledge to the incoming project team. (Ideally, key members of the bid team take up roles on the project team, but this won't always be practical.)

- *Weed out non-valuable information*. Go through the bid files (both electronic and physical) and discard early drafts, rough notes, storyboards, etc. Obviously, only weed out items that have no conceivable benefit to the project team and might otherwise cause confusion. The point of this exercise is to ensure that what remains is clearly labelled, accessible and meaningful to the project team. If in doubt as to an item's worth, given it a meaningful label and store it under a miscellaneous heading; better safe than sorry. There may be quite a bit of work involved in sorting through material, filing and labelling and generally tidying up the mess left behind in the rush to complete the proposal. It is a chore, but it prevents valuable information being lost to the incoming project team.

- *Archive all bid materials carefully*. Not just key documents (i.e. the bid itself) but working papers, research notes, minutes of design meetings, lists of key themes – paying particular attention to the estimation and cost models.

- *Hold briefing sessions between the bid and incoming project team*. Cover items which aren't obvious from reading the bid. (Assume that the project team will have already read the bid.) What was it like working with the client during the bid? What aspects of the project particularly interest the client? Where are the risks? What are the critical assumptions? Are there weak points in the bid? Don't hold back on any negative aspects – the project team's best chance of dealing with problems is to know about them as early as possible.

SIGNING OFF

There has been a lively debate amongst scientists since the very earliest days of genetics about its importance in shaping the destiny and life chances of individual human beings. Some believe that the genes we inherit from our parents determine many aspects of our appearance, health, intelligence and emotional make-up. If true, a large part of what makes us who we are is predetermined at birth and has lasting influence on our educational achievements, standard of living, ability to form lasting relationships, predisposition to disease and illness, etc. In other words, significant parts of our lives are 'programmed in' at birth.

An alternative view supposes that the environment we live in has equal (if not greater) influence. The surroundings in which an individual is raised, their exposure to experiences and opportunities – these lead to life choices which in the right circumstances can overcome genetic predisposition or build upon it. External influences and freedom of choice are ultimately what shapes the individual.

In all probability, the answer lies somewhere between the two. Is a gifted pianist born so because of some random combination of inherited genes or is the child inspired and encouraged from an early age to develop their talent? Surely both must play a part. This is the 'nature versus nurture' debate.

This leads to an obvious comparison with the 'life chances' of a project. A successful project requires an experienced and talented project manager, well versed in management practices and capable of steering the project around the unforeseen obstacles in its path. The project team has freedom of choice to achieve the project's goals, but the project's genetics are determined during the bid stage. The project may be 'born' with every chance of success, thanks to the diligent work of the bid team in establishing a sound project framework. Conceivably, the project may be predisposed at its start-up to problems of such magnitude that no amount of clever management will truly be able to resolve them.

Bid-writing, like any sales activity, is a challenge. Writing a winning bid that also predisposes for a successful project is doubly so. I hope that this book has helped with both these challenges. Good luck and good bid writing!

Summary: The Transition to a Project

- *Good organization* is the key to the final stage of producing the proposal. Use the checklists and plans created earlier to guide you through the final stages.

- Bid submission isn't the end of the work. *Prepare in good time* to negotiate or present to the client or follow up with a final submission.

- *Trade-off discussions need to be handled with objectivity*. Make good use of your estimation and cost models, i.e. if a requirement changes, you should be able to model the effect of those changes in terms of scope of work, cost and price.

- *Understand the basis on which you are negotiating* with the client. For instance, a cost reduction means waiving or relaxing requirements. A price reduction means squeezing profits.

- *Always ask for a debrief*. No matter the outcome, there are always valuable lessons to be learned and fed back into your next proposal.

- *Set actions arising from a lessons-learned review*. A lesson isn't truly learned unless it is translated into an action to improve things next time round.

Appendix A

A Bid Checklist

The following example of a bid checklist is intended as a guide. You may need to modify it to suit your own particular proposal writing process.

The point about a bid checklist is that is will save time and prevent costly mistakes. It will help establish the project framework and thereby put the resulting project on the best possible footing. But a checklist can be no more than a guide; it will need to be carefully interpreted each time a proposal is written.

DOs AND DON'TS

Do use a checklist as an aide memoire throughout the bidding process and particularly in the latter stages when time is short and important tasks can get forgotten.

Do omit steps from the checklist which don't apply to your particular bid, but make sure your reasons are valid.

Do make sure you have planned well enough to leave sufficient time to complete the end stages of the bid.

Don't rely on the chronological sequence of tasks in the checklist. Every bid is unique and sometimes tasks need to be done in a different order (but make sure you have valid reasons before you stray too far).

Don't ignore any explicit instructions the client has given you about preparing the bid. These must take precedence over the bid checklist.

Note: Items shown in italic should ideally exist as document templates. Using these will save time during a bid and will bring consistency to the bid process. Some of these are discussed in more detail in Chapter 3.

Before you receive the ITT (or pre-qualification questionnaire):

- Keep your market knowledge uptodate (clients, competitors, prospect lists, opportunities, etc.).

- Keep your archive of ITTs and proposals up to date. (Useful for reference and ideas.)

- Find out as much as you can about a forthcoming ITT *before* it is issued.

When you receive the ITT (or pre-qualification questionnaire):

- Skim-read the ITT to establish whether it is a strong prospect for bidding.

- Review what you know of the client and their requirements *before* you read the ITT in detail.

- Establish who needs to influence your bid/no-bid decision.

- Schedule a time for the bid decision and get copies of the ITT to the right people. You may also want to supply briefing notes based on your prior knowledge of the client's requirements.

Bid/no-bid decision:

- The decision makers must review the ITT.

- Complete an *ITT evaluation scorecard*.

- Assess the implications of bidding and identify critical factors. (Note: Should any of these factors change, you may need to revisit the bid/no-bid decision.)

- Seek approval or authorization to proceed with the bid.

- Complete the *bid/no-bid decision sheet*.

If you are going to bid:

- Create a *bid timeline* with the key external dates (e.g. presentations to suppliers, last date for submitting questions, the submission deadline, BAFO completion date, anticipated award date, contract signature, etc.).

- If instructed by the ITT, notify the client of your intention to bid.

- Create (and store securely) a master copy of all the ITT material, in case working copies are mislaid.

If you are not bidding:

- If the ITT was sent at the client's instigation, write a polite letter stating your intention not to bid, as a courtesy. You don't necessarily have to give a reason.

- Archive the ITT, evaluation scorecard and no-bid decision sheet.

Bid strategy:

- Assemble or research any knowledge relevant to the bid, e.g. knowledge of the client, market place, competitors, etc.

- If there are complex contractual terms and conditions, have someone from your legal department begin that review as soon as possible.

- Re-read the ITT and any supporting documentation thoroughly.

- Record the key phrases and recurring themes used by the client on a *client hot-buttons sheet*.

- Put yourself in the client's shoes and think about their desired outcomes, constraints, starting point and any worries they might have.

- Review your offering. How will it need to be tailored for this client?

- Write down your *key themes*.

- How would you expect your bid to differ from the competition? Write down your *discriminators* and *differentiators*.

Bid planning:

- Record all the client's instructions about the structure of your proposal and how it should be produced in a *bid production worksheet*.

- Identify who needs to contribute to the bid. Confirm their availability and check for other commitments (e.g. other assignments, holidays).

- Produce a *high level structure* for the proposal (i.e. major section headings). If the ITT mandates a structure, make sure you follow it.

- Check what the ITT says about how proposals will be evaluated. Where do you need to place most emphasis? Draw out any evaluation guidelines into a *marking scheme*. You might want to ask your own reviewers to evaluate the draft proposal against this marking scheme later on.

- Create and maintain a *task list*. Use this to record all major jobs that need to be done to get the proposal finished. Subdivide into sections for each member of the bid team. (Don't forget to include those who will need to authorize the bid for submission, review technical content, quality review the bid and sign off the costs.)

- Working back from the submission deadline, add internal deadlines to the bid timeline.

- Create a *budget outline* – what do you know about the client's budget for the work? How is this apportioned against work packages?

- Prepare a *review plan* and schedule the key review stages with appropriate staff:

    - Bid Strategy Review
    - Draft Contract Review
    - Costing Review
    - Draft Bid Review
    - Pricing Review
    - Business Sign-off

Building the structure:

- Develop a *detailed proposal structure* to an appropriate level (heading, subheading, sub-subheading, etc.).

- Create a *storyboard* for each section of the bid, or use some alternative form of outlining.

- Review the storyboards. Is the emphasis going in the right place? Does the outline structure and page count tally with the marking scheme?

- Identify at least one section of the proposal where each key theme is addressed as a major topic.

- Assign key themes as minor topics to other parts of the proposal.

- Work on any parts of the solution which need development, e.g. the design for a bespoke solution, feasibility analyses, etc.

Check compliance with requirements:

- Create a *compliancy matrix*, or use the matrix supplied with the ITT.

- Review the compliancy matrix to make sure there is a section of the proposal which properly addresses each requirement.

- Modify the detailed proposal structure accordingly.

Research:

- Identify areas where more information is needed and formulate a plan to obtain or research this information.

Risk assessment:

- Hold brainstorming sessions with the team to identify project risks. Think about the client's perspective as well as your own.

- Evaluate and prioritize the *risk list*.

- What opportunities are there for modifying the solution to minimize some of the high-priority risks?

- Write up the risk list for inclusion in the management section of the bid.

Bid strategy review:

- Prepare and distribute the following in advance to the bid strategy reviewers:

  - Client's ITT
  - ITT evaluation scorecard
  - Bid/no-bid decision and justification
  - Client's hot-button sheet
  - Your key themes, discriminators and differentiators
  - Proposal document outline
  - Budget outline
  - Risk list
  - Any other pertinent materials (e.g. research, market knowledge, etc.)

- Conduct a Bid Strategy Review and document the key points raised.

- Act upon any major concerns raised by reviewers, and incorporate agreed actions into the relevant documents (e.g. the task list, detailed proposal structure, etc.).

- Agree and document the internal business case for pursuing this work. What are your organization's objectives? What is the expected business return? Is this primarily a strategic opportunity – perhaps a chance to gain experience in new areas?

Assembling off-the-shelf materials:

- Identify what off-the-shelf materials will form part of the bid and organize copies well in advance (e.g. product specs, company policies, etc.).

Writing the bid:

- Check that the bid-writing team understand their assigned tasks and the timescales for doing the work.

- If a *document template* is not already available, create one. Check that you are complying with any style or formatting requirements specified in the ITT.

- Create a *master proposal document.* Incorporate the detailed proposal structure.

- Agree how the master document will be updated by the team. How will update conflicts be avoided? How will the master be backed up?

- Decide where diagrams and other visual elements can be used to greatest effect (and perhaps save on writing text).

- Refer to the *drafting guide* when writing each section of the bid to ensure consistency.

- As each section is completed, update the compliancy matrix with a cross-reference to the relevant section in the body of the proposal. Make use of cross-referencing tools in your word processor wherever possible.

- If time allows, have the draft sections of the proposal independently reviewed by peers.

- Request clarification from the client on any vital issues, but think carefully to avoid exposing insightful thinking to competitors.

- Periodically, check progress against the bid plan. Are you on target or falling behind?

- Revisit the task list regularly. You may need to apply the 80/20 principle.

Estimating and costing the bid:

- Break the solution down into sensible work packages.

- Compile the list of products to be delivered in the project and then work backwards to see what tasks are required to deliver these products. Check back against the work package breakdown and refine as needed.

- Use good estimation techniques and build up the estimation model.

- Involve the right people in the estimation work.

- Use metrics from previous work as a guide where relevant.

- Build a cost model. Ideally this should be directly driven by the estimation model. Any changes to assumptions or requirements then feed through automatically into the costs.

- Check that the costing breakdown can be traced back to the work breakdown in the proposal. Make sure there are no work elements missing from the cost model and that all planned work is adequately described in the bid.

- Update the cost model as the detailed bid is written. Watch for 'over-engineering' of the solution which might exceed the client's budget.

- Calculate a bid price based on cost but taking into account other business-related factors such as mark-ups, contingency, profit margins, etc.

- Check that the emerging price is still within the client's budget. If not, you will either need to find a more cost-effective (but compliant) solution or consider discounting the price.

Building the master version of the bid:

- As each section of the proposal is drafted, review it for completeness, consistency and style. Does it address all the necessary points? Does it emphasize key themes or state discriminators and differentiators in the right places?

- Keep the master proposal updated with each quality-reviewed section.

- Periodically, review the master proposal to see if any structural changes need to be made. Look for repetition and inconsistency.

Executive summary:

- Check that the Executive Summary contains all of the key themes, discriminators and differentiators.

- Does this section exceed the planned page count? Edit ruthlessly if necessary. Remember the Executive Summary will be the most-read part of the entire proposal.

- Is the Executive Summary a true summary and doesn't just repeat large chunks of material elsewhere in the proposal?

Contract review:

- Conduct a Contract Review.

- Confirm any amendments which are required to the contract terms and conditions.

- Clarify any urgent issues with the client.

- Document minor issues (e.g. rewording of clauses). These can be addressed during final contract negotiations.

Costing review:

- Conduct a Costing Review. (Note: it should be possible to finalize costs before the bid itself is finished).

- Document the key points raised in the Costing Review.

- Agree with the reviewers what actions are needed to respond to the points raised in the review.

Draft bid review:

- Conduct a Draft Bid Review. Note: at this stage the bid should be near completion with the key sections fully completed. Review the proposal against the following questions:

  - Executive Summary – if read in isolation, does this contain all the main messages of the proposal?
  - Does the proposal demonstrate that you have understood the requirements?
  - Is there a clear statement of what is being offered to the client?
  - Have you addressed the feasibility and practicality of the offered solution?
  - Are the principal messages clearly stated?
  - Is the material complete (including appendices and supporting material)?
  - Is the proposal compliant? Has a compliance matrix been completed and cross-referenced to the proposal?
  - Does the proposal contain full pricing information? Does it follow the pricing structure or other guidelines which the client defined in the ITT?
  - Will the presentation and style of proposal impress?
  - How will the proposal be scored against the marking scheme?

- Agree what remedial action is required and update the task list. This must be feasible with the resources and time available.

- Get internal signoff of the draft bid.

Pricing review:

- Review all costing and pricing assumptions.

- Check that the cost model has been kept in step with the proposed solution and estimates.

- Make sure all price stakeholders understand if there are price elements not supported by costs (i.e. where discounts are being applied).

- Get internal agreement and sign off the bid price.

Generate the master:

- Complete any outstanding tasks on the task list.

- Combine any stand-alone sections into a single master document. For large bids, the document may be split into several files. Make sure there is a master directory which contains only the master source files.

- Spellcheck the master proposal.

- Print out a master copy of all sections of the proposal, including appendices, cover letter, inserts, etc.

- Have the master printout proof-read to spot any incomplete sections, typographical errors, inconsistencies or duplications.

- Take back-ups.

Proposal production:

- Check that you have all the necessary resources to generate the required number of proposal copies (e.g. paper stocks, binders, brochures, toner cartridges, etc.).

- Confirm that the dispatch arrangements will meet the client's deadline (e.g. couriers have been booked, the delivery destination is clearly understood – or alternatively that the electronic submission process has been tested).

- Review the bid production worksheet to be clear on the client's submission instructions. Double-check that the proposal meets these requirements.

- Print out the required number of copies, plus at least two copies for internal reference. Make media copies (e.g. CD-ROM) as directed by the ITT.

- Bind printed copies. Perform a final quality check (e.g. misprinted or blank pages) and dispatch to the client via secure means.

- Notify the client of the dispatch and, if possible, confirm safe receipt with a time and date-stamp.

Transition to a project:

- Sort out bid material, clearly labelling documents that may be relevant to the incoming project team.

- Archive all bid materials for future reference.

- Establish and plan for activities in support of the submitted bid, e.g. responses to questions on the bid, presentations or follow-up meetings with the client.

- Thoroughly brief the incoming project team. What are the key assumptions? What are the main risks? What have you learnt during the bid process that isn't necessarily written down?

- Make sure the project team are aware of all elements of the project framework created during the bid.

- Consider scheduling key stage reviews during the project start-up stage where members of the bid team can comment on the emerging project plan.

- Review the effectiveness of the bid process. What are the lessons to be learned?

Appendix B

Glossary

BAFO

Best And Final Offer. Final version of the bid submitted to the client at the end of the negotiating period.

bid

(Or proposal). The set of documents submitted to the client comprising a binding offer of work.

bid checklist

A guidance sheet to ensure that key elements of the bid process are carried out. See Appendix A for an example.

bid/no-bid decision

Key decision point early in the bid life cycle which assesses the commercial feasibility of bidding.

bid process

The formal process governing the analysis, preparation, creation, production and submission of the bid.

bid production worksheet

Checklist used to record the key checks and steps needed in the final stages leading up to the submission of the bid. All members of the bid team have visibility of this to make sure nothing is overlooked.

bid timeline

Summarizes the schedule for when key tasks need to be completed, e.g. review dates, final submission date, contract award date, etc.

bottom-up	A method of analysing the breakdown of work or cost estimates beginning with the most detailed activities first and aggregating up into more generic headings. See also *top-down*.
client hot-button	A subject, idea or problem which is particularly important to the client. Often a recurring theme in the ITT.
commitment	A commercially binding promise made by the supplier to achieve a project milestone on the specified date. Cf. *estimate* and *target*.
compliance matrix	A document which shows the detailed mapping between the client's requirements (as stated in the ITT) and the elements of the solution (as documented in the bid) where the fulfilment of those requirements is described. This is the main tool for demonstrating that the bid is compliant.
cone of uncertainty	A concept which states that the degree of planning uncertainty increases the further ahead we try to forecast project events, i.e. as risks and project issues become less clearly defined.
consensus expert judgement	An estimation technique reliant on a group of knowledgeable specialists reaching agreement (via an unspecified number of iterations) on estimates for a particular aspect of the project.
cost model	A tool used to capture the costs, drivers and costing assumptions at a detailed level. Ideally, cost elements are directly based on figures held in the estimation model.
count and calibrate	A simple estimation technique based on identifying a suitably representative metric which can be summed across all project elements and converted into the desired units for estimation purposes.

critical path	The set of tasks on the project schedule which cannot overrun without causing key delivery dates to be missed later in the project.
debrief	The process by which the client provides feedback on the submitted proposal to the supplier enabling bid processes to be improved.
decomposition	The act of breaking down project tasks into progressively smaller and more manageable activities which can then be estimated and assigned to individuals more easily.
deductive reasoning	A logical structure for presenting an argument based on a set of statements from which a new statement of fact can be derived. Cf. *inductive reasoning*.
dependencies (external)	Circumstances or events beyond the immediate control of the project manager or team which may influence the project (often significantly).
dependencies (internal)	Circumstances or events under the control of the project team but which require careful management to avoid undesirable consequences for the project schedule or budget.
differentiator	A tangible element of the solution which will make a bid stand out when evaluated next to competitors.
discriminator	A tangible element of the solution which is unique to a bid, i.e. something which competitors cannot offer.
down-selection	The process by which a client reduces the number of credible bidders through a series of competitive selection stages.

drafting guide	A document prepared by the bid manager to achieve consistency of style (i.e. format, tone, presentation) in a proposal being worked on by multiple authors.
due diligence	The process of verifying estimates or costs during the pricing of the bid.
estimate	In a planning context, a date for a key milestone or delivery based on the most realistic estimates prepared by the bid team. This corresponds to a 'most likely' assessment, taking into account the various risks, issues and assumptions. Cf. *commitment* and *target*.
estimate bias	A consideration or unsupported opinion which exerts influence on an estimate (e.g. presupposing the outcome of the estimate, or applying unwarranted pressure to the estimator).
estimation granularity	The smallest working unit used in the estimation process, e.g. a working day.
estimation model	A tool used to capture and maintain estimates (and underlying assumptions) across all elements of the project.
executive summary	A key section of the proposal which introduces the bid and summarizes the main messages of the proposal. Since this is the most-read section of the proposal, it requires significant attention.
expert judgement	An estimation technique which relies on a knowledgeable specialist to analyse a set of tasks and arrive at an estimate based on their judgement of the work entailed.
high level structure	The breakdown of section and subsection headings to be used in the proposal (or similar information held in an outlining tool).

inductive reasoning	A logical structure for presenting an argument based on a sequence of statements which logically imply some new statement of fact. Cf. *deductive reasoning*.
innovative bid	A bid which offers an alternative approach to satisfying the business objectives. This may mean the bid is non-compliant with the ITT because the goals are achieved in a different way to that envisaged by the client.
ITT	Invitation To Tender. The set of documents issued by the client which specify what the requirements are, the contractual details, and how the bid is to be produced and submitted.
ITT evaluation scorecard	A document template used to assess the relevance and fit of the client's requirements to the supplier organization. This supports the bid/no-bid decision made early in the bid life cycle.
key theme	An important message conveyed by the bid, typically relating to the supplier's ability to deliver an aspect of the project. Key themes have both factual and persuasive elements.
management solution	The section of the proposal which specifies how the project will be structured and managed in order to deliver all of the client's requirements.
marking scheme	The approach to be used by the client when evaluating a number of competitive bids. The marking scheme will typically indicate the weighting attached to individual sections of the bid.
MILI	Make It Look Important. The temptation when writing the bid to use complex and important-sounding words and terminology. This sacrifices clarity and simplicity and obstructs effective communication with the client.

offering   A supplier's standard products, services and solution – before they have been tailored to meet the needs of a specific client. Cf. *solution*.

PQQ   Pre-Qualification Questionnaire. An initial (and briefer) form of proposal designed to establish bidder credibility and assist in the down-selection of suppliers who will go forward and submit a full proposal.

project framework   The preliminary planning activity carried out during the bid life cycle. This helps to ensure that the proposal is based on a feasible plan and that there is a smooth transition into project initiation at the end of the bid phase.

proposal   (or *bid*). The set of documents submitted to the client comprising a binding offer of work.

proxy   Objects or properties which can be counted during the process of estimation. The count can then be converted (using historical metrics) into an estimate of time, cost or materials. For example, the number of functional elements in a system design can be used to calculate the number of lines of software to be written.

Red Team review   A key stage review conducted by independent reviewers at the point where the draft bid (including costs) has been prepared.

requirements   The key features of the solution which the client has asked for. These include both functional elements (e.g. system features or services) and non-functional elements (e.g. performance criteria, service levels, etc.).

review plan   A part of the bid plan which specifies when key stage reviews are carried out and who the independent reviewers are (and their availability).

solution	The customized offering which has been tailored to meet the needs of a specific client. Cf. *offering*.
stakeholder	An individual with a vested interest in the contents or the outcome of the bid but who is not part of the bid team (e.g. a budget holder).
storyboard	A detailed outline for a section of the bid. The storyboard is a writing guide, specifying what messages should be included, section length and other key parameters. Reviewing storyboards allows important changes to be made in structure and emphasis before the writing task begins.
target	A delivery milestone which is determined by the outcome of the estimation process, representing a realistic and achievable goal. It is an output of the planning process rather than being imposed by the client. Cf. *estimate* and *commitment*.
task hierarchy	The logical decomposition of work from the highest most abstract level down to detailed (and more manageable) tasks.
technical solution	The element of the proposal which specifies the products or services to be provided by the project (but not necessarily the way in which they will be delivered). Cf. *management solution*.
Tender or *bid*	The set of documents submitted to the client comprising a binding offer of work.
top-down	A method of analysing the breakdown of work or cost estimates beginning with the highest level (or summary) activities and successively breaking them down into more detail. Cf. *bottom-up*.

trade-off   The process of negotiating with the client
                               following bid submission to arrive at a solution
                               which is mutually satisfactory. This often means
                               descoping or relaxing certain requirements in
                               order to bring the bid cost within the client's
                               budget.

Index

80/20 principle 226

A
accountant 21
acronym 170
active sentence 148, 160, 203
activity 98
added-value 27, 51
advisory 196, 200
affordability 138
analyse the opportunity 22–23, 28, 36
analysis 21, 150
analyst 20
annotation 164–165, 188
approval process 205
archive 212, 215, 220–221, 230
artefacts 38–41
assertion 169
assumptions 70, 95, 104–107, 115,
        123, 127, 135, 138–142, 171, 178,
        183, 189–190, 194, 209, 226, 230
audit trail 140

B
background material 147
back-ups 229
bad habits 176
bean counter 21
Best And Final Offer 4, 105, 209, 221,
        233
bias 107–109, 112, 116, 127, 236

bid 4–5, 233, 239; *see also* proposal
    artefacts 38–41
    assembly and dispatch 22, 26, 28,
        37, 230
    checklists 67, 207, 219, 233
    instructions 60
    life cycle 21
    non-compliant 6
    overview 152
    planning 29, 43, 200, 222, 226
    process 5, 13, 31, 35–38, 41–44, 233
    production worksheet 39, 222,
        230, 233
    resources 144, 154
    review 30, 195, 205, 223, 228;
        see also review
    size 154
    strategy 60, 221, 223–224
    structure 158
    team management 30
    timeline 39, 221–222, 233
    weaknesses 172
    writer's toolkit 38
bid manager 30
    responsibilities 29
bid/no-bid decision 30, 38, 135–136,
        210, 220, 224, 233
    sheet 221
bidders' briefing 50
big picture guy 21
bottom-up 131, 151, 234

brevity 147, 163
briefing sessions 215
budget 31, 142, 222, 224
business
    benefits 93
    case 93, 225
    context 50, 59, 64, 145
    objectives 47, 63
    writing 15

C
captive audience 150
Chaos Report, The xv
Churchill, Winston 166
clarification 50, 58–59, 70, 208, 210, 226
client 21
    goals 47, 145
    hot-buttons 39, 221, 224, 234
    objectives 31, 145
    research 57
    stakeholder 5, 47
    themes 49
    trust 69
coherent 137
commercial agreements 3
commercial bid 4
commitment 87, 95, 110, 135, 234
common problems 11–12
comparison factor 123
comparison method 111, 119–123
competitors 58, 172
completeness 41
compliance 6, 17, 22, 26, 28, 37, 146, 223
    criteria 22
    matrix 40, 223, 225, 228, 234
complexity 114, 181, 186
comprehensive 137, 145
Conan Doyle, Arthur 97
concept diagram 73
conceptual framework xvi–xvii

concluding paragraph 170
cone of uncertainty 103–104, 234
conformant 137
conjecture 168
consensus expert judgement 110,
        115–117, 234
consistent 137, 175
constructive criticism 196
content 162
context 166, 171
contingency 76, 79, 125, 227
    cost 136, 138, 140–141
    plan 179
continuity 215
contract review 223, 227
contractual dates 47
contractual issues 183
convergence 210
core competencies xvi
cost 82, 130–142, 211, 226, 229
    drivers 136, 139
    elements 132
    model 31, 40, 82–83, 93, 129,
        131–135, 138–142, 209–211, 226,
        229, 234
    reduction 211
    scrubbing 135, 139–140
    target 138
cost-effective 137
count and calibrate 111, 118–120,
        127, 234
create a feasible proposal 22, 25, 28,
        36
creative thinking 26, 42, 44, 69
credentials 68
credible bidders 16
critical path 185, 234
cross-reference 171, 225
culture 181
custom-built 146

D

deadline 32, 44
debrief 30, 212–214, 217, 234
decomposition 98, 235
deductive reasoning 167–169, 235
delegating 30
deliverables 47, 184, 226
delivery
    dates 47
    mechanism 184
    processes xvi, 68, 93
    strategy 31, 68
dependencies 82, 84, 183–185, 188, 194
    external 46, 185, 188, 190–191, 235
    implications 192
    internal 188, 190–191, 235
    ownership 191
designer 21
detailed structure 40
diagram 182, 225
dialogue 149
differentiators 39, 53–55, 61, 222, 224,
        227, 235
direct address 149
discount 141
discriminators 30, 39, 53–56, 61, 156,
        222, 224, 227, 235
distraction tasks 35
document outline 180
double counting 89–90, 111, 134
down-selection 208, 235
draft text 157
drafting guide 40, 225, 235
Drucker, Peter F. 207
due diligence 236
duration 84

E

early review 31
editing 30, 175

editor 20
efficiency 41
electronic submission 230
empathy 55
emphasis 145
empty sentences 204
ending 170
enthusiasm 163
entry requirements 60
error bars 102, 123, 125–126
error margin 76, 78–79, 92, 94, 104, 116
estimate 75, 78–95, 236
    best-case 115, 118, 126
    characteristics 91
    most-likely 115, 118, 126
    off-the-cuff 90
    poor 125, 127
    worst-case 101, 114, 118, 126
estimation 26, 76–95, 226
    context 89, 114, 121
    due diligence 123–126
    manipulation 88
    methods 97—127, 226
    mindset 89
    model 93, 95, 210–211, 226, 236
    precision 100–101
    processes 91, 95
    range 100–101
    reference project 119–122
    relevance 100–101
    scope 121
    sources of error 89–91, 95
    target project 119
    units 114
evaluating the ITT 30
evaluation criteria 49
evidence 52, 156, 172
executive summary 31, 56, 145, 150
        192–194, 199, 227–228, 236
expert judgement 110–114, 236

extension 32–33, 44
external factors 76
extras 209

F
facts 16, 94, 164, 166, 176
factual writing 165, 167–168
failure 10–11
feasibility 3, 209, 228
feedback 212–214
financial issues 183
financial review 134–135
first draft 206
five Cs 137, 142
fixed price contract 141
flexibility 152
Ford, Henry 195
formulate a strategy 22–23, 28, 36
foundations 3, 13
fulfilling requirements 17

G
Galilei, Galileo 1
gatekeeper 196, 200
generic material 147
go the extra mile 34, 72–73
von Goethe, Johann Wolfgang 45
good communication 161
granularity 98, 131, 236
graphics 30, 157

H
Harvey-Jones, John 29
heading
     active 148–149
     passive 148
     section 150–151
hidden themes 49–50
hierarchy 145, 150
high-level structure 40, 222, 236
highest-value tasks 33

hitting the wall 32, 44
holistic view 188
Holmes, Sherlock 97
honesty 172, 194
human resources manager 20

I
Iacocca, Lee 63
identify the need to change 65–69
illustrator 20
implement a change 65–67
implications 171
improving the process 30
inconsistency 227
inductive reasoning 167—169, 237
inertia 120
informative 144
influence 107
ingenuity 86
innovation 21, 55, 71–72, 237
interpretation 70
invalid comparison 109
Invitation To Bid 4; *see also*
          Invitation To Tender
Invitation To Quote 4; *see also*
          Invitation To Tender
Invitation to Tender xvii, 4, 31, 34,
          45–46, 64, 69, 93, 221, 237; *see*
          also tender
ITT analysis checklist 59, 61
ITT evaluation scorecard 38, 220,
          224, 237
ITT review 135–137

J
jack of all trades 20
jargon 173, 203
judgement 76, 107

K
key message 166–169

key output 183
key themes 31, 35, 39, 46–56, 60–61,
    153, 156, 159, 164–165, 222–224,
    227, 237
keywords 50
knowledge transfer 30, 215

L
lead author 154, 156
learning lessons 30, 211–214, 217
library of bid components 212
logical 144
logical sequence 162

M
macro level 158
Make It Look Important 173, 176, 237
management planning 178
management solution 146, 177–194, 237
management summary 192
managing the bid team 30
margin of error 75
market knowledge 220
marketing collateral 158
marking scheme 39, 222–223, 228, 237
master proposal 225, 229
McConnell, Steve 75
meaningful titles 144
messages 162
method conformity 115, 123
methodology xvi
metrics 92, 114, 119, 133, 135, 226
micro level 158
milestones 47, 185, 188
mind map 151–152
mindset 73, 78–79, 114, 174
mini-theme 148
von Moltke, Field Marshall Helmuth 77
Monte Carlo method 100
Morecombe and Wise 143
MSP xvi

multidisciplinary challenge 20
multidisciplinary skills 27

N
need to know 58
negotiation 208–209, 211, 217, 228
nice to know 58
non-compliant bid 6, 34, 210

O
objectives 8, 47, 156
objectivity 172
obligations 185
offering 23–25, 27–28, 58, 94, 238
Ogilvy, David M. 15
openness 172
opportunist 21
opportunity 21
options 70, 73
organization 9, 13
outline 144, 154, 156, 158, 160, 224
outlining tools 151
over-engineering 226

P
padding 147, 173, 203–204
page
    budget 154, 173
    count 157, 223
    limits 147
paragraph
    closing 157
    opening 157
patterns of argument 166
payment dates 47
perfectionist 21
persuasion 9, 12–13, 16,143, 162, 175
plain-speaking 149
planning the bid 29, 41, 78–79
planning
    date 47

documents 179
fact 94
product-based 181–182, 194
task-based 181–182, 194
polishing 30, 147, 192,194, 202–205
pomposity 173
positive discrimination 35
post-submission 208
pragmatism 21, 44
pre-qualification questionnaire 4,
    220, 238
preconceptions 107, 110,112, 116
preferred supplier 211
preliminary planning 6
presentation 55, 162, 209
Previn, André 143
price 31, 68, 93, 129–142, 146, 210–211,
    227–229
price-to-win 141
pricing
    decisions 141
    model 141–142
    review 135, 223, 229
    section 158
    sheet 133
    strategy 135–136, 138, 140, 141
    structure 133
PRINCE 2 xvi, 6, 181, 188
prioritizing 33–34, 41, 43, 180
problem category 65
product group 98
production 230
professionalism 193
profit margin 130, 141–142, 211, 227
profitability 130, 140
project
    control 178
    framework 6–7, 9–10, 12–14, 63,
        77–78, 81, 238
    objectives 7, 93; *see also* objectives

plan 31, 177, 180
schedule 183–188, 194
start-up 215, 231
project manager 20
proposal 4, 93, 238
    evaluation 33–34
    feasible 22, 25, 28
    highlights 192
    package 30
    structure 30, 150–160, 223
    winning 19, 47
    workmanlike 47
proprietary methods 111
proxy 118, 238
Putt's law 177

Q
qualifications 146
quality
    control 22, 26, 28, 37, 195–206
    plan 183
    standards 22, 47
quality writing 174
quantity 84

R
re-estimating 112
recycled material 147, 174–175
Red Team Review 135, 138–139,
    198–199, 238
reference documents 60
reference projects 69
relevance 145
remedial action 229
repetition 144, 203, 227
reporting 183
request for proposal 4; *see also*
    invitation to tender
request for quote 4; *see also*
    invitation to tender

requirement 60, 93, 238
    analysing 46, 48, 50, 64, 67
    change 209
    costing 131
    fulfilling 17
    misunderstood 3
    research 57
    tracking 92
research 30, 57, 221, 224
researcher 20
resources 8, 60, 82, 84, 157
responsibilities 6–7, 183
    bid manager's 29
reusability 42
reverse-engineered 110
review
    affordability 197
    approval 196
    arrangements 202
    checklist 159–160
    comments 202
    commercial 197
    compliance 197
    cost 228
    deliverability 197
    feasibility 197
    formal 184
    independent 171
    output 196, 198
    peer 203
    plan 40, 197, 200, 205, 223, 238
    presentation 197
    process 201
    strategic 196, 198
    structural 197
    timing 199–200, 202
reviewers 157, 159
    external 154
revision 174
reworking 202

risk 46, 60, 104, 135, 138–141, 179, 181,
    194, 230
    analyst 21
    assessment 209, 224
    list 224
    management 8, 26, 183, 191
    mitigation 68
roles 41, 183
RUP xvi

S
sales message 15
salesman 20
salesmanship 27
Schumacher, E.F. 143
scope 144
    writing tasks 153
scoping 26, 59, 140
second guessing 108
second opinion 116
section title 156
seeds of failure 2
selection 17
selling 78–79
Shaw, George Bernard 161
shortlist 4
showing 17
Sign of Four, The 98
sign-off 30, 202, 223, 229
    sheet 41
slack 79, 185
solution 23–25, 27–28, 63, 93, 223, 239
    alternative 172
    compliant 17
    cost 136
    design 77, 78
    development 55, 135–137
    feasible 60, 135
    review 135–138
stakeholders 6, 59, 239

client 5, 47; *see also* client
supplier 5; *see also* supplier
Standish Group xv
statement of requirements 34
storyboard 40, 153–159, 203, 223, 239
    template 154–157
strategy
    formulation 22, 28, 66
strong writing 161–162, 175
structure 30, 143–160, 223
    macro 163
    micro 163
submission deadline 9, 33, 44, 207
submission timetable 60
subsections 145, 150, 157
success criteria 60, 66
superlatives 172
synergies 137
systemic error 116

T
target 87, 95, 239
task 98
    duration 82
    hierarchy 7, 239
    list 99, 222, 226, 229
    prioritization scheme 34
    sub-task 98–99
technical jargon 170
technical solution 146, 239
technologist 20
telling 17
tender 4, 239; *see also* proposal
throughput 82
time and materials 141
time-cost-quality triangle 84–86
time pressure 14
tolerance 104
tone 159, 163, 171, 203

tools 38
top-down 131, 150, 181, 239
top-level headings 145
trade-off, 240
    analysis 137, 211
    discussion 210, 217
transition 22, 27–28, 37, 207–217, 230
Twain, Mark 129

U
unconscious themes 50
undiscovered themes 51

V
value-added elements 18
value for money 66, 138
verbosity 173, 203
version control 133
vision, lack of 3

W
weak writing
win–lose gap 17–18, 27
win themes 30
winning proposal 19, 47
word count reduction 204
work allocation 160
work-day 98
work package 99, 226
    definition 183
work time 82
working hypothesis 169
workmanlike proposal 47
workshare 154
workstream 98–99
writer 20
writing 30
    pattern 168–169, 176
    template 166–167

If you have found this book useful you may be interested in other titles from Gower

The Bid Manager's Handbook
David Nickson
Paperback: 978-0-566-08847-6

Making the Business Case:
Proposals that Succeed for Projects that Work
Ian Gambles
Paperback: 978-0-566-08745-5
e-book: 978-0-7546-9427-4

The Project Manager's Guide to Purchasing:
Contracting for Goods and Services
Garth Ward
Hardback: 978-0-566-08692-2
e-book: 978-0-7546-8129-8

Strategic Negotiation
Garth Ward
Hardback: 978-0-566-08797-4

Visit **www.gowerpublishing.com** and

- search the entire catalogue of Gower books in print
- order titles online at 10% discount
- take advantage of special offers
- sign up for our monthly e-mail update service
- download free sample chapters from all recent titles
- download or order our catalogue